COVENANT AND CREATION

An Old Testament Covenantal Theology

COVENANT AND CREATION

An Old Testament Covenantal Theology

William J. Dumbrell

The Paternoster Press

Copyright © 1984 William J. Dumbrell

First published 1984 by
The Paternoster Press, Paternoster House,
3 Mount Radford Crescent, Exeter, Devon
and
Lancer Books, P.O. Box 115,
Flemington Markets, New South Wales, NSW 2129

SOUTH AFRICA:
Oxford University Press, P.O. Box 1141, Cape Town

British Library Cataloguing in Publication Data

Dumbrell, W.J.
    Covenant and creation.
    1. Bible.   O.T.——Criticism, interpretation, etc.
    2. Covenants (Theology)—   [1]Biblical teaching
    I. Title
    231.7'6   BS1199.C6

ISBN 0-85364-346-6

Australian ISBN 0-85892-249-5

Photoset in Great Britain by
Photo-graphics, Honiton, Devon
and printed for the Publishers by
A. Wheaton & Co. Ltd., Exeter, Devon

CONTENTS

CONTENTS

1

The Covenant with Noah – a Recall to a Basic Pattern of Creation

A. THE COVENANT WITH NOAH IN THE GENERAL CONTEXT OF THE FLOOD

i. *The immediate Context of Gen. 6:17–18*

'For behold, I will bring a flood of waters upon the earth, to destroy all flesh in which is the breath of life from under heaven; everything that is on the earth shall die. But I will establish my covenant with you; and you shall come into the ark, you, your sons, your wife, and your son's wives with you' (Gen. 6:17–18 RSV).[1] In this reference we meet for the first time in its some two hundred and ninety occurrences in the Old Testament the Hebrew word $b^e r \hat{\imath} t$, normally translated as 'covenant' in most English versions. Whether this translation is an accurate one is a matter to which we shall later have to give some attention. At present however we may postpone that question. The speaker in Gen. 6:17–18 is God, while the person addressed is Noah. What is being said in these two verses reflects immediately upon a decision which has just been taken. God plans virtually to bring to an end all forms of human and animate life in the universe with the account of whose origins the earlier chapters of Genesis have been concerned. A series of divine interventions had resulted in the creation of a world which God had then pronounced as 'very good', i.e., as conforming to the divine intention in every way. The successive episodes in the Book of Genesis which have brought us to the threat of Gen. 6:17–18 have witnessed progressive and increasing attempts by the human race to thwart divine purposes. The result of all this has been the content of these verses which is the divine decision taken and now announced to blot out every living thing from off the earth. Apart from Noah and his immediate family all animate life is to cease.

The surrounding context explains why God appears to have given up on the human situation and to have decided upon this cataclysmic course of action. God had seen that 'the wickedness of man was great in

---

[1]. Quotations are from the Revised Standard Version unless otherwise indicated.

11

the earth, and that every imagination of the thoughts of his heart was only evil continually' (Gen. 6:5). That reference follows, seemingly, as a direct response to the somewhat curious and difficult narrative of Gen. 6:1–4. There we find a bizarre account of intermarriages between parties who are respectively described as 'sons of God' and 'daughters of men'. No real explanatory detail is supplied and the account is altogether tantalizing and allusive. The nature of these alliances so offensive to God is not known. The explanations of the strange phrase 'sons of God' range from angelic beings to antediluvian kings to members of the 'godly' line of Seth, a son of Adam, whose descendants where particularly renowned for their fidelity. Yet the episode of Gen. 6:1–4 appears to have been the final human assertion of arrogant independence which prompted the divine response of the flood.

In response to the coming flood preparations are then put in train. Noah is chosen as one man through whom the human race is to be preserved, a command is issued to build an ark in which Noah and his family and species of living creatures etc., are to be housed and in chapter 7 the immediacy of the flood is foreshadowed. Yet a prior warning of one hundred and twenty years seems to have been given (cf. Gen. 6:3). Noah and his entourage enter the ark and after a short waiting period a forty day flood occurs, its waters cover the earth for one hundred and fifty days, after which time God causes the waters to abate over a period of one hundred and ninety days. Noah successively sends out two birds and the return of one of these indicates by what it brings that the waters have finally subsided from the earth. After a short further waiting period, Noah and his family leave the ark. The flood account concludes in chapter 8 with Noah's grateful and responsive sacrifice to God, who announces in turn that never again will a flood of such a character trouble the earth.

ii. *The Question of Extra-Biblical Parallels to the Flood – the Distinctive Character of the Biblical Account*

The student of ancient Near Eastern literature and history will quickly note a broad familiarity between the biblical flood narrative and parallel flood stories from cultures contemporary to the biblical records. The extra-biblical materials are well known in fact and well documented. Common to them all is the theme of the preservation of one man, either alone or with his family or companions and it is such a preservation which provides for the future of the human race. A common framework of creation, the rebellion of man, the technical achievements of men and then the flood argues for the interconnection of the biblical account with such comparative materials. This, however, gives no concern to the biblical interpreter who is predisposed to argue for the uniqueness of the biblical materials, for it comes as no surprise to find that the biblical record cannot be treated in isolation from the world around. Of course parallels of such a detailed character raise the question of possible literary dependence either way, as does also the existence of parallel creation accounts in the various ancient Near Eastern cultures. This is an issue which does not need to be taken up in detail here, beyond observing that the differences between the biblical and non-biblical accounts in each case make direct borrowing either way extremely improbable if not impossible. It is not however the existence of non-biblical parallel accounts of creation or the flood which is important in itself. What is important in each case is the particular use and theological exploitation made by the bible of the common materials.

This is very clearly the case in the biblical flood account where in contradistinction to any parallels, the biblical narrative advances ethical reasons for the divine action. We have been confronted in the early chapters of Genesis with the notion of a created universe backed by ethical principles which imply a moral response and we should in any case have expected this. But the flood account appears to assert that there are universal moral laws which are intended to regulate the conduct of men. If we had been left in any doubt by the narrative, since it is God who brings the flood, we are clearly reminded that these moral laws reflect the mind of the creator God who stands behind our world. A notion of such an accountability of man for moral faults introduces into the biblical flood narratives ideas which would have been generally revolutionary in the ancient world and lends to them, as we have already indicated, a theological distinctiveness.[2] Perhaps, however, the language of the narrative as it bears upon the moral domain permits us to be even more precise.

iii. *Noah and his Age – Noah as 'Righteous' in an age of 'Violence'*

When Noah is introduced into the narrative at Gen. 6:8 the contrast is drawn between him and his generation. It is at once said in v. 8 that Noah was the object of divine grace. That the application of such grace was not arbitrary is made clear by the subsequent verses in which Noah is described as a 'righteous man, blameless in his generation; Noah walked with God' (Gen. 6:9). Such a description must not be thought, however, to have provided the ground for divine action for the term 'righteous' (Heb. ṣaddîq) in the Old Testament primarily refers to conduct within a relationship. Only secondarily or derivatively is it a forensic or legal word defining status. That is to say, the term 'righteous' in the Old Testament generally refers to conduct logically arising from the prior establishment of a relationship. Such conduct would be appropriate to and consistent with the relationship established. Of

---

[2]. As Nahum M. Sarna, *Understanding Genesis*, (New York: Schocken Books, 3rd ed., 1974), pp. 52–53, notes.

course conduct of this character where the relationship is one which involves God should and could be described as moral since actions follow attitudes. The ethical ground upon which the conduct is based, however, is the prior relationship established. So verse 9 in continuing the description of Noah as righteous notes that he 'walked with God'. We may take it that such a phrase is simply an alternative description of Noah as righteous. We should understand therefore that Noah had been characterized in his age uniquely by his conduct. This had recognized and given expression to the structure of relationships ordained to exist between God and man. It is this attitude towards the Creator who stands behind the structure which constitutes his righteousness. We shall not be far wrong, indeed, if we describe such conduct as loyalty or fidelity. The nature of the relationship, however, between Noah and God as creator is not empirically verifiable, and in the final analysis we should have to term it therefore belief or trust. The further note in verse 9 that Noah was 'blameless', is merely comparative, as the following prepositional phrase, 'in his generation', makes clear. Successive Jewish commentators have noted this.

By contrast to the divine attitude to Noah, verses 11–12 show us the divine attitude to the world. The earth is described as corrupt in God's sight and as filled with 'violence' (Heb. hāmās). The consequent comment in v. 12 that, 'God saw the earth, and behold, it was corrupt; for all flesh and corrupted their way upon the earth', seems designed to refer to and reverse the favourable comment of Gen. 1:31 in which divine satisfaction with the world as created was expressed. The Hebrew term hāmās is regularly used in the Old Testament to denote the flagrant breach of a just order and particularly of an order divinely constituted.[3] The further observation in v. 12 that all flesh had corrupted their 'way' seems to be merely a slightly wider underscoring of the same reality. The entire structure of animate nature, animals as well as men ('flesh' in v. 12 is obviously used in this wider sense, cf. v. 17) had perverted natural relationships. They had overstepped the parameters of their orders (i.e. 'their way' – the basis upon which appropriate conduct should proceed) and had disturbed the boundaries within which natural laws had operated.[4] Thus, what is on view in this picture of total corruption is not merely naked human aggression which may be subsumed under the general term 'violence', with man set against man. Rather, this is a picture of the total rupture of created relationships on the part of the creature. An appropriate punishment, the flood, results and a virtual reversal of Gen. 1 follows. The basic distinction between heaven and earth effected by Gen. 1:6–8 is obliterated (cf. Gen. 7:11).

---

[3]. Cf. H. J. Stoebe in E. Jenni and C. Westermann ed., *Theologisches Handwörterbuch zum Alten Testament*, (München: Kaiser, 1971), Vol. i, p. 583b.

[4]. Note the comments by D. J. Clines, 'The Theology of the Flood Narrative', *Faith and Thought* 100 (1972–3), pp. 128–142.

The windows of heaven open to bring this about together with the other disturbing phenomena which 7:11 reports. This brings a deluge of such magnitude that it progressively engulfs the earth, then affects birds, cattle, swarming creatures and finally all men (vv. 19ff). By this order which reverses the original creation pattern the world is effectively put back into the Gen. 1:1 situation.

B. COVENANT AT GENESIS 6:18

i. *The Meaning of* B^{e}rît – *Is 'Covenant' a Suitable Translation?*

This is the general context in which the particular theological statement of Gen. 6:18 with which we commenced is made, namely, 'but I will establish my covenant with you'. There are many imponderables in this short statement. What, for instance, is the precise meaning of the verb 'establish' here and why is the verb future? Why is the notion of covenant, which will later become a pervasive biblical concept, introduced here without prior introduction and thus seemingly as an assumed reality or as a known term? What is the sense of the possessive pronoun 'my' as attached as suffix to the Hebrew word *b^{e}rît*? Further, has the covenant to be established with Noah a general theological application, so that Noah is to be construed as the general representative of humanity at large? Is he a representative figure with whom God will begin again, or is the notion of covenant in this context confined to the personal fortunes of Noah alone? And what of the meaning of the word 'covenant'? Can we take it that the use in this context is consistent with the general Old Testament use of the term. Conversely, is there no such general usage and does the term in this reference bear the stamp of a particular authorial significance so that in effect it is used in some specialised or technical sense confined to this narrative?

For the development of our argument it may be most helpful if some discussion is advanced at this point on the highly significant Hebrew term *b^{e}rît*. As has been indicated, the customary translation of this word has been 'covenant'. In recent years however, in a number of technical studies, the adequacy of that rendering has been called into question. Basically, the notion conveyed by the English word is that of agreement, with the nuance of legal agreement whereby rights and privileges, commitments and obligations are set up between two parties, an agreement which may have involved extended or protracted negotiations. Admittedly, the English word can also bear the note of an undertaking or a pledge advanced by one party and thus can mean substantially a unilateral vow or a promise. Most naturally, however, the English word embodies the idea of an agreement which has involved mutual consent. This latter meaning would not fit at Gen. 6:18, for there the divine announcement appears to point to a one-sided arrangement. We are quite in the dark as to what set of preliminaries, if any at all, constituted it or formally called it into being. The material in the context immediately adjacent to Gen. 6:18 moreover, is of little help either in determining the content of the covenant or in providing any help towards establishing an absolute meaning for the use there of *beʳît*.

Etymology often provides some help, though we should have to be cautious for we seem to be dealing at Gen. 6:18 with a term which, for the author, has already acquired considerable theological significance. The word thus may well be used there in some specialized or detailed sense. Etymology, moreover, has only a limited function and will probably do no more than suggest possibilities for meaning or the semantic range of the particular word. So that even if we could establish absolutely the etymology of the word *beʳît*, we should still be forced to come to terms with the particular contexts in which the word occurs. The case could be additionally complicated by the fact that we have no guarantee that different biblical authors would have used the word in quite the same sense. Indeed any one biblical author could have used the word differently in different contexts. Thus if the ambivalences which the English word covenant contains may be transferred to the Hebrew equivalent, then one or different writers may choose to use *beʳît* as 'mutual agreement', 'unilateral commitment', 'solemn obligation', 'vow', 'promise' or the like.

The task of determining the etymology of *beʳît* is made more difficult by the fact that there is no final consensus as to the origin of the word. However, the derivation which has most commended itself and probably ought to be adopted[5] is that which takes its meaning back to the Middle Assyrian noun *birītu*, a word whose sense is 'bond' or 'fetter'. This is the more probable, since in the Old Testament, *beʳît* when used in contexts where relationships are established or confirmed, seems usually to carry with it the note of obligation, whatever else may be implied at the same time.

ii. Bᵉrît – *Does the Term Initiate or Confirm Relationships?*

If the use of *beʳît* at Gen. 6:18 seems theologically specialized we may balance that by looking at other contexts in Genesis where the word is used in what appears to be a more secularly neutral context. We ought also to bear in mind that at the very least we may expect the Book of Genesis to display a final editorial unity. We might expect therefore some general relationships between secular and theological use of *beʳît* in Genesis. We might also expect at least some working relationship in meaning between the secular or profane use of the word in the Old

---

[5]. A survey of the possible etymologies of *beʳît* is offered by E. Kutsch, *Verheissung und Gesetz*, BZAW 131, (Berlin: De Gruyter, 1973), pp. 28–39.

Testament and its theological use since the Old Testament appears to have been very carefully theologically edited. What is more, the secular contexts in which $b^e r \hat{\imath} t$ is used in Genesis seem to be fairly representative of its very widespread use in the Old Testament as an inclusive term for economic, political or social arrangements which have been concluded on a quasi-legal basis. This is irrespective of whether the particular arrangement described as a $b^e r \hat{\imath} t$ is negotiated from a position of superior advantage or whether it is petitioned for by a weaker party.

Thus in Gen. 21:22–32 a dispute over water rights relating to the well of Beersheba is settled between Abraham and Abimelech, the Philistine king of Gerar, by a public declaration of respective rights which takes the form of an announced covenant (v. 32). A declarative oath is bound up with the conclusion of this formal contract, but the oath is clearly ancillary to the covenant itself. It is obviously an important ingredient in the total arrangement, but it is not the covenant itself. The oath appears to be confined to and to regulate the way in which the agreement is reached and to have reference to the conditions which surround it. The word 'covenant', however, appears thereafter to delimit and express the relationship existing between the two parties as a result of the agreement. Importantly and representatively of major Old Testament contexts the archaic expression for covenant conclusion, 'to cut a covenant' (Heb. $k \bar{a} r a t \ b^e r \hat{\imath} t$), is used at v. 32. We shall later have occasion to note the significance of this expression for Old Testament covenant conclusion in the light of comparative ancient Near Eastern examples.

In the two other contexts in Genesis a similar secular undertaking is concluded. In chapter 26:26–33, under circumstances remarkably similar to those of 21:22–32, Isaac reaches an accommodation with the same Abimelech, and at 31:43–54 Laban initiates and then carries through a covenant with Jacob whereby in addition to the outstanding property matters which are resolved, a delimitation of the border thereafter to exist between them is determined. The terminology and the regulative details are virtually identical with those of Gen. 21:22–32. That is to say, the covenant is 'cut', oaths are formally taken and given. There is additionally, a solemnity of the transaction in all three episodes which takes it out of the sphere of merely chance or natural relationships. In all three episodes this is made clear by the virtual parallelism in each of the three accounts of the verb 'to swear' with the phrase 'to cut a covenant' (21:27,31; 26:28,31; 31:44, 53). As well as underscoring the permanency of the arrangement, such a parallelism emphasizes, as we have indicated, that the nature of the transactions involves agreements which transcend normal or natural, social or even legal relationships. Additionally, in two of the three accounts (Isaac with Abimelech, 26:30; Jacob with Laban, 31:46), the covenant is followed by what appears to have been a sacrificial meal (certainly this is the case at Gen. 31:54). Such a feature, however, seems to witness to the new relationship so

formed rather than in itself being a constituent element of the formation. Perhaps, as D. J. McCarthy has pointed out, the meal was a symbol
of the newly created solidarity and functions thus as a type of acted
sign. Certainly, signs of one character or another seem to have been
associated with all three covenants. Moreover, the concept of a recall of
the arrangement by the designation of visible material objects as
'witnesses' occurs in two of them.[6]

Yet none of this terminology occurs in the context of Gen. 6:17–18,
and nothing other than the notion of the sign in the context to which v.
18 seems to refer, namely Gen. 9:9–17. It does not follow, however that
such terminology would have been appropriate in secular contexts but
would have been avoided as inappropriate in theological contexts. For
we should most naturally expect that a theological usage would have
developed from secular practice. The biblical usage would then invest
secular contexts with particular significance. We shall not be surprised
therefore to find all the terminology encountered in the three secular
Genesis sections to which we have referred, occuring, by such a process
of cross-fertilization, frequently, and usually within most of the divine
covenant episodes reported in the later biblical materials. The implications which the absence of this expected terminology in the related
contexts of Gen. 6:17–18 and 9:9–17 give rise to will therefore have to be
detailed and examined. But before that is done, there is a further and
most important conclusion to be drawn from the three secular covenants in Genesis to which we have made reference. This will have
considerable bearing not only upon our understanding of what is
involved in the matter of covenant conclusions, but also upon our
understanding of the nature of the covenant relationship itself.

We are not speaking here of the status of the parties involved. In the
three Genesis accounts this aspect is not given particular prominence
and the issues are left somewhat open, though as we might have
expected in each of the three cases, the respective patriarch appears to
have occupied the more elevated position. Moreover, since in the
ancient world covenants were regulative of affairs between man and
man and nation and nation we should most naturally expect that the
nature of the parties concerned would be a variable. So, in the Old
Testament the reported covenant arrangements include parity, master/
servant and suzerainty types. Rather, as McCarthy has pointed out,[7]
what is of extreme importance to note is the function that the actual
covenant conclusion, the making of the formal agreement, performs in
each episode. The very evident fact in each case is that the role of the
agreement is not to initiate a set of relationships. What the covenant

[6]. Cf. D. J. McCarthy, 'Three Covenants in Genesis', CBQ 26 (1964), pp. 179–189.

[7]. D. J. McCarthy, 'Covenant-relationships', in Questions Disputées d'ancien Testament, C.
Brekelmans ed., (Gembloux: J. Duclot, 1974), pp. 91–103.

does is formalize and give concrete expression to a set of existing arrangements. In Gen. 21 it is clear that the contacts between Abraham and Abimelech have been prolonged and extensive. Abimelech (v. 23) talks of a 'loyalty' for his part (Heb. *ḥesed*) which has characterized his dealings with Abraham in the course of the long relationships which the patriarch has had with Gerar and in particular in the matter of the associated land relationships. The point of the covenant which he now seeks is the maintenance of those relationships, i.e., the covenant will give firm quasi-legal backing to an arrangement which is already in existence. Equally in Gen. 26:23ff., the prior understanding in the matter of water access to Beersheba is to be regulated by a covenant between Abimelech and Isaac. Isaac is plainly normalizing an agreement which had formerly existed between Abraham and the Philistines (cf v. 15, 18). In 31:43 ff., the quarrel between Laban and Jacob, settled by covenant, hinges upon Laban's acquiescence to rights which are already Jacob's, namely his rights to his wives and children, livestock, etc.

This point is an important one and apart from the Genesis contexts it is supported in general principle by an examination of similar secular covenant conclusions which McCarthy has undertaken on the historical books.[8] In the case of covenants concluded between Joshua and the Gibeonites (Jos. 9), the men of Jabesh Gilead and Nahash the Ammonite (1 Sam. 11:1–3), David and Jonathan (1 Sam. 18:3), David and Abner (2 Sam. 3:12–21), David and Israel (2 Sam. 3:21; 5:1–3), Ahab of Israel and Ben Hadad of Syria (1 Kgs. 20:31–34), Jehoiada the High Priest and King Joash of Judah (2 Kgs. 11:17), though the terminology is not constant and though the constituent elements differ, and though equally the status and nature of the parties to the conclusion is not uniform, what remains the same in each case is that the covenant concluded refers to and involves a final solemn commitment by which a state of existing relationships is normalized.

One may plausibly infer from all this that covenant in the normal secular practice of the ancient world appears to have been a device whereby existing relationships which time, circumstances or other factors have brought into being, were given the semblance of legal backing in the form of a ceremony whose major thrust was that of solemn commitment. To this was given the added force of the self-imprecatory nature of the associated rites and language and associated with it was the further powerful and personally binding factor of oaths given and taken. Though not the covenant itself, the oath was a very closely related feature and its effect was to pronounce upon the undertaking parties a conditional curse should the arrangement be violated. By synecdoche the oath becomes the point of reference for the

---

8. D. J. McCarthy, 'Bᵉrît and Covenant in the Deuteronomistic History:' *SVT* 23 (1972), pp. 65–85.

total arrangement and was thus used extra- and intra-biblically as a virtual synonym for covenant.[9]

Let us now summarize our findings to this point. To judge from secular biblical examples – and these are more than likely representative of the general ancient world picture – covenants presupposed a set of existing relationships to which by formal ceremony they gave binding expression. They operated between two parties, though the status of the parties varied considerably. The language of covenant was carefully prescribed by convention. One 'cut a covenant', oath and witnesses were moreover involved, and often there was an associated sign. But in the context of Gen. 6:18 to which we now turn no one of these features is present and absences of this character in what is a passage of critical, though often undervalued importance, require explanation.

iii. *Why is the Terminology of Covenant Initiation Lacking in Gen 6:18 and 9:9ff?*

(a) Is the absence a 'source' peculiarity?

The explanation which is most commonly offered is that Gen. 6:18, like the associated passages in Gen. 9:9–17, offers us a technical use of $b^e r \hat{\imath} t$ which has developed theologically, and that the theology which supports this development and which finds expression in such Genesis passages is characteristic of the authorial strand of the Pentateuch commonly designated the Priestly source. Here it will be necessary to refer briefly to the Pentateuchal 'documentary hypothesis' of literary source criticism, whereby the first five books of the Bible are suggested to be an editorial compilation consisting of at least four identifiable strands.

> Usually they are denominated J, E (in both cases the sigla were adopted because of the source preference for a particular form of the divine name, Yahweh in the case of the J source, Elohim in the case of the E), D (predominantly Deuteronomy but the final editorship of this book is reflected elsewhere in the Pentateuch), and P (a Priestly-school composition whose interests were heavily theological and cultic and which on the usual view was a product of the exilic or the immediate post-exilic period. Customarily it is held that the school responsible for this source gave final editorial shape to the Pentateuch). The refinements which this source hypothesis has undergone in the course of this present century need not concern us. It is still widely held, though it is expressed more tentatively than it was by its nineteenth century proponents.
>
> The implications of such an approach to the Pentateuch are clearly important and can be dealt with only summarily here. If we were to concede the possibility of historically identifiable sources then the results

---

[9]. Cf. M. Weinfeld, 'B^{e}rît', *Theological Dictionary of the Old Testament*, Vol. ii. (Grand Rapids: Eerdmans 1974), p. 256.

which source criticism has offered might well seem quite plausible. These are that the sources were in fact theological interpretations of Israel's past and were delivered at significant points within its history (J is normally suggested to have written in the early post-Davidic period and in magnification of the still intact Davidic empire. E is seen as the interpreter of the older traditions for the Northern kingdom after the division of the kingdom following upon the death of Solomon. D is usually viewed as the editor of a corpus of literature running from Deuteronomy to 2 Kings, the total body of which is then suggested to offer a rationale of Israel's history in an endeavour to account for the position of Judah in exile. P is considered to have been the interpreter of Israel's theological traditions for the re-emerging post-exilic community.) The effect of all this is to make a homogeneous approach to the literature of the first five books of the Bible impossible. What emerges from the Pentateuch on this view are different (and indeed competing) theologies, each arising from different cycles of tradition or different policies of selection of details, each representing different historical and socially conditioned interests. On this view the construction of a theology of the Pentateuch would be a complicated and tortuous process which must first proceed by way of theologies derived from the individual sources. Hopefully some final common factors might emerge from them. Since in modern biblical criticism the approach to the Pentateuch finds its complement in a similar atomistic view of the individuality of other biblical books, the prospect, given this approach, of erecting a biblical theology for the whole of the Old Testament is equally remote.

Issues of this character are not capable of simple resolution, and since they are bound up so pervasively with most modern approaches to the Old Testament, they cannot be ignored in our exposition. Certainly it cannot and should not be suggested that biblical materials should not be exposed to literary critical examination. One may even go so far as to agree that in a complex document like the Pentateuch, embodying materials spread over an identifiable historical period of something like six hundred years from Abraham to Moses, the existence of some source material, primary documents of some character, must be supposed. The point of departure would, however, come on the question of their identification in terms of strands and thus also their precise dating. But, leaving aside reservations of this character, it is now becoming increasingly evident that whatever may have been the nature of source materials underlying the Pentateuch, the individual books have been so carefully edited as to make any source theory impossible of precise verification.

Leaving to one side such obvious issues as the dating of individual books and the identity of authorship, questions on which a consensus would not be forthcoming, the way forward in biblical scholarship might well be the simple construction of a theology of the Old Testament on the assumption that the thirty-nine canonical books have at least some literary association. Of course, this would still leave open questions such as the relationship of this derived theology to the history of Israel which it is supposed to reflect. This is a thorny issue on which there is bound to be continued disagreement. But it would be a significant forward move in Old Testament studies if less attention were paid to the fruitless and inevitably subjective task of attempting to construct a history or a typology of the development of Israelite religion, and much more emphasis were to be directed towards the construction of an Old Testament theology from within the framework of traditionally received components, namely the Canon.[10]

We cannot leave this general question without making particular reference to the flood narrative to illustrate the difficulties which confront the source critic. This is *the* narrative which has often been supposed best to exemplify the way in which details from two of the classic sources, 'J' and 'P' have been carefully woven together to provide a final unit, within which, however, the doublets and overlaps are still evident to the reader.

> Usually Gen. 6 is said to exhibit a twofold introduction to the flood (6:1–8 J, 6:9–22, P) while Gen. 7 – 8 is thought to provide a careful editorial construction of two combined sources, 'J' and 'P'. Two examples of recent reservations about such traditional critical views will be sufficient to indicate the fragility of such source approaches. In an examination of Gen. 7:6–17, a section traditionally dissected between 'J' (7:7–10, 12, 16b) and 'P' (7:6, 11, 13–16a, 17), Francis I. Andersen has demonstrated that the whole is a single grammatico-syntactical unit in which stylistic and elaborate syntactical constructions bind the whole together.[11] Careful work of this character in the usually supposed doublet areas would probably lead to similar conclusions. Turning to the flood narrative as a whole, Gordon Wenham has argued for the tightly constructed palistrophic unity of the entire narrative. He has demonstrated the chronological consistency of the whole, a point of frequent dispute, and he has, moreover, pointed to the need of the whole for the purpose of drawing parallels with other Mesopotamian accounts.[12]

(b) And thus is the language technically characteristic of the Priestly Writer?

All this makes any emphatic assertion that Gen. 6:18 is Priestly a little less convincing than it may once have been. Such an assertion is normally backed by the appeal to the use of $b^e r \hat{\imath} t$ in Gen. 6:18 and the associated Genesis references as technical and characteristic of the Priestly source. Particularly characteristic of this source, it is claimed, is

---

[10]. The need for biblical theology to take this direction is emphasized by B. S. Childs in *Biblical Theology in Crisis*, (Philadelphia: Westminster, 1970).

[11]. F. I. Andersen, *The Sentence in Biblical Hebrew*, (The Hague: Mouton, 1974), pp. 126–6.

[12]. G. J. Wenham, 'The Coherence of the Flood Narrative', *VT* XXVIII (1978), pp. 336–348. Wenham admits that skilful redaction could have blended sources together, but the force of his work is to make discernible sources less likely, if not improbable.

the use of the Hebrew expression *hēqîm bᵉrît* in the verse (to establish a covenant, cf. also Gen. 9:9, 11, 17; 17:7, 19, 21; Exod. 6:4), which is used, so the assertion continues, in the highly individualistic sense of 'taking an oath'. S. McEvenue, who has recently systematized the evidence for this approach,[13] notes that the phrase *hēqîm bᵉrît* occurs only four other times in the Old Testament (Lev. 26:9; Deut. 8:18, 2 Kgs. 23:3; Jer. 34:18), all in the consistent sense of fulfilling an oath which had been taken earlier.

If McEvenue is correct that the language of Gen. 6:18 is both Priestly and technical then an explanation has been offered for the remarkable absence of normal covenant terminology in almost all of the divine covenant sections in Genesis,[14] with Gen. 15:18 providing the only exception. There the normal terminology of 'cut a covenant' occurs. But we have argued that there is no certainty that Gen. 6:18 could or need be assigned to any defined source and we will now suggest that the stylistic reasons which are advanced for the occurrence of the peculiar covenant vocabulary in this verse are neither a necessary nor a sufficient explanation for their appearance.

The four additional cases to which McEvenue appeals do not indicate that *bᵉrît* is used in any one of them in the peculiar sense of 'oath'. Deut. 8:18, it is true, brings together the two notes. It is necessary to 'establish' (*hēqîm*) the covenant which has been previously 'sworn' but there is no need here to give *bᵉrît* McEvenue's suggested sense of oath. Deuteronomy is well aware of the distinction between to 'swear an oath' and to 'swear a covenant', as a comparison of the texts Deut. 7:8 and 8:18 will demonstrate. The closeness of the relationship of oath and covenant has already been admitted and this no doubt accounts for the fluidity of the terminology that we find in Deuteronomy. But the two concepts are distinct in Deuteronomy as the evidence of 29:14 clearly indicates, where the expected terminology of covenant conclusion *kārat bᵉrît* occurs together with the addition of an oath, a conjunction of terms which has led to the RSV translation of 'sworn covenant'. Leviticus 26:9 offers no support since the occurence of the phrase *hēqîm bᵉrît* there is unaccompanied by any reference to an oath, while 2 Kings 23:3 is positively unhelpful to McEvenue since in that context Josiah 'cuts a covenant' with the people to 'establish (*hēqîm*) the words of this covenant that were written in this book'. The same may be said for Jer. 34:18, for not only is there no specific reference to an oath in that verse, but what is there 'established' is a covenant which the parties addressed had previously 'cut' (Jer. 34:8). McEvenue does not mention a further occurrence of the phrase *hēqîm bᵉrît* at Ezek. 16:62 where in the same context at Ezek. 16:59 oath and covenant are held as distinct. McEvenue's major appeal is to the supposed P context of Exod. 6:4–8 in which the opening and closing

---

[13]. S. E. McEvenue, *The Narrative Style of the Priestly Writer*, Analecta Biblica 50, (Rome: Biblical Institute Press, 1971), p. 74.

[14]. Apart from the occurrences of *bᵉrît* referred to, the remaining instance is in the secular context of Gen. 14:13.

verses do offer some connection between covenant and the notion of oath. There is no necessary equation between these two elements, however, and that passage seems best taken as a reference to divine fidelity to the Abrahamic covenant as subsequently repeated in the experience of Isaac and Jacob and as reinforced by the swearing of an oath. It might be pointed out that the New Testament was aware that the patriarchal covenant and oath were two separate items. In a context in which the trial of Abraham's faith is referred to, the writer to the Hebrews (Heb. 6:17) avers that an oath was added to the previous promises and thus there were constituted the 'two unchangeable things' (Heb. 6:18).

The suggestion, therefore, that $b^e rît$ is used at Gen. 6:18 in the special sense of oath does not commend itself. This suggestion, moreover, makes the verse merely anticipatory of the later covenant context of Gen. 9:8ff in which the covenant with Noah is supposed to be concluded, and thus brought into being as a new thing. McEvenue[15] has rightly noted that Gen.6:18 with its reference to 'my covenant' which is to be 'established' is enigmatic and provides us with no indication of what the substance of the covenant referred to may be. He is further correct in noting the very close connection between the contexts of Gen. 6:17–18 and 9:8ff where specific details of the established covenant arrangements are provided. Yet what is not clear from Gen. 9:8ff is whether the detail there advanced refers to the beginning of the covenant with Noah or whether alternatively, the context here tells us what will result from divine adherence to the arrangements already referred to as 'my covenant' in Gen. 6:18. Indeed, the most natural interpretation of this verse is that an existing arrangement to be preserved is referred to, to which no more specific appeal is required than the denomination of it as 'my covenant'. Of course, the manner in which it will be preserved may well be specifically designated in Gen. 9:8ff in this sense Gen. 6:18 could be said to be anticipatory. But both passages will then refer to some definite arrangement, prior to both, which is being upheld.

(c) Absence of the terminology 'cut a covenant'

McEvenue has additionally suggested that the P author had carefully avoided at Gen. 6:18 the normal term for covenant conclusion, $kārat\ b^e rît$ in his theological presentation of covenant as sworn oath. If he is correct, and since on his view the inauguration of the arrangement of Noah as future is being referred to at Gen. 6:18, then the phrase $h\bar{e}qîm$ $b^e rît$ would be merely one of the many alternative expressions which are customarily thought to have been available to biblical writers to introduce the notion of covenant inception.[16]

---

[15]. McEvenue, op.cit., p. 46.

[16]. Weinfeld, op.cit., p. 260.

A perusal of the Old Testament evidence makes it clear, however, that the phrase *kārat b^erît* is universally used throughout the Old Testament period by biblical writers to describe the point of covenant entry. Thus, the expression is used to indicate the initiation of the Abrahamic covenant (Gen. 15:18), the Sinai covenant (Exod. 24:8), the Davidic covenant (Ps. 89:3) and the Jeremianic new covenant (Jer. 31:31). The position is the same in the case of Old Testament secular covenants and the other expressions which are often cited as the equivalent of *kārat b^erît* and thus as offering an indication of covenant point of entry are not to be so understood. Thus Heb. *^ābar* ('enter') at Deut. 29:12 ('that you may enter into the sworn covenant of the Lord your God') refers there to the adoption by the community of the Mosaic covenant already existing. At 1 Sam. 20:8 Heb. *hēbî* ('bring') is used, but the reference there is to the covenant between David and Jonathan concluded with the formula *kārat b^erît* at 1 Sam. 18:3. At 2 Sam. 23:5 the covenant with David is referred to as 'made' ('He has made with me an everlasting covenant'), i.e. Heb. *sîm*, but this seems a reference to the covenant previously established at 2 Sam. 7 and which is elsewhere described as having conventionally been 'cut' (Ps. 89:3). At Jer. 34:10 certain 'who have entered into the covenant' (Heb. *bô'*) are mentioned, but the covenant in mind is that which has been 'cut' between the parties at Jer. 34:8. 2 Chr. 15:12 which describes the response to King Asa's reform movement and his overtures to the North and which speaks of those 'that entered (Heb. *bô'*) into a covenant to seek the Lord, the God of their fathers' is seemingly difficult. It must be pointed out, however, that the reference has the Heb. definite article attached to the noun covenant, and this then probably suggests that what is in mind is the renewal or the re-enactment at a gathering of North and South, of the older arrangements which had characterized the undivided kingdom.

(d) Is the covenant with Noah established or confirmed?

In short, outside the Book of Genesis the terminology of covenant entry appears to have been consistently maintained.[17] Such a consistency must cause us to reflect whether by the use of *hēqîm* with *b^erît* in the contexts of Gen. 6:18; 9:8ff (and Gen. 17) – all of which refer to covenants as 'established' or 'given' (Heb. *nātan* Gen. 17:2) – the beginning of a new covenant arrangement is being referred to, or whether in each case the continuation of some prior understanding is in mind. A decision here is bound up with the way in which the Heb. verb *hēqîm* is to be taken in these references.

This verbal element is a causative theme of the verb, derived from the primary verb *qûm*, an intransitive verb meaning to 'arise', to 'stand'. Thus, in a causative sense this verb will mean to 'cause to stand' and

---

[17]. The only apparent exception to the consistent use of this terminology is Ezek. 16:8. The context there is that of a marriage union between God and Israel in which the legal formulary may have been thought to be inappropriate. Ezekiel is no stranger to the traditional usage (cf. Ezek. 34:25, 37:26).

therefore to 'erect', but also equally frequently to 'establish' (by causing
something to stand) and hence to 'maintain'. In theological contexts in the
Old Testament the sense of 'maintain' is frequent. So the causative is used
of covenant requirements which have been adhered to Deut 27:26, 2 Kgs.
23:3), or commandments which have been kept (1 Sam. 15:11; 2 Kgs.
23:24) or by this construction the fidelity of God to his word is asserted
(Neh. 9:8). The causative of the verb is also familiar and frequent in the
sense of 'carry through', and thus, depending upon the context, 'establish'
or 'fulfil'. So God 'confirms' the word which he swore to the patriarchs
(Deut. 9:5; cf. similarly 1 Sam. 1:23; Isa. 44:26; Jer. 28:6). At 2 Sam. 7:25
David prays that God might 'confirm' the prior promises of that chapter
(similarly, 1 Kgs. 2:4; 6:12; 8:20). At 1 Kgs. 12:15 the divine word given to
Ahijah of Shiloh and bearing upon the division of the kingdom after the
death of Solomon, is 'fulfilled'. At Jer. 11:5; 23:20; 29:10; 30:24; 33:14, the
verb expresses a divine intention to carry out or refers to the divine
execution of what has previously been promised. At Gen. 26:3 God
appears to Isaac with a repetition of the promises given to Abraham to
'fulfil the oath' sworn to his father and we may also mark Num. 30:14
where a husband 'establishes' his wife's vow by refusing to annul it.

Evidence of this character makes it more than likely that in contexts
where $h\bar{e}q\hat{i}m$ $b^e r\hat{i}t$ stands (Gen. 6:18; 9:9, 11, 17; 17:7, 19, 21; Exod. 6:4;
Lev. 26:9; Deut. 8:18; 2 Kgs. 23:3) the institution of a covenant is not
being refered to but rather its perpetuation. We have already virtually
suggested in passing that this was the case in regard to the citations
referred to other than those in Genesis. We may probably now surmise
that what is being referred to in Gen. 6:18 is some existing arrangement
presumably imposed by God without human concurrence, since it is
referred to as 'my covenant'. Despite the human sinful condition, he is
determined to maintain it. The nature and the details of this arrangement are not clear from Gen. 6:18, though they might with some
probability have been inferred from the course of the Genesis narrative
to that point. The details will become quite clear, however, when Gen.
9:1ff is reached.

C. AFTER THE FLOOD

i. *The New Beginning of Gen. 9:1ff*

When the flood had run its full course Noah is divinely commissioned
to leave the ark (Gen. 8:15ff) and a sacrificial response to the divine
deliverance follows. The divine commitment, given at this time, never
again to send a flood ushers in presumably the time of forbearance to
which St. Paul refers in Rom. 3.26. The reference to the heart of man in
Gen. 8:21 which remains unchanged by the experience of the flood
refers initially to the eight who have been saved and thus throws into
clear relief the nature of Noah's righeousness as something extrinisic to

him. Since we are virtually being told that a deluge would be an appropriate response by God to the sin of any age, mankind has been preserved by grace alone. Until the end of time the continued existence of the created order will thus be grounded simply in the gracious nature of the divine character.

It is under these circumstances that the new beginning which is the subject of Gen. 9:1ff occurs. The similarities between 9:1–2 and Gen. 1:28 are strikingly obvious and make the concept of this new beginning clear. Man is again, as he was in Gen. 1, commissioned to be fruitful and multiply, to fill the earth and to repopulate, he is assured that his status and role in the order of creation as the divine image (9:6) remains preserved, and the formularies of 6:18 are then repeated and amplified in 9:8ff. The covenant is now seen explicitly to involve Noah's seed (9:9). That is to say, the implications contained in the salvation of the eight are now made clear. What is also now clear is that the covenant referred to in 6:18 was not with Noah personally but with Noah representatively. The covenant referred to is designed to provide for the future of the human race and is therefore universal in its scope. In the most general sense it is determinative for the history of mankind and there can thus be no question of conditions which may attach to it to control its acceptance. The providential care of God as Gen. 8:22 had indicated, will again be extended to all men. Such a concept of covenant does not therefore take into account particular historical circumstances under which it may have arisen, it is clearly not contingent upon human reaction to it nor even dependent upon human knowledge of it. In the most general terms it proclaims the lordship of creation and the care of the creator for what has been created. It is thus an indication that behind the unchanging laws of nature to which Gen. 8:21–22 made reference and whereby the sun will rise upon the just and the unjust there stands the personal Lord of creation himself.

ii. *Sequence of Thought in Gen. 9:1–17*

We now turn to Genesis 9, for a detailed treatment of vv. 1–13. With chapter 9 the set of covenant relationships which the preservation of Noah and his family maintained, but which the flood threatened to abrogate, is taken up again. The argument of the chapter is progressive and before the question of covenant itself is broached with obvious reference to Gen. 6:18, there is a return through Gen. 9:1–7 to Genesis 1. Noah is now set before us as a second Adam. Gen. 9:1–7, as the inclusive phrases at the end of v. 1 and in v. 7 indicate, is a clearly defined section whose purpose is to indicate to us that though Noah is invited to begin again and is armed with Adam's mandate, it is a changed world in which he is summoned to operate. He is still to function as the divine image (v. 6), but it is now a fallen world in which he moves. The tenor of Gen. 9:1–7 recognizes that the harmonious set of relationships which characterized the ordered world of chapters 1–2 is now sadly fractured. Now the animal world lives in fear and dread of man, for the conditions of paradisiacal peace which had previously prevailed among the creatures have been breached. The whole creation thus has begun to groan in travail. Man now becomes explicitly flesh-eating; formerly he had lived under a vegetarian regimen (Gen. 1:29). He himself now lives in a world in which he is under threat from his fellow men. The fact of life, present since Gen. 4, is now specifically legislated for (9:6). As the image of God, however, man is sacrosanct; an attack upon him is virtually an assault upon God.

Gen. 9:8–17 then appears expansively and progressively to restate Gen. 6:18. The Gen. 6:18 notion is widened in 9:9 to include Noah's descendants, thus making the representative position of Noah clear. We must pause here, however, and ask ourselves what is the nature of the possessive pronoun attached as suffix to the Hebrew noun $b^e r\hat{i}t$, i.e. what in fact is the force of the 'my' of 'my covenant'. If the term covenant on any understanding has inbuilt into it the note of obligation,[18] certain questions follow. Is this a covenant by which men are obligated, or does God bind himself and thus make mankind the beneficiary of the obligation so undertaken? The context of both chapters 6:18 and 9:9, 11, 15 strongly suggests that the latter view is to be supported. What is being maintained is upheld in spite of human failure, and in the Gen. 9 context specifically, independently of human knowledge. It is clear from this chapter that it is not required that man should understand the nature of the covenant; God simply obligates himself to maintain it so long as the course of history proceeds.

iii. *Covenant in Gen. 9:9–17 and the Sign of the Bow*

For our understanding of the biblical notion of covenant this point is an important one and it is fully borne out by the course of the continuing argument in Gen. 9:9ff. Gen. 9:10 widens our concept of covenant, for the arrangement is now seen to include every living creature, birds, cattle and the beasts of the earth from whom no response which could have prompted the initial covenant agreement, could have been expected. Clearly then, as the emphasis in Gen. 9:1–7 has already led us to expect, the stress in the covenant agreement is upon man by virtue of his role in the created order. Equally clearly v. 10 informs us that though man is a necessary ingredient in the total plan, the overall blueprint is much more extensive. In Gen. 9:12, a verse to which we must return, a gracious assurance in the form of a sign is given to that part of the covenant circle which had been threatened by the flood (i.e. man and all living creatures). However, it is a fair inference from v. 13 that the parameters of covenant must be drawn even more widely in this section

---

18. The thesis of E. Kutsch, *BZAW* 131, is in fact that $b^e r\hat{i}t$ means obligation.

than they have been so far. In that verse the arrangement is said to stand between God and all the earth, i.e., between God and the fullest and final sphere in which man, around whom the covenant has been structured, will move. We may take it that the aim of this covenant is total harmony between man and his world. It may be a further and a warranted inference, however, that the position of the bow as over-arching, as it were, heavens and earth, speaks for the potential harmony of all creation under this arrangement.

Before drawing more general inference from all of this, we direct attention to the role of the sign in Gen. 9:12–17. We note that the promise of the enduring nature of the renewed structure is fortified by an appeal to what, from this point onwards, will be the tangible evidence for its continuance. The sign of the bow in the clouds is a comprehensive guarantee of the perpetuation of creation. Implicitly the nature of this covenant renewal sign carries with it the endorsement of the aims of the original creation and the certainty of their fulfilment. In all of this human response is, in effect unnecessary, as it was in the initial establishment of the order in Gen. 1.

Verses 12 and 17 by the inclusion of common material delimit the section and by this reiteration stress the importance of the sign. Verse 12 names the form of the sign as the rainbow to be set in the clouds. We are not told whether we are to understand the rainbow as now for the first time introduced, or whether an outstanding point of natural phenomena is being invested at this stage with new significance. But its purpose is to offer an appropriate assurance that never again will the earth be destroyed, and as a nature sign it is clearly as suitable as it is extensive. The term 'bow' is, other than in the rainbow contexts of the Old Testament, always used for an offensive weapon, and this has occasioned expositors to take their cue from some extra-biblical para-llels and to suggest that the hanging of such a bow in the sky was a divine declaration of peace. Parallels are adduced between this action and that which occurs in the Babylonian creation epic Enuma Elish, where Marduk, the champion of the gods and the vanquisher of the chaos dragon Tiamat, (after his victory) hung up his bow in the heavens as a constellation. There is, however, absolutely no trace of any mythological parallels relating to divine combat in the flood account. Like the infrequency of the phenomenon in Palestine itself, [19] the rainbow is rarely alluded to in Scripture and where it does appear it is always associated with 'cloud' as a naturally assumed connection. It is referred to in the judgement vision of Ezekiel 1 (Ezek. 1:28) where it is intimately connected with the manifestation of the divine glory, another judgement feature in that narrative. The only other and suggestive scriptural mention is at Revelation 4:3, where the judgement

---

[19]. Cf. P. A. H. DeBoer, "Quelques remarques sur l'Arc dans la Nuée", *Questions Disputées d'ancien Testament*, C. Brekelmans ed., p. 110, n. 11.

nature of that vision seems again to connect it with Ezekiel 1, though it should also be noted that the doxology with which the heavenly scene concludes in Revelation 4, celebrates God as creator and sustainer of the universe. In any case the significance of the bow in Gen. 9 is as the witness to the introduction of a stable era of order in the world, and an indication that the providential care of God for his creatures will not thereafter cease.

Verses 14–16 explain in some detail the function of the sign. Broadly speaking, the function of any sign in Scripture where God is concerned, is to indicate a divine revelatory action which is meant to convey the certainty that what the sign points to will either continue to exist or has now come into being. Clearly the bow of Gen. 9 is this type of faith sign. Thus, it is not a natural sign whereby one would inferentially be able to pass at once from the sign to what has been signified. It is a conventional sign which depends for its understanding upon the revelation which accompanies it. It does not identify the covenant, let alone establish it, it rather serves to confirm a faith in what is known to have been established. Divine signs are most often used in Scripture this way, namely not to capture the attention of the viewer, but to indicate to him that he must pass on from the sign to the substance of the sign. In this way Deut. 11:3 reminds the hearers that the signs (and deeds) which God performed in Egypt were not merely a demonstration of power in their own right, but were designed to motivate Israel to love God and to keep his commandments. Yet the signs were not themselves sufficient to achieve this. Words were required, to explain their function, as Deut. 11:8 thus indicates. Likewise the twelve stones erected by Joshua at Gilgal immediately after the crossing of the Jordan (Josh. 4:3ff) had no value apart from the interpretation of their significance given by Joshua, and the historical event to which they were attached.

Signs of some character or other, as we have seen, were often attached to secular covenants and similarly faith signs are frequently found in the Old Testament as linked with divine covenant ratification or renewal. So, apart from the bow of Gen. 9, circumcision is added at Gen. 17:11 and later the Sabbath (Exod. 31:13, 17, cf. Ezek. 20:12, 20). These three signs are not, however, uniform in their significance. The purpose of the rainbow in Gen. 9 is to indicate God's intention for the future; it operates thus by way of reassurance. We are told that its major function is to remind God of the obligations to which he has committed himself and that it is really addressed to a wider circle than those to whom the word accompanying the sign has been committed. Thus v. 13 indicates that the bow is a sign of the covenant existing between God and the earth and it is clear that the sign is not essentially tied to human cognition of it. It is rather for God, and he will 'remember' it (v. 15), and it is he who will look upon it and be reminded of its nature.[20]

---

[20]. On the function of the sign in Gen. 9 cf. Michael V. Fox, 'The Sign of the Covenant', RB 81 (1974) pp. 557–596. Mention should be made here of the use of Heb. zōkar, 'remember',

Of course, we must not think that something additional to and outside of the divine nature is necessary to stimulate God to provide for the obligation to which he has committed himself, for one would hesitate to ascribe memory lapses to the Creator of the universe! For the use of 'remember' in the Old Testament is hardly ever, as it invariably is with us, simply a reference to the power of the psychological recall of the past. Biblically, when the past is 'remembered', what is often meant is that what is done in present experience is logically dependent upon some past event. This is what is meant in Genesis 9. Similarly, when God 'remembered' Noah at Gen. 8:1, what is being said is that he activated his intention to rescue him by causing a wind, at that time, to blow upon the earth to assist the waters to subside. Likewise, when God 'remembered' Hannah (1 Sam. 1:19) he took action to carry out his promise to her, to provide her with a son. In short, the rainbow as a 'sign of the covenant' (Gen. 9:12), does not identify the covenant or locate it, nor point to its existence. Its function as a permanent sign is to operate independently in the service of the covenant as a reminder to God of its existence. The permanency of the sign is in effect a guarantee of the permanency of the covenant.

iv. *Summary of the Argument to this Point*

Our examination so far of the notion of $b^e r \hat{\imath} t$ in Gen. 6:18 and Gen. 9:8–17 has pointed to the unilateral character of the covenant referred to. The initiative has lain entirely with God. Responses of course have been and would have been demanded, but they are responses which would have brought with them the blessings which attached to the covenant on the one hand, or the curses which the rejection of the covenant would have invoked on the other. They are no part of the covenant itself, but rather results of attitudes taken to the covenant. We would therefore agree that $b^e r \hat{\imath} t$ in its theological use as far as we have proceeded denotes 'obligation' or 'commitment' and would agree, further, with those who have suggested[21] that covenant, though an established translation, is a somewhat misleading rendering. There is nothing in the background of the word which would argue otherwise, in spite of a comment such as that of W. Eichrodt whose Old Testament Theology proceeds from such a strong covenant base:

> The use of the covenant concept in secular life argues that the religious $b^e r \hat{\imath} t$ was always regarded as a bilateral relationship; for even though the burden is most unequally distributed between the

---

in the *Qal*, of God, in the O.T. The point is important in relation to both the present context and Jer. 31:34. Cf. B. S. Childs, *Memory and Tradition in Israel* (London: S.C.M., 1962), p. 33 for the observation that although the divine memory is not identical with action, it is not divorced from it.

[21]. E. Kutsch, op.cit., p. 206.

two contracting parties, this makes no difference to the fact that the
relationship is still essentially two-sided.[22]

This takes too little account of the entire biblical presentation, since
Eichrodt has focused essentially on the Sinai covenant almost to the
entire exclusion of other Old Testament divine covenant material.
Naturally, under the circumstances with Eichrodt presumes to prevail,
namely that of 'two contracting parties', there must be mutuality, but
we are certainly confronted in Genesis with a sequence in which there
can be no question of two parties being involved.

Again, we have noted so far that the appearance and the use of the
word $b^e r\hat{\imath}t$ succeeds the set of relationships by which it was brought into
being. Our examination of the flood narrative has sent us back to Gen. 1
to examine the nature of the relationships which are set up there. There
is a reservation, however, which must be raised at this point. Secular
covenants in the Bible appear to have come about because of the
discovery of mutual concerns, or the recognition of mutual interests, or
the expansion of personal trust. Here there was room for mutuality,
even in the case of suzerain/vassal arrangements. In the religious use of
the word in the Old Testament it is difficult to see how these could have
provided an analogous case. A pledge of divine obligation does not
follow the development of mutual relationships, discovery of personal
interests, etc.; by the very nature of such a pledge it must be co-
terminous with the onset of the relationship itself. In this way the
absence of the term $k\bar{a}rat\ b^e r\hat{\imath}t$ in the Gen. 1–11 context is explained. It is
difficult to see how it could have been used. 'Cut a covenant' implies
two identifiable parties who are concerned in the ceremony. In fact the
phrase $k\bar{a}rat\ b^e r\hat{\imath}t$ is only very rarely used in the Old Testament without
a connecting preposition which serves to indicate the nature of the
arrangement as it affects another party or to indicate the other party
precisely involved. There could, however, in the nature of the case, be
no question of two parties involved in any basic arrangement which is
entered into by God by virtue of creation itself. If then, as we have
suggested, the first reference to a covenant as already existing (Gen.
6:18) refers to a divine relationship established by the fact of creation
itself, the absence of the standard terminology of covenant initiation
from the early Genesis narratives is explained. Likewise the presence of
the expected terminology when new initiatives are made by God at
various stages of Israel's history is equally understandable, since an
historical entity with whom a covenant may be 'cut' is in those cases
identifiable (i.e. Abraham, Israel, David, etc.). And it would further
have to remain a matter of dogmatic assumption – though verified
clearly in the case of the renewed pledge to Noah – that the divine
purposes which the initiation of relationships by God was designed to

---

[22]. *Theology of the Old Testament*, vol i (London: S.C.M., 1961), p. 37. Eichrodt is singled
out for special mention here, because of the heavy covenantal emphasis of his theology.

achieve, would be fulfilled. This point will be elaborated later, but it will be sufficient for the moment to observe that God could not have been expected to rest content with the frustration of the intentions which he so plainly endorsed in Gen. 1:31 and the progressive unfolding of the account of Gen. 1–11 shows us that this indeed proved to be so.

v. Details of the Covenant with Creation – Gen. 1–3

(a) The divine image and kingship

Gen. 9:1–2 had begun the post-flood era with the renewal of the mandate given to man in 1:28. The remainder of the covenant renewal material of Gen. 9 has been concerned to guarantee the order over which man will exercise his mandate. But the substance of the covenant with which we are concerned is clearly a commitment implicit in the total creation account of Gen. 1:1 – 2:4a. Such a commitment was intended to achieve the purpose of creation. As the emphasis in 9:1–7 by its position in the renewal narrative suggests, it is through man that divine purposes will be realised. Man is set over the created order, yet his future cannot be considered separately from the world over which he is set. The refusal of the Creator to permit the divine purposes to be frustrated, either in regard to man himself or his world, must necessarily therefore have redemptive consequences which will concern not only man, but finally his world as well. For the redemption of the creature will involve nothing less finally than the redemption of all creation and we are well aware that this is the goal towards which biblical revelation progressively moves.

We are required at this point to offer some brief exposition of Genesis 1 – 3, to note the nature of the obligation laid upon man, the way in which man defaulted, and what, in fact, was the significance of that lapse. Our most natural starting point will be the question of the divine image in man since in the context of Gen. 1:26–28 it is closely bound up with the dominion over creation which he is to exercise, and moreover, it is the point to which Gen. 9:1–7 returns. There would be general agreement among expositors that the older notions which viewed the divine image as something innate, i.e. as original righteousness forfeited as a result of the fall, or similar positions which regarded the image as natural reason or some other intrinsic property which identified man as man, did not do justice to the biblical terms used (i.e. 'image' and 'likeness') in Gen. 1:26. Insofar as such approaches failed to take account of the 'visibility' of man to which the concept of Heb. ṣelem ('image') most certainly refers[23] they were unsatisfactory. Man, moreov-

---

[23]. Claus Westermann, *Genesis 1–11*, Biblischer Kommentar altes Testament (Neukirchen-Vluyn: Neukirchener Verlag, 1974), pp. 201–14 provides a summary of opinion offered on the question of the 'image'.

er, is defined in Ps. 8:5 (with obvious reference to Gen. 1:26) in terms of his relationship to God, and in kingship language. There is much therefore to be said for the view that the notion of the image of God in Gen. 1 is primarily to be understood in terms of function and as referring to the whole man.[24] By creation, man is then the visible representative in the created world of the invisible God. If we may anticipate the course of later Old Testament development, we may say that man stands over against God in terms of the function that man will exercise in the world in almost the precisely analogous representative sense that the Messiah or king of Israel does as the national representative of divine rule.

If man in the image is thus being viewed in terms of a representative but derived kingship role in Gen. 1, then standing behind the representation, and being the reality of which the image is but the shadow, is the kingship of God. It has often been noted that the mode of expression in which the creation account of Gen. 1 proceeds is that of royal fiat (cf. 'Let there be light!'). This is simply a further allusively associated indication that it is with the theology of God's kingship that the Bible so transparently begins. Clearly the kingship of God is not a theological awareness which is patiently developed by Israel as a result of analogies which have been read out of Israel's political development; rather it was the theological datum from which the basis of Israelite faith proceeded. It would provide a theological understanding of all Israelite social and governmental relationships as they would develop. It would further give direction to the projections of the final world order which became in the later Old Testament the subject of prophetic and apocalyptic expectation.

(b) The goal of the covenant – 'rest'

The creation account, however, does not conclude with man and his mandate, for man is not the consummation of the account, though he is the agent through whom the aims of creation will be realised. Gen. 2: 1–4a forms the conclusion to the account of creation. The symmetry of the eight creative acts spread over the preceding six days, and set in what seems to be an inner parallelism and progression between days one to three and four to six, receives its real significance from the addition of the seventh day. By the divine rest on the seventh day the goal of creation is indicated, a goal which will be maintained notwithstanding sustained human attempts to vitiate it. Not only does the

---

[24]. Phyllis Bird has shown that behind the term 'image of God' lies the royal ideology of the ancient Near East (cf. the use of *salmu*, cognate to Heb. *ṣelem* 'image' in Akkadian). Not relationships or essence is so much on view in Gen. 1:26 as man as the possessor of royal power. cf. P. Bird, 'Male and Female He Created Them; Gen. 1:27b in the context of the Priestly Account of Creation' *HTR* 74 (1981) p. 142, n. 34.

seventh day rest note the goal to which creation points, but it is the call to man to begin history holding firmly in view that 'the goal of creation, and at the same time the beginning of all that follows, is the event of God's Sabbath freedom, Sabbath rest and Sabbath joy, in which man, too, has been summoned to participate.'[25]

This notion of divine rest which man is thereafter invited to share becomes a dominant one in the later Old and New Testaments and the institution of the Sabbath (Exod. 31:13–17) becomes the particular covenantal sign of the concept. So the sabbath, which brings to an end the week, becomes for Israel an invitation to enter into, and rejoice in, the blessings of creation. It is noteworthy that when the sabbath is legislated for (Exod. 20:8–11), it is brought not only into a framework of redemption, but also into particular connection with creation. On the sabbath, therefore, Israel is to reflect upon the question of ultimate purposes for herself as a nation, and for the world over which she is set. For in pointing back to creation, the sabbath points also to what is yet to be, to the final destiny to which all creation is moving. We may note in this connection the perceptive remark of Claus Westermann regarding the nature of the sabbath: 'What is peculiar to the holy day in the course of every day happenings is that it points to the goal of the creature which God has created in his image. The work which has been laid on man is not his goal. His goal is the eternal rest which has been suggested by the rest of the seventh day.'[26]

The remainder of Genesis 2 seems primarily an exposition of chapter 1:26–28 in which the creation of man as a species has been discussed and where the dominion given to man is thus conferred upon mankind. In Genesis 2 we are in effect told how this dominion mandate which is his within the covenant structure, is to operate. Here we note that it seems to be the intention of the writer in 2:8 to indicate that man was created outside Eden and then placed within the garden. The garden is presented as a centre of world blessing. In it arose the world river which divided outside the garden into four systems. The garden also operates as a divine sanctuary, the point where the immediacy of the divine presence was encountered and enjoyed. In short, created in the world with dominion over it, man is immediately abstracted from the world and placed directly in the divine presence. What is being said in all this is surely how the dominion mandate was to be exercised. What is stressed is that the command of Gen. 1:28 can function only within the set of divine/human relationships which chapter 2 proceeds to construct. Thus in Gen. 2 we are offered a model of how man thereafter is to

---

[25]. Karl Barth, Church Dogmatics, iii/1, (Edinburgh: T. & T. Clark, 1958), p. 98.

[26]. C. Westermann, Creation, (London: SPCK, 1974), p. 65. The developed Old Testament theology of 'rest' employed different terminology to that used in Gen. 2:1–4. The close link, however, between such 'rest' and the Sabbath which epitomized the concept was always maintained. (cf. Exod. 20:11 where the two concepts of 'sabbath' and 'rest' are brought together).

regulate the world over which he has been set. Man's abstraction from the general world does not thus vitiate 1:28; rather it makes it implementation possible. The complete congruity between man and his garden environment (cf. 2:19) as well as the idyllic male/female relationships to which the latter half of the chapter points, function as illustrations of the manner in which dominion over ordered nature was to proceed. In the opinion of the narrator (2:24) the marriage relationship ought to be the perfect reflection of this harmony. Man was to control his world, not primarily by immersing himself in the tasks of ordering it, but by recognizing that there was a system of priorities by which all of regulated life was to be controlled. If he were rightly related to his Creator, then he would rightly respond to creation. In this manner also, we should note, male and female relationships were set within the covenant. There is an order of priority here which the New Testament expresses by its doctrine of headship, which is to be exercised by man over woman (1 Cor. 11:3; Eph. 5:23, both with reference to Genesis 2). What this headship means should thus be clear from Genesis 2 and the evidence which we have assessed suggests that headship within that relationship, like dominion within the wider relationship, entails the obligation to understand the nature of the relationship and the duty to maintain it by exercising a God-centred life.

In passing, we note that it is interesting to observe in Genesis 2 the sense of values which the author of the account exhibits so acutely; namely that the objects upon which man in our present world places extreme value (i.e. the gold and precious stones of Gen. 2:12) and towards which his energies are bent in the endeavour to secure them, were to be found in the world outside the garden but not within it. Too much capital should not be made out of such an aside, but it is at least suggestive that in the Eden situation the total blessing focus is thrown upon the experience of the divine presence, from which material enticements of any character must not detract.

(c) The demand of the covenant and its breach

There was in the garden a very vital element of condition within the relationship and to this reformed theology has very correctly drawn constant attention. In the garden two trees were singled out for special mention, the tree of life which was in the 'midst of the garden' (Gen. 2:9), where the phrase used seems designed to underscore the accessibility of that tree, and the tree of the knowledge of good and evil. It is described simply as being in the garden, and its fruit was forbidden. Since no such prohibition attached to the tree of life, but on the contrary, permission to eat of it seems to be entailed in the general permission granted to eat of every tree, apart from the tree of the knowledge of good and evil (Gen. 2:16), we may take it that in the

garden man had eaten of the fruit of the tree of life. Only after the fall
was access to it prohibited (Gen. 3:24), and the motive advanced for that
decision is that the knowledge of good and evil acquired by the fall
made it expedient that man should be barred from the garden 'lest he
put forth his hand and take also of the tree of life, and eat, and live for
ever' (Gen. 3:22). That is to say, the divine prohibition placed on entry
to the garden is an act of grace designed to ensure that man's fallen
condition would not be perpetuated eternally.

The conditions by which fellowship in the garden was to be regulated, were, as we well know, not met. When the fruit of the forbidden
tree was eaten, we were all somehow involved (Rom. 5:19). What
happened in Eden affected for ill the future of the human race. It will be
necessary for us to review briefly at this point what constituted this
infraction of covenant to which we have referred, for clearly any future
renewal of the covenant arrangement would carry as inbuilt the same
regulative conditions, and we should thus need to recognize as fully as
we may the nature of this initial transgression.

We need first to recognize the transgression of Adam as a free act. The
prohibition of Gen. 2:17 presupposes the ability to choose between
alternatives, as well as an understanding of the consequences which
ensue from disastrous choice. There is no evidence within the biblical
account to suggest that prior to the fall the position of man was
determined, either from within himself, or in virtue of his situation in
the garden. He had been created as an autonomous moral being and
stood presumably on the threshold of an advance towards fuller and
more perfect moral personal expression. The story suggests that prior to
the fall he was able to determine the course of action to be adopted;
subsequent to the fall, as we are well aware, he is in the grip of the
consequences of the course of action which was chosen.

What then was involved in the act of eating from the fruit of the tree
of knowledge of good and evil? Often, the prohibition on eating is
construed simply as a test of obedience arbitrarily imposed. There is
surely truth at this level, though simply to reduce the significance of the
tree to that of a visible reminder of what was to be avoided does not do
justice to what is pleaded by the serpent (Gen. 3:5) and confirmed after
the fall by God (3:22). In the eating of the fruit, enlightenment would
follow and they would be 'like God knowing good and evil' (Gen. 3:5).
To regard the tree simply as a touchstone by which obedience was to be
measured, is thus to leave us in doubt as to how the eating of its fruit
could enable the eater to be 'like God'. Similarly, the familiar interpretation of the terms 'knowledge of good and evil' as reflecting sexual
understanding of each other in inadequate. True, the first reaction of
the pair after the fall seems to support such a view. But to adopt this
view is firstly to read into the narrative misplaced comparative material
at that point from the ancient Near East bearing upon the mythical
notion of a 'sacred marriage'. In such a ritual a primeval union was

thought to be reenacted whereby human well-being, agricultural fertility and general fecundity was thought to be ensured. Secondly it also fails to explain how the acquisition of such knowledge could make the acquirer 'like God'. Again, the interpretation of the phrase 'knowledge of good and evil' as inclusive of total knowledge by references to opposite poles, is attractive, but it does not come to terms with the realities of the human situation after the fall. In our world we simply do not see man in possession of profound knowledge of the character that this interpretation would imply.

The phrase 'knowledge of good and evil' is better taken, following W. M. Clark,[27] as referring to the exercise of absolute moral autonomy, a prerogative which the Bible reserves to God alone. Clark is able to illustrate the point from a wide range of Old Testament contexts. Solomon, for example, prays (1 Kgs. 3:9) for an understanding heart to govern his people that he 'may discern between good and evil'. This is an absolute for the task before which he is placed, since he continues in the text, 'for who is able to govern this thy great people?' The latter half of the same chapter offers a parade example of Solomon's judicial wisdom, and when Israel acknowledges the astuteness with which the matter of disputed motherhood of the child has been resolved, they perceive that 'the wisdom of God was in him, to render justice' (1 Kgs. 3:28). What is clear from this passage is that final authoritative decisions of this nature, which affect the whole shape of life, require the mind of God. For the human being, wisdom of this character is derivative, not natural. It must be sought from God and its source must be acknowledged. The regulation of the decision making processes for life on all levels will not proceed satisfactorily unless the limitations of human knowledge are recognized.

Clark's point that the determination of what was good and what was evil was ultimately a divine one is important and elucidates the context of Gen. 3, for it permits us to note what was the essential character of the fall. By eating of the fruit man was intruding into an area reserved for God alone, and the violation of the command is tantamount to an assertion of equality with God, a snatching at deity.[28] The decision of Adam to be self-legislating brought with it diverse consequences. Although thereafter he was the possessor by use of tremendous determinative power, and thus 'like God', yet he was 'unlike God' in that he would constantly be uncertain of the nature of the issues before which he was placed. He would never be able to foresee the consequ-

---

[27]. 'A Legal Background to the Yahwist's Use of "Good and Evil" in Gen. 2–3' *JBL* 88 (1969), pp. 266–278. On the general relationship of Gen. 2:4–3:24 and the view that sin was an attack upon and a breach of the harmony of the created order cf. also Jerome T. Walsh, 'Gen. 2:4b–3:24 A Synchronic Approach', *JBL* 96 (1977) pp. 161–177.

[28]. A counterpart of Adam's action is clearly the attitude of Jesus referred to in Philippians 2:6.

ences of the choices which he would make. Having power to choose, he would continue throughout life and history to be the captive of his choices. Putting himself in a position of moral defiance to his Creator, he plunged himself into a life of tension and absolute moral uncertainty. Thus the command of Gen. 2:17 was not merely probative. In refusing to submit to the moral government of God, he refused to know God (Rom. 1:28). A reprobate mind resulted and as a consequence of the fall man became assertive, but was unable to control himself or his world.

D. THE COVENANT WITH NOAH AS REDEMPTIVE

i. The Old Testament use of the Flood Imagery

The results of the fall are recounted in the ensuing early chapters of Genesis in terms of the progressive spread of sin. Chapters 4 – 11 are given over to illustrating this spread, with the flood account the major pause in the narrative movement of Gen. 1 – 11. We have seen that God pledges himself at Gen. 6:18 to maintain his commitment and we have noted that the rescue of Noah puts man, and thus his world also, on the threshold of a new beginning at Gen. 9:1ff. Too often expositors have seen the covenant with Noah as limited to a pledge of stable order in the post-flood era and thus merely providing an example of God's general providential care. The use of the Noah material in the subsequent course of Scripture argues, however, for more than just a pledge of enduring stability.

A complete review of the use of the Noah traditions in Jewish and Christian writings is not planned here.[29] One or two uses within the Canon, however, do call for comment. In Isaiah 54:7–10 God announces his everlasting fidelity to the generation of the exile. While they may have been inundated by overflowing wrath (Isa. 54:8), God will gather them with everlasting compassion so that the old alliance will be again established after the exile, which like the flood period of Noah, will then be seen to have been merely a brief interlude within the everlasting covenantal framework. The general summons to the exiles is to begin again. In what appears to be a general reference to Gen. 9 and the covenant renewal theme there, as God had sworn to Noah, so God's anger will turn from the exiles. His covenant of peace will stand firmer with them than the immutable mountains or hills (v. 10).

As Westermann has noted,[30] in an effort to provide a suitable analogy, the prophet has gone back beyond the history of Israel, to a

---

[29]. Jack P. Lewis, A Study of the Interpretation of Noah and The Flood in Jewish and Christian Literature, (Leiden: E. J. Brill, 1968), offers this.

[30]. C. Westermann, Isaiah 40–66, (London: S.C.M., 1966) pp. 275–6.

turning point in the history of the human race with which the return from exile would be comparable. The further comparison which the prophet makes here of redemption with creation, or rather the depiction of redemption as a new creation, is entirely consistent with the force of his argument throughout Isaiah 40–55. The salvation promised is clearly a return to what had been previously experienced, as the use of the flood imagery plainly indicates. The permanency of the prospect in store for the returned exiles is underscored by the use of $b^e r \hat{\imath}t$, as is the eschatological significance of the return, by the addition to $b^e r \hat{\imath}t$ of Heb. *shālôm* ('peace'). Continuing community, well-being and eschatological certainty are thus held out by the prophet here as the consummation of God's saving action, an action for which in the Old Testament as Westermann notes, covenant is not the foundation, but rather the confirmation.

ii. *The covenant connection of 1 Peter 3:19–21 – The Flood as redemptive*

While in later Jewish thought Noah assumed an increasing importance, for our purposes it is the striking connection which is made in the important New Testament passage of 1 Peter 3:19–21 in somewhat similar analogy to that of Isa. 54:7–10, between the flood and a new or renewed covenant, that is enlightening. In Peter 3:19–21 the new era in human history inaugurated by the resurrection and ascension of Jesus is placed in parallelism with God's primeval activity as seen in the salvation of Noah.[31] The comparison is drawn between the waters of the flood by which Noah was saved and Christian baptism of which the flood is seen to have operated as a foreshadowing. Just as Noah and the seven who were with him were rescued from a general human sinful condition, so by means of baptismal water Christians are drawn out of the world. The parallel in both cases is not the few who were saved but the water by which they were saved. Not, however, adds Peter, that the operation of water by itself in the case of baptism effected salvation. Baptism serves only as a 'removal of dirt from the body', if its exterior effects are considered. What is meant, Peter goes on to explain, is that baptism which is an 'appeal to God for a clear conscience'.

The interesting word in this last quotation is Greek *eperōtēma*, translated as 'appeal'. Such a translation, however, hardly seems to do justice to a New Testament theology of baptism, since this would reduce baptism to no more than an acted prayer. The word *eperōtēma*, however occurs in the contemporary legal terminology in the technical sense of 'entering into a contract'.[32] This would make a translation of

[31]. A very full treatment of this important context is provided by W. J. Dalton, *Christ's Proclamation to the Spirits*, Analecta Biblica 23, (Rome: Biblical Institute Press, 1965). Note especially p. 208.

[32]. Dalton, op.cit., p. 225.

'commitment' or 'pledge' a possibility, with the thought perhaps of that undertaking made at the time by the candidate for baptism which would correspond to a baptismal confession. Equally possible and doubly attractive is the contractual sense that the word is well able to bear. In this case baptism is being regarded as an acknowledgement of covenantal obligations, and thus at the same time a commitment which is intended to be a moral witness to the world. By itself baptism is merely a water rite which cannot save, for nothing is effected by the rite itself. But baptism can be the means by which the world is renounced, just as by committing himself to the waters, Noah condemned the world and became an heir to the righteousness which is by faith (Heb. 11:7).

Whatever our views on the 1 Peter context may be, the section makes it clear that Noah's deliverance was regarded as a type of Christian redemption.[33] This in its turn means that we shall not do justice to the covenant renewal passages in Gen. 9 if we see them merely as an arm of general revelation at that point with no redemptive application. Genesis 9 has made it clear, as we have seen, that the covenant with Noah had the preservation of the created order in view, but this in itself is a redemptive exercise on the widest scale. The restoration of man is bound to affect his world and consistently with this, the New Testament asserts strongly that the redemption of the creature must involve the redemption of creation.

E. A Comprehensive View

Our survey of the nature of the relationship with man and his world begun by God in Genesis 1 is now complete. We have seen that in the contexts of Gen. 6 and 9 the term $b^e r\hat{i}t$ is applied to this arrangement. The very fact of creation involved God's entering into relationships with the world, and it is therefore insufficient to side with Karl Barth[34] and others who would regard creation as merely the ground of covenant, the basis upon which a covenant with man can proceed. A biblical doctrine of covenant in the light of the evidence adduced cannot be merely anthropologically related. The world and man are part of one total divine construct and we cannot entertain the salvation of man in isolation from the world which he has affected. The refusal to submit in Eden meant a disordered universe and thus the restoration of all things will put God, man, and the world at harmony again.

---

[33]. The covenant connections in 1 Peter 3:19–21 and the importance of *eperōtēma* in this context, are well drawn out by David Hill, 'On Suffering and Baptism in 1 Peter', *Nov.T.* 18 (1976), pp. 181–189.

[34]. *Church Dogmatics* iii/1, p. 218ff.

It would follow from our analysis of Gen. 1 – 9 that there can be only one divine covenant, and also that any theology of covenant must begin with Genesis 1:1. All else in covenant theology which progressively occurs in the Old Testament will be deducible from this basic relationship, and we shall have occasion to note the chain of connection which having moved from creation to Noah, leads us from Noah to Abraham, from Abraham to Sinai, to David, to the Jeremianic new covenant and thence to Jesus its fulfiller.

In postulating a unity for biblical theology in covenant, the older reformed theologians were entirely correct. The arrived at this conclusion by postulating a unity between the Testaments derived from the unfolding of divine purpose. In this they were again correct. Our knowledge of the ancient Near Eastern world has brought us in recent years into contact with comparative materials which have been of immense value for Old Testament covenantal studies. None of this can be ignored and constant reference will be made to it in this study. Yet, finally, biblical theology is a discipline internal to the Canon. It will recognize that the Old Testament society constantly demonstrates cultural affinities with its contemporary world. But it will show that there is a marked distinctiveness in the use to which such materials are put, or that they are always wedded to a set of presuppositions with which they are received. All this will mark off the Old Testament from its background. So in regard to covenant we should expect to find the Old Testament material has been influenced by comparative parallels. We shall, however, be aware also of the limitations of the comparative approach, for by its very nature the Old Testament society never tolerated a simple transfer of comparative concepts.

There is one more point which will assume growing importance as this study develops. So far we have referred only briefly to the supposition that the account makes reference to the idea of divine kingship standing behind the Genesis 1 material. But in view of this, we should expect an interrelationship of divine kingship and covenant as the biblical notion of covenant develops. We shall see that from Sinai on this is particularly so, for the goal of covenant is divine rule over the world, recognized by mankind. The presupposition of covenant is the present kingship of God. That is why it is impossible to construct a total theology of covenant by resorting simply to the Old Testament. The parameters are fully outlined there as we shall see. But to note the complete equation of covenant and kingly rule, and the divine image displayed in man's function within that relationship we shall need to turn to the New Testament and to the gospels in particular. It will not be possible within the compass of this present study to reach that point: however when Jesus confronted his contemporaries with a demand to return to their covenant base, it was backed by the claim that in his ministry the kingdom of God had confronted men.

Summary

We began the chapter by drawing attention to the distinctive character of the first biblical mention of $b^e r \hat{\imath} t$ (Gen. 6:18). We turned our attention to the manner in which $b^e r \hat{\imath} t$ is used, firstly, in Genesis and then, biblically, more widely. We noted that $b^e r \hat{\imath} t$ when theologically used in the Old Testament (and indeed when secularly so as well) refers to backing of a quasi-legal nature given at the stage of the conclusion of the $b^e r \hat{\imath} t$, to a prior relationship. The argument that the language of Gen. 6:18 was technical and 'Priestly' was examined and dismissed, and the absence of the expected terminology of covenant initiation ($k\bar{a}rat\ b^e r \hat{\imath} t$) was to be explained, we suggested, by the fact that the verse dealt with confirmation of what was in fact an existing covenant.

Gen. 9:1ff clearly returns in thought to 1:26–28, with correspondences between Noah and Adam intended. The notion of the Noachian covenant as continuing an implied 'Covenant of Works' concluded by the Deity with Adam was rejected, since the evidence of Gen. 9:9–17 strongly implied that the covenant which was confirmed with Noah had been brought into existence by the act of creation itself. God's refusal to let the creation intentions lapse was then contrasted with man's default and the narratives of Gen. 1 – 3 were examined. The eschatological notion of 'rest' was seen to be demonstrated by the nature of the relationship between man and God to which Genesis 2 had pointed. Since 9:1ff pointed to a recovery of the original purpose for man and his world, the covenant confirmed to Noah could not be seen as merely a divine commitment to providential care. The use of the Noachian covenant materials in the Bible appeared to justify the assertion that in the post-fall era the notion of covenant contained the aspect of redemption of creation as well as the maintenance of the order.

The implications of a covenant implied by the fact of creation itself were then drawn out. There could be only one biblical covenant, of which the later biblical covenants must be sub-sets. This is the way in which the later argument of this work will proceed. Finally the correlation of covenant and the kingship of God was made.

Excursus

NOAH AND ADAM AND THE 'COVENANT OF WORKS'

In Gen. 9:1ff there are obvious points of correspondence which the narrative intends us to draw between Noah and Adam. These, and the representative position occupied by Noah in the covenant with which he is connected, and the renewal of the blessing of life in Noah after the flood, have all provided substance for what had been the view of traditional reformed theology, namely that a divine covenant with Adam operated and that it should be explicated in terms of a federal headship of the human race which Adam exercised. In the terms of this exposition the promissory element of this covenant lay in the offer of life in Eden, conditional however – and thus the note of obligation was imported – upon Adam's obedience. Noting the existence of such implied conditions, reformed theology most usually attached to the covenant it supposed to have been bestowed upon Adam the title, 'Covenant of Works'. In this vein the Princeton theologian, Charles Hodge, argued that the Genesis 2 narrative (cf. Gen. 2:17) contained the ingredients of both promise and condition. The reward promised to Adam was life on the condition of obedience, a position which Hodge found to be consistent with the whole tenor of scripture, and one in fact which found expression on many scriptural levels. 'God', he wrote, 'having created man in his own image in knowledge, righteousness and holiness, entered into a covenant of life with him, upon condition of perfect obedience, forbidding him to eat of the tree of knowledge of good and evil upon pain of death.'[1] A probationary period having been completed, Adam would have entered into the life which had been promised.

On this view the Covenant of Works was something established by God with man after creation, something additional to the act of creation, and not given with creation itself. That is to say, the covenant was not an end in itself, but the means to an end. Adam had possessed a form of life but not life in its highest form, namely eternal life. He had possessed a limited freedom but it was a lapsible freedom. The elements of this covenant were the promise of eternal life, the penalty which default would impose, death, the stipulation which was imposed, perfect obedience. When the probation period under which the

---

[1]. Hodge, *Systematic Theology*, II, (Grand Rapids: Eerdmans, 1946), p. 117.

44

covenant had placed Adam had ended, Adam would have enjoyed that transformed immortality which will be the possession of believers at the Second Coming. Further, as with Noah, this covenant was not effected with Adam alone, but involved the whole human race whose federal head he was.

Hodge's nineteenth century formulation was very representative of reformed traditions and continues to enjoy conservative support apart from some minor reservations. Herman Hoeksema in a fairly recent work has voiced reservations on the score of inferences such as Hodge's, in regard to man's potential for higher blessing, drawn solely from the narrative of Gen. 2 and he is unwilling to locate the covenant conditions as precisely at Gen. 2:17 as Hodge did.[2] He does not doubt that Adam had stood in some covenant relationship, though he rightly has difficulties with the concept of a covenant with man which was something additional to creation itself. Rather, he prefers to suggest that the covenant with Adam was something constituted by creation, and consisted in a relationship of living friendship and fellowship, a relationship which had been brought into being when Adam had been created in the image of God, which whatever else it involved, meant a knowledge of God.[3] In such a covenant Adam was God's representative in creation, God's prophet, priest and king. Organically, the entire human race was in Adam, and legally he represented them. By virtue of this connection it was inevitable that death should pass upon the entire human race, as St. Paul in fact observes (Rom. 5:12–19).

Hoeksema justifies his argument by general but not specific scriptural argument, with the exception of an appeal to the contested reference of Hosea 6:7, 'But like Adam they transgressed the covenant' (RSV margin), where the parallel verse member continues, 'There they dealt faithlessly with me.' A theological breach of some covenant is suggested by this verse, yet most commentators (and translations) prefer slightly to modify the text and Hos. 6:7 (though with no real support from textual witnesses) and read Adam as the place name of the conquest traditions (Josh. 3:16). The implication is thus drawn that Israel had been unfaithful ever since the actual crossing of the Jordan itself. Certainly this would suit Hosea's heavy emphasis upon the role of the land as bound up with covenant blessing and thus retention, or as bound up with covenant curse and thus expulsion, though a particular reference to these possibilities finds no place in Hosea 6. It is possible that the reference to Adam in Hosea 6 is to be taken generically, i.e. 'like men' Israel had transgressed the covenant, treating it as though it had been an ordinary human arrangement. Yet, given the fondness of Hosea for allusively referring to Israel's early history (cf. Hos. 11:8; 12:4),

[2]. Hoeksema, *Reformed Dogmatics*, (Grand Rapids: Reformed Free Publishing Association, 1966), p. 217.

[3]. Hoeksema, op.cit., p. 222.

Hoeksema and others may be correct in seeing a reference to the first men at Hos. 6:7, but the context is too uncertain and cannot itself carry the weight which such reformed commentators have placed upon it.

The difficulty, however, which confronts one in approaches such as those of Hodge and Hoeksema, which may be fairly taken to be representative of the reformed movement, is that they do not take sufficient account of precise biblical content. The strength of such dogmatic approaches lies mostly in a careful depiction of the conditions under which the relationship in which Adam was involved, were to be exercised. Their weakness, however, lies in the inadequate grounding of the covenant concept itself, which largely becomes a matter of general biblical inference. There is a tendency in most such approaches to read the total flow of biblical revelation back into Genesis 1–3. However generally correct in the final analysis deductions of this character may be, most often there is the failure to note what is precisely being said in Gen. 1–3, since whatever conclusions are drawn from these chapters, they cannot be separated from the entire course of the total presentation of Gen. 1–11. Unless account is taken of this continuous context, inferences drawn from particular sections may not do justice to the direction that concepts are assuming on the whole. In regard to covenant specifically, we shall certainly not provide an adequate coverage of any 'Covenant with Adam', or 'Covenant of Works' or links with 'Creation', unless we first note the covenant interrelationships which are operating throughout Gen. 1–11, drawing our conclusions from specific reference to the use of covenant terms themselves.

---

[4]. Walter Vogels, *God's Universal Covenant* (Univ. of Ottawa Press, Ottawa, 1979) returns to the idea of a primitive universal covenant to be found in the early chapters of Genesis. He finds the ingredients of the vassal treaty scattered throughout Gen. 1–11. But his approach is highly selective and not in our judgement related either to form or semantic occurrence.

2

The Covenant with Abraham

A. THE ORDER OF THE ARGUMENT

The concept of the covenant with Abraham brings into prominence the biblical doctrine of redemption. The material associated with the Abrahamic covenant is not, however, easy to systematize. Not only is it dispersed over different chapters but also it often seems repetitive in its presentation. Careful evaluation of the accounts is required and particular matters relating to the order of the presentation of the material need to be discussed. Since the first mention of the term *bᵉrît* occurs at Gen. 15:18 it seems logical and necessary to commence at that point, and, continue with the detail of that chapter. Yet it will become clear in doing so that the real content of the Abrahamic covenant has been given in chapter 12:1–3, a passage to which we shall then turn. In doing so, however, we must not lose sight of the fact that the call of Abraham in this passage is a redemptive response to the human dilemma which the spread of sin narratives of Gen. 3–11 have posed. Prior then to discussing Gen. 12:1–3 in detail we shall need to refer to the earlier narratives of Genesis, especially to the Tower of Babel narrative of Gen. 11. Chapter 12:1–3 will itself require careful, detailed explanation, with particular attention being paid to key terms and sequences. After this ground has been cleared away we shall be free to devote the remainder of the chapter to the way in which the Abrahamic covenant operated within patriarchal experience. Then we shall look at the essential restatement of the Abrahamic covenant that Gen. 17 provides. Let us therefore now begin with Gen. 15:18.

B. GENESIS 15:18 AND ITS CONTEXT

i *The Covenant ritual of Gen. 15:18*

The circumstances which surround the first mention of a covenant with Abraham in Gen. 15:18 are remarkable, and quite without parallel in the rest of the Old Testament. In a general context of a vision received by Abram, the bizarre rites by which the covenant is concluded are narrated. They demand some detailed attention. Since they come before the reader without any prior parallel, though they bear the marks of great antiquity about them, it is to be inferred that what is to us such an oblique reference would have presented no difficulties to the ancient readers whose social context would presumably have supplied sufficient explanation.

Verse 18 informs us that the content of the ceremony was covenant determinative ('on that day the Lord made a covenant with Abram saying'), and that the covenant itself related to promises involving descendants. It also located them in a specific area, as the details of Gen. 15:18b–21 indicate. It is of interest also that later Jewish exegesis saw the ceremony as accompanied by sacrifice[1] and certainly the total rite incorporated the five clean sacrificial animals of the later system. Extra-biblical parallels able to be adduced point in the same way.[2]

There is doubt as to the function of the five clean animals in the rite. Normally the imprecatory features of the incident have been stressed and the extra-biblical parallels from Mari and Alalakh have been adduced. God passes, in mysterious terms, (v. 17) through the severed animals, giving substance to the parallels between Gen. 15 and Jer. 34:18 which are often drawn. In Jer. 34 a covenant was concluded between the Judean king Zedekiah and leading citizens, aimed at freeing slaves during the Babylonian siege of Jerusalem, by the passage of the participants in the ceremony (from the princes of Judah and downwards) through the dismembered parts of a calf. In its context the imprecatory character of Jer. 4:18–20 seems clear. We may, however, be dealing with something different in Gen. 15. Gerhard Hasel[3] has recently argued that Gen. 15:9–11 deals merely with covenant ratification and not imprecation, suggesting that the imprecatory formulas which invoke destruction upon the participants would not have been applied to Yahweh by the author of Genesis.

There is no doubt substance in his contention but if covenant ratification *alone* is on view here, the details of this bizarre rite of Gen. 15:9–11,17 remain unaccounted for. Here, the more recent suggestion of Gordon Wenham,[4] though extremely hypothetical, does attempt to

---

[1]. Jubilees 14:11, 19.

[2]. M. Weinfeld, 'The Covenant of Grant in the Old Testament and in the Ancient Near East', *JAOS* 90 (1970), p. 197, draws attention to some extra-biblical parallels. We might note at this point Weinfeld's thesis of support for the antiquity of the Abrahamic covenant drawn from the similarity of the arrangement to the so-called *kudurru* documents of the Kassite period in Babylonia (c. 16th cent. B.C. onwards). These were, in effect, a deed of gift signifying a royal grant. Parallels of this character cannot be overpressed, however, because of the long currency of the *kudurru* practice. On the whole question of 'royal grant' type parallels to the Abrahamic covenant cf. additionally M. Weinfeld, *Deuteronomy and the Deuteronomic School*, (Oxford: Clarendon, 1972), pp. 74–76.

[3]. In his 'Meaning of the Animal Rite in Gen. 15' *JSOT* 19 (1981), p. 70.

[4]. 'The Symbolism of the Animal Rite in Gen. 15: A Response to G. F. Hasel *JSOT* 19 (1981), pp. 61–78' *JSOT* 22 (1982), pp. 134–137.

relate the details to the context. Wenham rightly notes the 'clean' character of the five animals involved in the ceremony and suggests that their number emphasizes the solemnity of the occasion. The total incident is conceived by him to prefigure Israel's future. The sacrificial animals, he suggests, may represent Israel while the unclean birds of prey which Abram repels are suggestive of foreign aggression thwarted. Following upon Gen. 15:6 the total scene thus depicts the protection given to Israel by the nature of the Abrahamic covenant. In this connection the divine passage through the pieces (v. 17) is not imprecation but a theophanic assurance of Yahweh's protection in terms somewhat reminiscent of the later 'pillar of cloud' wilderness guidance.

On this view the incident foreshadows Israel's later history and operates by way of added reassurance in a chapter which is devoted to this topic. While the issues must still remain open, Wenham's view does at least attempt to gather the substance of the chapter together. In any event the details present a daring anthropomorphism whereby God involves himself in an obligation whose nature is dramatized by an acted oath of self-commitment, (cf. Heb. 6:13). In any case, no undertaking is exacted from Abram; God alone is bound.

ii. *Content of the Covenant – Land and People*

As to the question of the content of the covenant, we are somewhat at a loss since no definitive new content is attached to the covenant which is 'cut' at Gen. 15:18. We might have expected that a statement on content would follow in this verse but instead we have a reference to what has been the subject of attention previously within the chapter, namely 'this land' which is brought into immediate connection with Abram's 'seed'. But the indication which is given in Gen. 15:18 is that the land which will belong to Abram's descendants has *already* been given. The Hebrew verb *nātattî* ('I have given') must be allowed in this context its full preterite force (as the Revised Version correctly recognizes), since a reference to the land as a gift has already been made at Gen. 13:15 in the same terms. Even if we admit the force of the RSV translation at this point ('I give'), we should still be required to contend that nothing new by way of content is being introduced by the notion of covenant here. We should further suggest that 'give' in this context must bear the sense that it does in Gen. 17:2 of bringing into effect an arrangement already concluded. We shall however, return to this point later.

For the purposes of the later biblical material it is important to note the careful delimitation of the land in Gen. 15:18–20. The boundaries are firstly described in general terms whose archaic character seems indicated by the unusual phrase occuring only here (Heb. *n^ehar Miṣrayim* 'river of Egypt', for the expected *naḥal Miṣrayim*, 'wadi of Egypt'). Within this broad geographical area, which is hereafter to be retained as the ideal border in outline of the promised land, a list of ten inhabitants of Canaan is given. Since, like most of the material in Gen. 15, the contents of this list are often thought to reflect the stylized impressions of a much later historical period, some further reflection on its detail is warranted.

Though the book of Genesis gives us no firm list of the pre-Israelite inhabitants of Canaan, and thus betrays no real interest in this question, we cannot conclude axiomatically that the incidental geographical details of this character are unhistorical. The narrower list of seven (Gen. 15:20–21) differs from the usual presentation of pre-Israelite inhabitants by its inclusion of the Rephaim (mentioned previously in Gen. 14:5), and by its omission of the Hivites. It seems, therefore, difficult to agree with suggestions often made, that such detail is fabrication.[5] On the other hand it would be too much to suggest that it is complete, or that it suggests total geographical extent. It is doubtless intended to convey no more than that Israel is to become the dominant power in the region,[6] and one must add that the omission of the Philistines from this list, a people with whom the patriarchs in the early narratives are seen to be in frequent contact,[7] shows in itself some ability to distinguish between indigenous inhabitants and later occupants.

Admittedly, the presence in Gen. 15:19 of the Kenites, the Kenizzites, and the Kadmonites seems to display an area interest. The Kadmonites, which may be a general term for 'Easterners', are found only here, though the Kenites (1 Sam. 15:6) and the Kenizzites through Caleb's connection with them (Num. 32:12; Josh. 14:6, 14), are both found later

---

[5]. Cf. the view of R. E. Clements, *Abraham and David: Genesis 15 and its Meaning for Israelite Tradition*, Studies in Biblical Theology, Second Series 5, (London: S.C.M., 1967), p. 21, n.25, who argues that the geographical detail is composite. Mention is made here of Clements's basic argument that the Abrahamic traditions, preserved at Hebron in the south and taken to Jerusalem by David, offered the pattern for the promissory covenant with David which Clements sees in 2 Sam. 7. In his view the Abrahamic covenant is a reworking of older materials in a very free fashion and was designed to offer support for the Davidic claims. No detailed argument on this point is offered here except to note that the basic improbability of this view which asserts the dependency of the Abrahamic covenant on the Davidic. Such a view, which is representative of many modern approaches, fails to take account of the essentially Sinaitic thrust that the Davidic covenant has in 2 Sam. 7. Moreover, why are the obscure tribes, the Kenites and Kenizzites, mentioned in Gen. 15:19 if this narrative is designed to legitimize the already established boundaries of the Davidic empire? Thirdly, Clements's thesis that the original Abrahamic material concerned a compact between the patriarch and a local deity of Mamre is an hypothesis which finds no support from the patriarchal narratives which are admitted to contain a very lofty monotheistic conception (cf. B. Gemser, 'God in Genesis', *OTS* XII (1958), p. 11).

[6]. So A. van Selms, 'The Canaanites in the Book of Genesis', *OTS* XII (1958), p. 192.

[7]. It need not be axiomatically assumed that the Genesis references to the Philistines are an anachronism. Though they did not arrive in force until c. 1200 B.C., sporadic colonies of these Aegean settlers could have been placed earlier.

in the deep south, in the Hebron area where David was located prior to his rule from Jerusalem. To suggest from all this that David took Abrahamic traditions with him from Hebron to Jerusalem which were there amalgamated with wider Israelite material, with the results being reflected in the supposedly strange connection that we now find in Gen. 15:19–21, is to ignore the probable significance of the sequence of ten peoples in these three verses. By the mention of the first three, stress is probably being laid on an occupancy of a location in the south, for that is the area at that time of especial Abramic interest. After his entry into the land he is first found north at Shechem (Gen. 12:6). There he builds an altar after a divine manifestation to him. Thereby the gift of the land is reaffirmed, and he subsequently moves to Bethel and thence to Hebron, having successively built altars. It is quite possible that the building of such altars reflected not so much patriarchal worship responses or life-style, but was rather a public assertion of ownership of the land as a result of a divine grant.[8] Abram may have been compelled to move progressively south as a result of pressure exerted by the city state inhabitants of the areas, for there is particular mention at Gen. 13:7 in connection with the Bethel area, of Canaanite and Perizzite occupancy of the land at that time. He may thus have moved south to Hebron, which area he made particularly his own.[9] In the south he seems quickly to have become an independent chieftain of great repute, as the general situation of Gen. 14 and the confederate alliance he there forms (14:13) suggest. In these circumstances, an affirmation of divine promises concerning the land, commencing from the deep south and bearing in particular view the contiguous peoples of that area at that time, is not only perfectly understandable, but would have doubtless proved to have been a very welcome note of divine assurance to Abram at an uncertain time.

iii. *The content of Gen. 15*

(a) The adoption of Eliezer

Gen. 15 begins without connection, though apparently the situation of chapter 14 which narrates Abram's victory over the coalition of five kings and what seems the submissive embassy of the strange biblical figure Melchizedek, seems presupposed. The divine word came to Abram in a vision (Gen. 15:1), a fact which has often led scholars to associate the material of Gen. 15:1–7 with the 'E' source (though the divine name Yahweh is almost exclusively used in that section), because of that source's supposed prophetic predilection. Visions,

---

[8]. D. J. Wiseman, 'Abraham in History and Tradition' (Pt. i. Abraham the Hebrew), *BS* 134 (1977) pp. 125–126, suggests this.

[9]. Van Selms, *OTS* XII, p. 194.

however, accompanying the language of divine assurance were often concomitants of divine revelation in the ancient Near East, from the third millenium onwards.[10] It may be mentioned here in passing that the attempt to apportion Gen. 15 between prior sources has now been largely abandoned.[11]

Though no connection with what precedes is provided, the language of divine protection at Gen. 15:1 (cf. 'I am your shield') suggests the presence of a threat in Abram's experience. Chapter 14 has witnessed Abram's growing power, yet it has at the same time exposed just how possibly tenuous his hold on the land actually was. One imagines then, that the mention of a divine 'shield' may have retention of the land in view. The further mention in that verse of a divine reward to be provided leads Abram to give the conversation a slightly different turn, as he puts the particular question relating to progeny (Gen. 15:2). Secure occupancy of the land will ultimately depend, as he knows, upon the realization of the divine promise of descendants who will occupy the land. He thus reverts in Gen. 15:2 to the tenor of promises previously given in this direction. It is possible that Abram, by his use of the phrase 'continue childless', is raising the prospect of his death.[12] This causes him to mention arrangements he has made for a successor, apparently his servant, Eliezer, who seems, though the textual position of Gen. 15:2 is uncertain, to have been an unwelcome one.

The nature of Abram's perceived difficulty is sharpened in 15:3. Eliezer, a slave born in his house, has apparently been adopted as a son. Such a practice of slave adoption was backed by widespread custom in the ancient Near East, and was a popular means of preserving the structure of family relationships. Evidence to support this Genesis use of the concept comes mainly from the east Tigris Hurrian site of Nuzi, of the mid second millenium B.C. The undertaking appears to have provided for a situation, where as a recompense for taking care of an aged parent, providing mourning rites, etc., a son so adopted would receive the family inheritance. Since from what we know of the ancient Near Eastern family structure, the only way for a stranger to gain access to a family was either by marriage or adoption, the usual inference drawn from Gen. 15:3 is that Abram is there speaking of the adoption of Eliezer.[13]

---

[10]. H. Cazelles, 'Connexions et structure de Gen. XV' *RB* 69 (1962), p. 326, cites the dream of Gudea of Lagash among others.

[11]. The assertion of parallel accounts in Gen. 15 is still maintained, but the identification of sources is left open, as Clements, op.cit. p. 17, admits.

[12]. The Heb. participle *hôlek* of v. 2 ('continue') can be used in the sense of 'decease' (cf. Josh. 23:14; 2 Sam. 12:23 1 Kgs. 2:2), though in those instances it is invariably accompanied by a preposition.

[13]. This inference may stand though admittedly the use of social parallels to explain the details of the patriarchal period has been overpressed, as T. L. Thompson, *The Historicity of the Patriarchal Narratives* (Berlin; De Gruyter, 1974), *BZAW* 133 and others have pointed out. However, M. J. Selman, 'The Social Environment of the Patriarchs', *Tyn. B* 27 (1976),

THE COVENANT WITH ABRAHAM

(b) The promise of Gen. 15:5 and Abram's response

Abram's uncertainty about the future of his line is now removed in the vision by a direct divine word. There is an explicit promise of a son and the divine assurance continues in v. 5. Abram's descendants will be so extensive as to be beyond human reckoning. We note that more than the language of national hyperbole is involved here, for the fulfilment of this promise can be finally understood only from the standpoint of a Christian perspective (cf. Rev. 7:9, where the assembled saints, gathered from every nation, stand around the throne of God, as a multitude which no man could number). Perhaps the lack at this point in the narrative of particular association with the land may suggest that this promise was not to be exhausted in the fortunes of political Israel. Equally, as this promise is finally fulfilled in the completed history of redemption, so the reaction of Abram in v.6 to the promise is seen by the New Testament writers to be a paradigm of the response to the divine promises which ought to characterize those of any period who stand in covenant relationship.

The New Testament interpretation of Gen. 15:6, particularly that of St. Paul in Romans 4, moved the verse into the area of justification. There is truth here, for Abram's response to the divine disclosure of the future is a personal credence given to the divine promises, a judgement that the divine word, independent of any human expectation, is deserving of confidence. The enigma of Gen. 15:6 concerns the precise meaning of the phrase which follows the belief statement, namely that he (i.e. Yahweh) 'reckoned it to him as righteousness.' The issue is not simple but the facts may be put as follows. The verb 'reckoned' (Heb. *ḥāshab*), where it is not used as a matter of supposition or opinion, is used broadly in two senses in the Old Testament.[14] In the first instance the sense is to impute to somebody something when the facts or the situation are otherwise (Job 13:24; 19:11; 33:10; 41:27; [Heb. 41:19]). This leaves open the possibility that the meaning in Gen. 15:6 is that Abram's faith was reckoned to him as righteousness when in fact it was not. In the second case, that which is reckoned to someone's account is imputed appropriately (cf. Lev. 7:18; 17:4; Num. 18:27; 2 Sam. 19:19; Ps. 32:2; Ps. 106:31; Prov. 27:14). Extremely close in sense to Gen. 15:6 is the

---

pp. 114–136, though judging that a number of the parallels customarily drawn are unconvincing, suggests that the slave adoption model may have force. Certainly slave adoption was not possible in later Israel. We note that the recent tendency to date the patriarchal material as late as the fifth century B.C. leaves unexplained firstly the fact that in the exilic period the role of the Davidic monarchy which was seen (2 Sam. 7) to be a political fulfilment of the Abrahamic promises, was being called into question. Secondly, in the exilic period there is a decidedly diminished interest in nationalism and thus in the concept of the promised land, questions with which the patriarchal narratives are primarily concerned.

[14]. I am indebted here to the work of J. A. Ziesler, *The Meaning of Righteousness in Paul*, SNTS 20 (Cambridge: Cambridge Univ. Press, 1972), pp. 180–185.

case of Phinehas, whose zealous act which stopped the plague at Num. 25:8 was reckoned to him for righteousness (Ps. 106:31). Admittedly, the difference between Ps. 106:31 and Gen. 15:6 is that the first involves an action, while the second demonstrates an attitude, but the point in both cases is that they exemplified the adoption of attitudes appropriate to an existing relationship. In the case of Phinehas the covenant nature of the act within the historical review of Psalm 106 is clear. The issue in the case of Abram in Gen. 15:6 is somewhat less clear. What is probably involved here, is the assertion by the narrator that Abram's immediate response of further trust was appropriate at this point. It might have been expected in terms of steadfast behaviour from one who stood within the ambit of the promises of Gen. 12:1–3, and to whom they had now been confirmed by a further divine revelation.

Our conclusion, therefore, is that what is being remarked upon in Gen. 15:6 is Abram's demonstrated example of covenant fidelity, for we have already noted that righteousness in the Old Testament basically indicates behaviour consistent with the nature of a relationship already established. In the later Old Testament the presupposition for behaviour response is universally the covenant relationship, understood as existing. By analogy, a similar approach to the difficult Gen. 15:6 seems to us as the most productive.

(c) Gen. 15:7–21 and the inauguration of the covenant with Abram.

The structure of Gen. 15:7–21 is similar in general outline to 15:1–6 and offers to Abram the same note of reassurance. This section emphasizes the gift of the land, as the earlier one had stressed the promise of descendants. But the dominant note in both halves of the chapter is that of inheritance (cf. vv. 2, 3, 4, 8). Both sections commence with a divine manifestation in which God identifies himself in a manner which provides for continuity with prior promises; in both, Abram expresses doubt as to the implementation of the promise; both sections conclude on a note of covenant affirmation, by Abram (Gen. 15:6) and by God (15:18). No explanation of the details of the experience of 15:12–16 is given. It seems possible, however, to draw some empathetic connection between the deep death-like sleep and the awesome experience through which Abram passed, and Israel's later sombre national experiences of slavery in Egypt. It is noted (15:13) that only after an oppression of four hundred years and then only as an act of divine redemption would Israel be placed in the land. In the intervening period God would forbear with the sins of the peoples whose land Israel will come to occupy.

Chapter 15, cannot, however, be considered as the inauguration of the Abrahamic covenant, for both halves of the chapter are bound together by the common theme of divine assurance concerning promises previously given.[15] Abram's question of v.2 presupposes the promise of issue, and the confirmation of it is given in terms thoroughly similar to those of Gen. 13:14–16, where multitudinous descendants and land are joined. Gen. 15:7, which introduces the affirmation of the promise of the land, takes us back to the point of original call, to Ur of the Chaldees, where the direction was given to Abram to go into the land which he would be shown. When the covenant is actually concluded, Gen. 15:18 links it designedly with descendants and territory. The covenant ritual of chapter 15 thus functions, as we have noted in regard to the covenant detail of chapter 9, as confirmatory of a relationship previously established. Since both halves of the chapter reflect the divine commitments given in 12:1–3, that section is therefore the point of departure to which we must refer for our understanding of the Abrahamic covenant.

C. GENESIS 12:1–3

i. The call of Abram and its relationship to Gen. 11:1–9

The patriarchal narratives preserve the record of a number of profound divine initiatives which are taken successively with Israel's ancestors, Abraham, Isaac and Jacob. These initiatives take the form of a covenant concluded with Abram, the substance of whose terms is endorsed in the experiences of his son and grandson. The promises of land and progeny to which this unilateral divine commitment will refer, are not intended by extension from Abraham to provide a link with the past. They are expected to provide the platform from which the historical Israel will finally emerge. By the end of the book of Genesis, we shall have witnessed the growth of a great and separate people of Israel. Its story began with a call to its forefather Abram in the land of Ur, to break with his ethnic, social and religious past. In regard to the last of these the nature of this significant spiritual enlightenment was not something to be inferred from within the course of history itself. Israel knew that within the loins of her forefather Abram and outside the future land of promise, a call had gone out to her to occupy the land. She was aware that her ancestors in Mesopotamia had worshipped other gods (Josh. 24:2), and within the Genesis narratives the pull of these other deities was always recognized. Thus, when Jacob returns from a long, self-imposed exile, from Haran, he is required to divest himself of 'other gods' (Gen. 35:2). Thus also Abraham's servant is quick to explain to the Nahor connections, the nature of the faith which is Abraham's (cf. Gen. 24:12, 27, 42, 48).

---

[15]. John J. Mitchell, 'Abram's Understanding of the Lord's Covenant', WThJ 32 (1969), pp. 24–48, correctly sees that Gen. 15 is confirmatory of Gen. 12:1–3.

Consistent with all of this is the emphatic presentation by the biblical narratives of Abraham as the founder of Israelite monotheism. The description of Israel's God as the God of Abraham, Isaac and Jacob, but never as the God of Moses,[16] perseveres until the end of the biblical period. While Moses may be brought into direct contact with the law,it is always Abraham who bears the promises which control the national or spiritual future of Israel. We have noted how Gen. 15 confirms the faith of Abram but does not begin it. We are now to take up the question of the origin of Abram's experience, so we take ourselves back to Ur of the Chaldees and the call of Gen. 12:1–3.

The narratives of chapters 1 – 11 properly end at 11:9, which concludes the Babel episode. The appearance at that point of a further genealogy alerts us to the fact that a significant new departure is about to occur, since this is the way in which the positioning of genealogies has so far functioned. After the sudden and seeming inconsequential end to the Babel story, we are all the more alerted to further possibilities about to unfold. This genealogy deals with a particular family stemming from the line of Shem, the point of whose blessing in Gen. 9:26 as elevated above the two other sons of Noah, had lain in the donation to the Shemites of the divine name Yahweh. That had been the first point in Scripture at which the divine name is associated with a particular group of peoples. For the intention of this blessing and its only result seem to be clearly attached to the posession of the divine name Yahweh itself. This is the name to be associated, as we know, with the redemptive history of Israel. It is doubtless for this reason that the narrator, having traced previously in Gen. 10:21–31 the family tree of Shem in broad outline, offers now a detailed presentation. In ten generations, the fortunes of that branch of the Shemites which will finally issue into the family of Terah are surveyed. From this clan Abram as the bearer of the divine name will step, by his call, into the arena of history.

The family tree of Terah, the father of Abram, then becomes the object of particular consideration (Gen. 11:27–32). Several of the names which occur appear to indicate the veracity of the later biblical generalization that 'your fathers lived of old beyond the Euphrates, Terah the father of Abraham and of Nahor; and they served other gods' (Josh. 24:2). Names such as Terah, Laban, Sarai, Milcah, appear to suggest some connection by the family with a lunar cult. If this reflects the probability that the Terah family stemmed from a centre at which the moon was worshipped then this would be confirmatory of Abram's connection with Ur. This city had as patrons until the end of its history, the moon god Sin and the moon goddess Ningal (a Sumerian equivalent of Sarah, with the

---

[16]. As M. Segal, *The Pentateuch and Other Biblical Studies*, (Jerusalem: Magnes Press, 1967), p. 125, points out.

meaning 'queen'), deities that were prominent also in the worship conducted at Haran.[17]

The migration of the family from Ur after the death of Abram's brother Haran, is recorded to anticipate the continued pilgrimage of Haran's son Lot with Abram later. Ur was a city in lower Mesopotamia, well known, from archaeology and from cuneiform texts, as a flourishing commercial centre from towards the end of the third millenium B.C. to about 1700 B.C. Ur was now left behind and the family move to Haran is recorded, but not before the text has informed us laconically of something of the personal circumstances of Abram with which a whole series of later problems would be compounded, namely that Sarai his wife was barren. The family settled at Haran, a further important upper Mesopotamian trading centre, though the destination in mind when Ur was quitted was Canaan. To bring the Terah history to a close, his death is mentioned at Gen. 11:32. This in itself did not provide the occasion for Abram's further move, for in actual fact, the death of Terah occurred some sixty years after Abram left Haran. The move from Haran was occasioned, as the narrative of 12:1 makes clear, by a direct call from God, received in Haran, though 15:7, together with Acts 7:2ff indicates that this was a second summons, dictated no doubt by the disposition of Terah to settle there.

ii. *The call as an elective call*

The call of Gen. 12:1 summons Abram to a series of separations from his country, i.e. the Mesopotamian background which embraces both Ur and Haran, from his kindred, i.e. from the Sethite base, and the clan structure with which he would have been socially comfortable, and, more narrowly from the Terahite clan, i.e., from his father's house. In short, the call was to abandon all natural connections, to surrender all social customs and traditions, to leave land, clan and family. These were the very areas of strong attachment which in the ancient world would have been thought to provide ultimate personal security. Whatever binds him to the past is to be discarded in this call which now comes to him to be the father of a new nation.

We may rightly term the call of God to Abram an elective call, and remind ourselves that such a sovereign act of God conferred greatness rather than rewarding it. Correspondingly, as H. H. Rowley has pointed out, the move of Abram was a response to divine guidance, rather than the result of a personal religious urge.[18] The particular vocabulary of election does not appear in Gen. 12:1–3, though the implications of those verses are clear. Of course, the Old Testament frequently refers to

---

[17]. Cf. R. de Vaux, *The Early History of Israel. From the Beginnings to the Exodus and Covenant of Sinai*, (London: Darton, Longman and Todd, 1978), p. 192.

[18]. H. H. Rowley, *The Biblical Doctrine of Election*, (London: Lutterworth, 1950), p. 29.

the election of Israel other than by the direct language of choice. Often it is with an appeal to the covenant, the conclusion of which had been grounded in choice. Sometimes it is to divine love expressed, or divine knowledge exercised (Amos 3:2) and at other times the vocabulary of creation is employed. In regard to Abram, the later Old Testament writers recognized the elective nature of the call. He is thus referred to as the friend of God (Isaiah 41:8), or the divine faithfulness to Abram is referred to in distinctively covenantal terms, by the use of the Heb. term *ḥesed* ('covenant fidelity', cf. Micah 7:20). In the case of Ps 105:5–10 we are, however, left in absolutely no doubt for there the phrase 'seed of Abraham' occurs in parallelism with the term 'the elect one, the children of Jacob'.

In dealing with the call of Abram, we are not dealing with the election solely of an individual. This much is clear when we note the significance in the preceding family narrative of the fact that Sarai was barren. In choosing the man, God is in fact choosing the seed yet to be. In demanding a break with the past, God is in this way bringing the future into the present. In commissioning an Exodus in response to the curse of Babel,[19] God thus brings onto the stage of history the associated ideas of a great nation and a land which they will occupy. The object of this divine election then, is the nation to stem from Abram, namely Israel, and of course, the seed which will finally proceed from that nation, namely Christ (Gal. 3:16).

iii. *The Call as a divine response to Gen. 1:1–11:9*

As St. Paul had pointed out (Rom. 4:17), the election of Abram involved the calling into existence of the non-existent. It is therefore appropriate that this redemptive call of Abram should be expressed in language which is tantamount to the language of a new creation. Thus the similarities between Gen. 12:1 and 1:3 where the actual work of creation was set in train) are not to be overlooked. So, as in Gen. 1:3, the form of 12:1 is that of a divine speech which includes a virtual imperative, calling a new phase of history into being, just as the words of Gen. 1:3 had called existence itself into being. In this way the absolutely free and unconditioned nature of the choice of Abram is emphasized, and thus the presence of the divine will as the power which shapes and directs all history is at this point made perfectly clear. There are parallels here for the believer also by which he may monitor his own experience. For Abram and for us, as Eichrodt has well noted, in the case of Abram,[20] commitment preceded understanding, a religious choice preceded a moral undertaking.

---

[19]. My indebtedness to the stimulating article of E. P. Nacpil, 'Between Promise and Fulfilment', *SEAsiaJT* 10 (1968), pp. 166–181 is acknowledged.

[20]. Theology of the Old Testament, vol. i, p. 286.

The call of Abram was a response to a human need, and the nature of that need had appeared very clearly in the post-flood history of the human race. Noah's handling of the renewed mandate appears in the sordid account of the second half of Gen. 9. Yet the distribution of general blessing continues, and this is seen in the table of nations (Gen. 10), with which the family of Shem is prominently connected. But though chapter 10 is the evidence of the spread of the human race, and thus a manifestation of blessing in terms of 9:1ff, it represents also the consequences of the sin of Gen. 11:1–9. The logical order of these two chapters (10 and 11) has been reversed. This seems to have been done to conform to the pattern of Gen. 3–11 whereby punishment is followed by grace extended. By doing this Gen. 9:1 operates as a new beginning, referring explicitly back to the divine mandate given to man at 1:28. To this family of man, scattered as a result of Babel, the call of Abram will finally bring blessing, and in this call is potentially the undoing of whatever barriers to final human unity Gen. 11:1–9 may have interposed.

(a) The implications of Babel. Redemption through Abram.

Gen. 11:1–9 concludes on a note of profound despair as to the prospects for the future of the human race. The narrative is a strange one, and commences on a seemingly innocuous note. At a time when men had a common vehicle of communication, they undertake what at first sight appears to be a promising effort at social co-operation. This capitalizes, not only on the linguistic unity which exists, but also on the absence of ethnic, social and economic barriers. In our modern world these have always been sufficient to negate every effort to promote a wider understanding between men. On the plain of Shinar (i.e. ancient Babylonia), this co-operative desire was to be translated into a common endeavour, and expressed through an appropriate symbol of human achievement. 'Come', they said, 'let us build ourselves a city, and a tower with its top in the heavens, and let us make a name for ourselves, lest we be scattered abroad upon the face of the whole earth.' What immediately follows would seem almost to have been an over-reaction of God. In response to what had appeared to be a very innocent and thoroughly human aim, he came down and confused the builders by importing language distinctions among them. In this way the spread of humanity which Gen. 10. has already narrated was begun.

The reasons for which this divine action was taken are not clear from the context, though we are given hints and these are now examined. The severity of the divine action would lead us to suppose that a gross and flagrant act of rebellion by mankind had been committed at Shinar. Some suppose that the ground for the divine action lay in the desire of the builders to 'make a name' for themselves, for it has been noted that the use of the Heb. verb *ʿāsāh* ('to make') with the Heb. noun *shem* ('name') is confined in the other passages in the Old Testament to the narration of the activity of a monarch (cf. 2 Sam. 7:9; 8:13) or to Yahweh who works wonders in Egypt (Jer. 32:20; Isa. 63:12; Neh. 9:10; Dan. 9:15). On this suggestion God intervenes to bring to an end the bid for power which the builders are making. There is some substance in this view, for human authority can result only from a divine gift. Moreover the promise given by God to Abram at his call that his name would be great (Gen. 12:2) seems an obvious reference to the tower builders for whose activities the call of Abram is to provide the real substitute. We must, however, be a little more precise at this point, and endeavour to locate the real nature of the tower builders' expectations. If we are able to see the character of such hopes clearly, then the nature of the divine response, and indeed the necessity for it, will be better understood. Correspondingly, we shall in this case be better able to perceive the purpose of Abram's call and the set of expectations with which he is to equip himself.

Particular attention in recent exposition of Gen. 11 has been paid to the place of the tower in the builders' plan. It is pointed out that the most natural construction to be placed upon the erection of a tower in the ancient world, is that it would operate, as indeed the use of the Heb. word *migdāl* ('fortress tower') suggests, as an instrument of city state defence. Since its top is projected to reach 'to heaven', some have suggested that this is the area from which a threat to the builders might eventuate, as they seek to protect their humanistic structure. To summarise, Gen. 11:1–9, seemingly so innocuous, represents in reality a last ditch effort by fallen men to build God out of his world. There is a difficulty for this suggestion in the shape of the addition, 'let us make a name', though this phrase might be contained within the lines of exegesis so far suggested if Heb. *shem* were to be taken in the quite acceptable sense of 'monument', though it does seem, by the use of that phrase, that the note of renown is obviously in the author's mind. This 'fortress tower view' is ingenious and adds weight to the position of Genesis 11 in the sequence of spread-of-sin narratives which commence with Genesis 4. But it is finally an unconvincing interpretation since the phrase 'with its top in the heavens' is, as we shall see, a semi-technical one, used of building operations generally, to depict their magnitude.

Simpler, and truer to the context, is the supposition that the account is concerned with man's search for security through city building, and with his desire to perpetuate his generation through monumental works of architecture. The grandiose character of the venture is underscored by the 'sky high' notion of v.4, for the use of that elaborate language is a fairly common way of describing structures in the ancient world which were thought to be impressive.[21] It would seem that the

---

[21]. Cf. Frank S. Frick, *The City in Ancient Israel*, SBL Dissertation Series 36, (Missoula: Scholars Press, 1977), p. 208.

semi-sedentary peoples of the period are beginning to drift, with the threatened loss of cultural unity. Yet, we must add here that the condemnation which the narrative brings cannot be on the score of misguided urbanization, for the city as such never stands biblically condemned. Rather, as Westermann has pointed out, [22] what seems to confront us in Genesis 11, is the search by society for a centre, which is, in fact, to be realised in themselves. In a God directed world, this is an arrogant human assertion to which at the very beginning of its manifestation, there must be an appropriate divine response. In passing, by the addition of the word 'tower' to 'city' the impressive Babylonian ziggurats, the famed Babylonian temple towers, could hardly have been directly in the writer's mind, for they were a response to a supposed endorsement of a site as 'holy' by a deity, while Babel is presented to us as a completely human initiative. It is the city state empire, potentially with its centre in itself, that is being condemned; it is the assumption of the substance of power without any God–based reality underlying it which prompts the divine action. The name which is to be given to Abram is certainly the offset to Babel, and the fame of the great centres of commerce in the Mesopotamian world can hardly have been far from the author's mind as God's promise of Gen. 12:2 is recorded. This is, at any rate, the contrast which the writer of the Epistle to the Hebrews saw in the arrangement of the material relating to Abram's call. With an obvious reference to the builders of Genesis 11, and doubtless also with Abram's point of departure in mind, he reminds us (Heb. 11:10) that Abram 'looked forward to a city which has foundations, whose maker and builder is God'.

(b) Gen. 12:1–3 as a response to Gen. 3–11

We have so far suggested that the 'name' to be given to Abram, the fame which he is to acquire, the reputation which his posterity will achieve, is a counter to the influence sought by the Babel builders. We have also suggested that the call of Abram in Gen. 12:1–3 contains in it an allusive reference to Genesis 1, and that therefore the redemptive purposes which are being expressed through the call of Abram are virtually couched in the language of a 'New Creation'. We have had earlier occasion to note that a connection is directly forged between creation and redemption by the Old Testament writers, especially within Isaiah 40–55, and that this connection is assumed by the writers of the New Testament and taken further. We have noted also that creation itself provides the grounds and warrant for all of covenant theology. It would be unfounded to suggest that creation itself necessarily implies redemption, just as it would be unfounded to suggest that commencing within a context of redemption as the biblical writers did, writing within a redeemed community, a doctrine of creation emerged as a sort

---

22. Genesis, p. 730.

of theological necessity. The truth is that divine revelation commenced with the unfolding of the fact of creation and its purpose, and from that purpose, as we have also noted, a general expectation of redemption would have taken its rise as a result of the fall. We do in fact see such an expectation expressed immediately after the fall in the 'proto-evangelium' of Gen. 3:15.

The expectation of a general redemptive purpose is, moreover, kept alive by the successive movements of divine grace which accompany every episode of the spread of sin in chapter 3 – 11. Each of the narratives of the fall, Cain and Abel, the 'sons of God', the flood and Babel, moves beyond a divine punishment which the act of sin provokes, to a divine act of forgiveness or a mitigation of punishment which follows.[23] Thus there is protective support for Adam after the fall (Gen. 3:21), Cain is marked lest he should be slain (4:15), a breathing space of one hundred and twenty years is (probably) given to the 'sons of God' before punishment came (6:3), and certainly the salvation of Noah is a mitigation of the absolute punishment on his age. Only in the Babel narrative does there appear to have been no divine act of grace extended. But it is appearance only, since in the Shem family genealogy which follows we have grace at work again, for the prospective redemption that Gen. 12:1–3 provides is in view.

More than all this, Gen. 11:1–9 presents the logical conclusion to a set of narratives whose purpose is to expose the total series of human failures and to treat the typical human situation collectively. To all this, 12:1–3 will be the divine response. The spread of sin in Gen. 3–11 is on an ascending scale, increasing both in its intensity and in its effects. This is obviously so from Gen. 4 to the flood, though some contend that the flood, not Babel provides a transition. The view has been expressed that Gen. 8:21–22, in which a divine pledge is given never again to curse the ground because of man, brings to a virtual end the period of the curse begun by the fall. It is suggested thus that a new beginning commences with 8:22 in which the unities of nature are again guaranteed. On this view the absolute of 8:21, 'I will never again curse the ground', should be understood as conveying the sense, 'I will never again regard the ground as cursed.' That the imagination of the heart of man is still evil from his youth is a factor which the flood has not changed. Now, however, a law of counteractive blessing will begin to operate, blessing will now stand alongside of the curse and undo its effects. The immediate results of this new beginning, it is contended, are first seen in Noah's fruitful use of the ground in Gen. 9:20–27 which in itself indicates that though the curse still exists and is active in this

---

[23]. D. J. Clines, 'Theme in Gen. 1–11', *CBQ* 38 (1976), pp. 483–507, building upon the work of Von Rad and Westermann, has traced carefully the theological interrelationships which characterize Gen. 1–11.

world, 8:22 has inaugurated a new age in which men need not rest under its power.[24]

Gen. 8:22, however, does no more than establish the natural parameters within which the activities of men will take place and without which, indeed, he will not function. The parallel phrase at the end of 8:21, 'Neither will I ever again destroy every living creature as I have done,' makes it highly improbable that the weaker sense of 'regard as cursed' ought to be adopted as the sense of the Heb. verb in the first half of 8:21.[25] The verse implies no more than that man's present lot will continue in a re-established world. We hear, moreover, nothing here about the removal of the particular curses (i.e., on child bearing) pronounced by God (Gen. 3:14ff) following the fall.

It can hardly be questioned that the Babel episode in its effects has had a wider influence than the flood. The results of Babel in its racial, social, economic and geographical divisions are still with us. So also are the very great divisions within the framework of human culture, and the impossibility of complete human co-operation that has been the continued result of linguistic barriers since Babel. The flood, on the other hand, was a severe punishment upon a generation only, after which a new beginning was made, and the creation covenant specifically reinaugurated. Hence, one is bound to see Babel as the logical end of the Gen. 4–11 narratives. Babel expressed a naive and total confidence in what human achievement could effect. It looked for one world, one common language family, one common social and economic platform from which human association could proceed. In short, it was the beginning of the utopian humanistic dream to which mankind has always subsequently aspired. We are fully aware that the unities which Babel sought will finally demand a full reversal of the results of the fall. Of that fall of man Babel was the logical social result.

We had noted previously the manner of God's beginning again after the flood, by a covenant re-enactment. We shall have occasion to underscore that in a somewhat parallel fashion, Abram's call is also a calling into existence of a new creation, of a situation after Babel in which God will begin again. Abram is thus, as we have earlier remarked, a new creature, summoned into being by the word. With the chaos of human history left behind, God begins again with Abram, as he will later begin with Israel in Egypt, by an exodus. Like Israel later, Abram will be moved out from the midst of a pagan environment, the

---

[24]. As R. Rendtorff, 'Gen. 8:21 und die Urgeschichte des Jahwisten' in *Gesammelte Studien zum Alten Testament* (München: Kaiser, 1975), pp. 188–197 has argued.

[25]. O. H. Steck, 'Genesis 12:1–3 und die Urgeschichte des Jahwisten', *Probleme Biblischer Theologie. Gerhard von Rad zum 70. Geburstag* (München: Kaiser, 1971), p. 530–531, notes 18–19, points out that Heb. *qillēl* used of 'curse' in Gen. 8:22 occurs again at Gen. 12:3 where the meaning to 'regard as cursed' would be as unsuitable as it is at Gen. 8:21.

call will come to him outside the land of promise. Like Israel he will be armed with a charter of blessing by which the future of the human race will be provided for and he will be placed, like Israel, in a promised land.

The continuity between Gen. 1 and Gen. 12 seems thus established. It will be therefore by the call of Abram that the general structure of the covenant which God has confirmed with Noah, will be carried forward. Gen. 1–11 has left us in no doubt that God's purposes for creation will be sustained. We could hardly have expected, however, that they would proceed in the way in which 12:1–3 envisage.

iv. *The content of Gen. 12:1–3*

(a) The structure of Gen. 12:1–3

What we have in this passage is a summary of relationships begun by God with Abram to which the title $b^e r\hat{\imath}t$ is later given in Genesis 15. The text runs: 'Now the Lord said to Abram, Go from your country and your kindred and your father's house to the land that I will show you (v. 1), and I will make of you a great nation, and I will bless you and make your name great, so that you will be a blessing (Heb. "be thou a blessing"), (v. 2), and I will bless those who bless you, and him who curses you I will curse; and by you all the families of the earth shall bless themselves' (v. 3). The syntactical structure of this passage is fairly clear, though there is some disagreement about the function of the Hebrew imperative with which v. 2 ends. The RSV translation of the final verb of verse three as reflexive ('bless themselves') is likewise open to argument.

GO (*imperative*) from your country and your kindred and from your father's house to the land that I will show you

v.2

----

and I will make (*imperfect*) of you a great nation
and I will bless (*imperfect*) you
and will make (*imperfect*) your name great.

BE (*imperative*) thou a blessing

v.3

----

and I will bless (*imperfect*) those who bless you
and him who curses you I will curse (*imperfect*)

And by you shall (*perfect*) all the families of the earth bless themselves

There is a major summons in v. 1 in the form of a Heb. imperative, followed in v. 2 by three Heb. subordinate clauses whose verbs are in the Heb. imperfect tense. Attached to them is the Heb. imperative with which v. 2 concludes. Then there follow two more subordinate clauses, again with Heb. imperfect verbs, and finally a main statement whose verb is in the Heb. perfect tense, concludes v. 3. It is agreed that the principal statement of these three verses is contained in the final clause of v. 3. The Heb. syntax indicates this and the clause is most probably to be taken as a result clause indicating what will be the consummation of the promises that the preceding verses have announced. That is to say, the personal promises given to Abram have final world blessing as their aim. Gen. 12:1–3 appears to be divided neatly by the use of the Heb. imperative at the end of v. 2 by which the imperatival announcement of v. 1 is concluded. This appears to suggest that just as v. 2 is dependent upon the introductory imperative of v. 1, so v. 3 takes its rise in the imperative by which v. 2 is terminated.[26] In short, the imperative of 12:1 issues into the promises of v. 2, while the situation of blessing or curse to which v. 3 points is the consequence of the command in v. 2 'be thou a blessing'. It is likely that v. 2 is to be divided effectively into only two clauses ('I will make of you a great nation,' and 'I will bless you by making your name great'). Verse 3a has two clauses before the final result clause of v. 3b ('so that all the families of the earth may win for themselves a blessing/be blessed in you') namely 'I will bless those who bless you', and 'him who curses you I will curse'. Verses 2 and 3 thus present a neat balance of two clauses both dependent upon a prior imperative, with verse 3b by its major statement concluding the sequence.

(b) Israel as a 'great nation'

The content of Gen. 12:1a–2 refers to Abram alone, and has in mind his relation to the land to which he is called and the nation which will stem from him. It thus appears to have Israel in view. The introductory imperative of Gen. 12:2b together with the content of v. 3, however, refer to Abram in relation to the remainder of the world. The syntactical division which we have suggested above clearly links land and descendants together, and we have noted that this link was stressed in chapter 15 when the prior relationship was confirmed by a $b^e r\hat{i}t$. Gen. 12:2 thus seems to involve a promise structure relating to political and social identity, divinely given here, as opposed to the social harmony sought without resort to God by the Babel builders. 'Nation' in v. 2 is a somewhat unusual term to be used in relation to Israel prospectively, since Heb. $g\hat{o}y$ ('nation') is usually reserved in the Old Testament for the world community excluding Israel. When used of Israel where continuity with the Abrahamic promises is not directly in mind, it is often used pejoratively (cf. Deut. 32:28; Judg. 2:20; Isa. 1:4; 10:6; Jer. 5:9

---

26. Cf. E. Zenger, *Die Sinaitheophanie*, Forschung zur Bibel 3, (Würzburg: Echter Verlag, 1971), p. 267, n. 122.

etc.).[27] The usual term applied to Israel is Heb. *ʿam* 'people', a kinship
term which expresses effectively the closeness of the relationship
between God and Israel which Israel's election had established. We
would thus need to ask ourselves why *gôy* would have been considered
an appropriate term here. It could be readily argued that what is in
mind is the emergence of Israel as a political unit at a later stage and that
the qualifier 'great' in Gen. 12:2 sets her off from her world. Certainly
gôy in the Old Testament is normally reserved for the description of a
political entity which can be delimited by appeal to geographical,
ethnic, social or cultural factors, and the use of such a governmental
term in this context could broadly have Israel's later political constitution in mind.

Perhaps more, however, is implied by the use of the term. We have
already stressed that Gen. 12:1–3 is the rejoinder to the consequences of
the fall and aims at the restoration of the purposes of God for the world
to which Gen. 1–2 directed our attention. What is being offered in these
few verses is a theological blueprint for the redemptive history of the
world, now set in train by the call of Abram. Thus it would not be too
much to suggest that not only the fact of redemption is contained in
these verses as an offset to the fall, but that we could probably expect to
find the goal of redemption here as well, even if only in allusive terms. If
Gen. 12:1–3 has in mind the complete recovery of the divine purpose,
then it will have in mind also the achievement of divine aims for man
and his world. We remind ourselves that Gen. 1–2 at this point unfolded
for us a system of divine government by which the life of man and his
world was to be regulated. In those chapters it was kingdom of God rule
for man and his world which was contemplated. Likewise we have
suggested that the goal of world redemption had as its aim the
restoration of kingdom of God rule, divine dominion established once
again over the world in which man functions once more as the
completely recovered divine image.

Bearing this in mind the choice of *gôy* in these verses may have been
a studied one. 'People of God', the usual designation later for Israel,
operates as a separative term, without reference in itself to the set of
wider purposes with which the call of Israel was bound up. But the
biblical plan of redemption does not finally focus upon a saved people
so much as it does upon a governed world. Thus the image of the
heavenly Jerusalem descending to earth in Rev. 21–22 functions as an
image of final political unity to be expressed through a redeemed
society. In short, the use of *ʿam* in this context may not have been an
adequate one. It may not in itself have been thought to emphasize
sufficiently the goal of redemption to which Gen. 12:1–3 directs itself.
For though Israel is certainly the nation which the Abrahamic promises

---

[27]. For the Old Testament sense of Heb. *gôy* ('nation'), cf. R. E. Clements, *Theological
Dictionary of the Old Testament*, vol. ii. pp. 426–433.

have immediately in view, Israel as a nation, as a symbol of divine rule manifested within a political framework, was intended itself to be an image of the shape of *final* world government, a symbol pointing beyond itself to the reality yet to be.

We may continue by pointing out that in some sense Babel was an attempt by 'peoples' to establish a world government centre and system. The failure of that experiment and the subsequent dispersion brought the 'nations' of Gen. 10 into being. The call of Abram poses then the real alternative. From that call a final world system will emerge, a 'great nation' will come into being of which the nation of Israel was but a mere anticipation.

If the choice of *gôy* here was dictated by considerations of this character then what follows in v. 3 makes sense. For the contrast which is offered in that verse is not with other nations of which the remainder of the world is comprised, and who must find their future in some relationship to Israel, but merely 'families', i.e. units with no real political structure, and in which no system of final governmental headship operates. Babel has alerted us to the fact that world government must be a God-given institution. If and when beneficial world government does come, God must impose it. Perhaps, then, this is the intended sense of the divine response to Babel which is found in Gen. 12:1-3. It may well be the case that in v. 2 Israel's history is not immediately being called into being, but the course of world history surveyed. Israel's later political system may be said to point to this divinely desired result. Old Testament eschatology tended very largely to be cast in particular political moulds and even when in the later Old Testament political Israel had vanished, such political symbolism continued to be used. Presuming such a framework, the New Testament emphasis was upon the saved people who would form such an end-time community. But the end-time community is seen as a saved entity within a very definite political structure and this is a point to which the Old Testament continually returns. Beginning with a notion of divine government, the Bible never fails to keep this ideal firmly before our gaze.

(c) The significance of 'blessing'

Before we turn to the evaluation of the content of v. 3 the significance of the term *blessing* in Gen. 12:1-3 now needs to be noted. The use of this term five times in this brief context is probably deliberate, playing apparently, as we shall shortly see, upon the notion of the power of the word. In Gen. 12:2a God blesses Abram and here the notion of blessing is bound up with nationhood and fame. As a result Abram is thus to be the embodiment of blessing, the example of what blessing should be (v. 2b). God will bless those who rightly recognize the source of Abram's blessing (3a),[28] and then finally in 12:3b Abram becomes the mediator of blessing for mankind.

In the light of the development of the Gen. 1–11 narrative, this sequence is impressive. Blessing is now the word with which the subsequent history of Abram and his descendants will be connected. It is usually argued that the origins of the concept of blessing (and curse) lay in the pre-biblical realm of sympathetic magic, but a connection between such origins and Old Testament use is not really apparent. There are, however, clear connections between the Old Testament and its environment on other levels. In the pre-biblical world it was conceded that blessings derived ultimately from the deity whose favour in blessing was sought. Likewise blessings in the Old Testament ultimately derive from God even though the intermediate donor may be at times a human agent (cf. Gen. 27:27–29). While at this stage we must generalise, the Old Testament evidence suggests that blessings in personal, national or natural spheres, are the manifestation of a solidarity in relationships whereby the natural or personal capacity for fulfilment of God's purpose is furthered. Thus at Gen. 1:28 when God blessed man and said, 'Be fruitful and multiply', this powerful word of God was bound to have its effects and to confer the beneficial power whereby man would be enabled to fulfil the potential for which he had been created. In Gen. 12:2 the concept of blessing is bound up with a theology of history which is there being presented. If our analysis of the syntax of 12:1–3 may be followed, God blesses Abram by enabling, through his call, the achievement of the goal of redemption, a great nation, i.e. God blesses Abram by making him potentially a great nation. Since there are ultimate goals to which blessing is directed in this section, it is a misunderstanding of the biblical concept of blessing to limit it in this context, as is often done, to power for life, accumulation of life, and thus to the promise of descendants alone.[29] Blessing here primarily has nationhood in view, a concept which in any case carries with it the notion of territory as well as descendants.

(d) Blessing as operative in the patriarchal narratives

Blessing in Gen. 12:1–3 thus encompasses the whole of humanity as well as the domain in which men will live. It is the whole world in its final redeemed form which is on view here and it is a matter of interest that when the narrative has occasion first to refer back to this passage,

---

[28]. An accepted sense of the Pual theme used in Gen. 12:3a ('those who bless thee') of the Heb. *bārak* ('bless') is 'recognized as blessed by God'. As we note in passing, in the Old Testament the primary action of *bārak* refers to divine initiative. In passive themes such as the Pual, God's action is acknowledged by men. On such a use of Pual cf. G. Wehmeier, *Der Segen im Alten Testament*, Basel: Friedrich Reinhardt, 1970), pp. 171–176.

[29]. Principally by H. W. Wolff, 'The Kerygma of the Yahwist', *Interpr.* 20 (1966), pp. 131–158.

explicitly to Abram as a carrier of blessing, it is Abram's relationship to the world which is referred to. In the episode relating to the destruction of Sodom and Gomorrah, Yahweh decides to divulge to Abram the shape of the coming destruction of Sodom, presumably to afford him the opportunity of interceding for Sodom and for Lot from whom the later Israelite neighbours of Moab and Ammon will emerge as nations. The reason for this is Abram's potential significance, namely that 'Abraham shall become a great and mighty nation and all the nations of the earth shall bless themselves by him' (Gen. 18:18). Thus, the subsequent intercession for Sodom is an indication of how blessing is to be mediated by Israel to a fallen world. Sodom was not spared, though it can be fairly said that men could later recognize the efficacy of this intercession since Moab and Ammon do result from the rescue of Lot through God's remembrance of Abraham (Gen. 19:29, 37–38).

The life style that is demanded of Abraham and his descendants is nowhere more clearly enunciated than in Gen. 22 as the blessing theme of chapter 12 is repeated in that context. It is an attitude of patient trust, a resignation even unto death, that will produce in Abraham the effectiveness of which the earlier promises had spoken. His willingness in chapter 22 to deliver up even the promise in the shape of his son elicits from God a remarkable confirmation that the blessing stands, and that it will have its full effect upon a wider world (22:16–18). The reason given for this is Abraham's obedience (v. 18). We may, however, translate this into the more general premise that fidelity to covenant promises and a life style which is consistent with them, i.e. the faithful maintenance of the covenant relationship, will bring blessing both to Abraham and to the world which he is called to serve.

The domain of blessing as a totally enriching life source finds a further illustration from the life of Isaac in Gen. 26. By that time something of the later range of Israel's influence is clearly beginning to take shape. Isaac sows the land and is blessed abundantly (v. 12), and is then envied by his neighbours (v. 14). This has been a consequence of a prior commitment by Isaac to the Abrahamic model. Warned against moving down to Egypt, and reminded with reference to the Abrahamic blessings that the promises were bound up with the land, and that upon the receipt of these promises obedience was displayed by Abraham (Gen. 26:2–5), Isaac 'dwelt in Gerar' (v. 6). When later in the same chapter the particular use of the land is a matter of dispute between Isaac and the Philistines, Isaac moves to Beersheba and the blessing is repeated there (v. 24). The immediate effect of this is that the nature of the blessing is seen by Isaac's Philistine neighbours as 'God with him' (Gen. 26:28–29). They then seek to relate themselves to Isaac by covenant. As H. W. Wolff has perceptively noted, the inference for the later reader is clear. Blessing for the nations is effected by a relationship with Israel as one who is blessed by God.[30] A somewhat

---

[30]. *Interpr.* 20, p. 149.

similar analogy is also provided by the Jacob-Laban accounts where
Laban the Aramaean is moved to confess to Jacob, 'I have learned ...
that the Lord has blessed me because of you' (Gen. 30:27).

The extent of the Gen. 12 blessings is thus displayed during the
course of these subsequent patriarchal narratives, and the content of the
blessing is essentially 'God with you' (Gen. 26:28, cf. 31:3 and note 15:7;
17:7–8; 26:3). This sense of the blessing is repeated in the experience of
both Isaac (26:4), and Jacob (28:4, 14 and cf. 27:27–29). How the
Abrahamic blessings were to be transferred to the nations is taken up
only allusively in Genesis, in the contexts to which we have referred
above, though it bears noting that the effecting of blessing was either
indirect (Gen. 18:18), or sought by others (26:28).

(e) Israel and outreach: Gen. 12:3b

That the nations are to be brought into direct contact with Israel as the
Abrahamic people is, however, the message of Gen. 12:3. How that is to
be effected has only allusively been foreshadowed, as we have noted, in
the subsequent Genesis narratives. The particular language of v. 3b may
prove to be somewhat more illuminating. It deserves close attention.
The RSV translation of the final statement of the verse, 'and by you all
the families of the earth shall bless themselves', leaves us with a
weakened concept of the nations merely invoking upon themselves
blessings of the character that attached to Abram. The RSV has taken
the concluding verb of 12:3b as reflexive ('bless themselves') in the
sense of wishing a blessing for oneself with reference to what had
happened to Abram. The construction of 12:1–3 is, however, climactic
and this RSV translation, which, to be fair, has enjoyed a good deal of
modern support, is decidedly anti-climactic. Already in v. 2b Abram
has been held up as an example and particularly as an offset to the tower
builders who had sought welfare for their world in their own way. One
would have most naturally expected that the flow of the context would
move on from Abram as an example of blessing to Abram as the focus of
blessing, the mediator through whom blessing will reach the world,
since in him, as the narrative has made clear, the Babel consequences
are to be reversed.

The issue of the translation of Gen. 12:3b is somewhat complicated by
the fact that in the Genesis contexts where the charter of 12:1–3 is
virtually repeated, the Hebrew verb is not always used in quite the
same sense as it is in v. 3b. Thus at Gen. 22:18 and 26:4 Heb. *bārak* ('to
bless') occurs in the Hithpael theme which is certainly predominantly
reflexive in its sense, though in the primary context of 12:3 as well as at
18:18 and 28:14 the verb is found in the more ambiguous Niphal theme,
a theme which in Hebrew is basically a medio-passive use. While the
reasons for this difference may possibly be bound up with the particular contexts, it is also possible that both themes of the verb are

alternatively used since neither in isolation quite conveys the precise sense intended. It may well be then, that neither a passive translation of 'be blessed', which older expositors advocated, nor a reflexive translation, 'bless themselves', which has more recently been popular, is adequate in itself. A combination of both, however, in the form of such a middle sense as 'win for themselves a blessing', 'find for themselves a blessing', would be more consistent with the differences in the verbal usage and with the development of the thought within Gen. 12:1–3. Such a sense would also be more congruent with the general Old Testament position on mission, whereby the nations are consistently presented as seekers, coming in to a reconstituted Israel. Finally, on the matter of the RSV translation of v. 3b, the rendering of the prepositional phrase in that half-verse as 'by you' clearly depends upon the adoption of the RSV reflexive translation. In itself the prepositional phrase could be more probably translated in a local sense ('in you') or in an instrumental sense ('through you'). The corporate notion of Gal. 3:28–29 where prominence is given to Abraham's seed suits either, though a somewhat parallel use of the phrase in Gen. 21:12 ('for through Isaac shall your descendants be named' RSV) tips the scales in favour of an instrumental sense.

(f) Blessing and Curse. The Abrahamic 'way'

The sense of the word 'blessing' in this context of Gen. 12:1–3 having been considered, the significance of its use must now be assessed. We have already noted the function of a blessing as a powerful word, as we have noted also the occurrence of the word five times within the three verses. It is noteworthy that the word 'curse' (Heb. '*ārar*) is found five times within Gen. 1–11 (3:14, 17; 4:11; 5:29; 9:25). In drawing our attention to this interesting parallel, H. W. Wolff[31] has pointed to the significance of the curse in Gen. 1–11. The operation of the curse had meant the loss of freedom (3:14), alienation from the soil (3:17), estrangement from society (4:11) and shameful degradation (9:25). Bound up with the notion of curse there has thus been a confluence of converging deprivation which has led man from Eden to Babel. The effect, as Wolff has stressed, of the fivefold re-iteration of the changed situation in Gen. 12:1–3 serves therefore to indicate that under the Abrahamic covenant, broken relationships are to be potentially and progressively repaired. Such broken relationships had led to the progressive series of distances which had been set in Gen. 1–11 between man and God and man and man. The new powerful word, which in Gen. 12:1–3 forms the substance of the Abrahamic covenant is to annul the curse of chapters Gen. 1–11. This new powerful word will find its fulfilment in the Word, for Christ would destroy the curse imposed by

---

[31]. *Interpr.* 20, p. 145.

the fall. He would also be the true seed of Abraham in whom the world will obtain a blessing. It is the function of the argument of Gal. 3 to make both of these facts clear.

Thus the dominant idea of the 'way' on which Abram is set in Gen. 12:1 is that it reverses the series of aimless human wanderings which have characterized 1–11. Men are still on the move in Gen. 11:2, but the centrifugal effect of these early Genesis narratives is now arrested by the centripetal potential movement of the world back to an Eden situation through Abram. Abram, however, only begins Israel's way. For Israel, her Old Testament history is a series of disappointing pilgrimages towards the goals which are never achieved. It is, in short, a combination of the elements of blessing and curse. Something of this ambivalent experience is clear even from the patriarchal narratives, for even though Yahweh himself is on the way there with Abram, leading Abram into a land which he 'will show' him, the fragile nature of Abram's response is seen once Canaan itself is reached. Almost at once Abram descends to Egypt and with the delivery up of Sarai to Pharaoh, puts at risk the promise of descendants. Curiously, having been 'shown' the land he then abandons it! The Abrahamic pilgrimage proceeds on a happier note in chapter 13, for there it seems the blessings of 12:1–3 have begun to operate. The surrender of territory to Lot in that incident suggests that the faith of Abram, as it is in Gen. 22, is forward looking. As a result, Abram is invited by God (Gen. 13:14) to lift up his eyes and survey the whole land. North, south, east and west, all is given to him and to his descendants. What land he has just surrendered is also his. In accepting the divine invitation to walk through the length and breadth of the land, he is in this way, as the customs of his age would have suggested,[32] taking legal posession of the whole. We have noted the increasing stature of Abram to which chapter 14 points. Gen. 15:1 – 18:15 are bound together thematically by the notion of the son in whom the promise of descendants will be taken further. Abram's attempts to rationalize this promise by obtaining an heir through Hagar is dealt with in chapter 16 and implicitly there rejected, as it is explicitly in chapter 21.

D. GENESIS 17

i. Analysis of the Chapter. Examination of specific details

For the course of the Abrahamic covenant chapter 17 is of essential importance. In Abram's ninety ninth year, at least fourteen years after the previous encounter (Gen. 16:16), when the issue had again been

---

[32]. As W. Zimmerli, *The Old Testament and the World*, (London: S.P.C.K., 1976), p. 69, remarks.

that of the son of the promise through whom descendants were to come, God reveals himself to the patriarch in the shape of the new deity term El Shaddai. The etymology of this divine name is still contested. Modernly, 'El the mountain One' is advocated. Function, however, rather than etymology must be our guide here. The use of this name in the patriarchal narratives from this point on is associated with the resolution of extreme difficulties between the content of covenant promises and the reality of the situation in which the respective patriarchs had found themselves at the time.[33] This note of powerful intervention which the name seems to imply is well brought out by the customary Greek Old Testament translation of 'God Almighty'.

The content of Gen. 17 as revelation bound with demand is virtually summarized in verse 1. Unqualified compliance with the terms of the relationship is demanded from Abram, a demand which is put by the expression, 'Walk before me, and be blameless' (cf. Deut. 18:13; Josh. 24:14). The content of the revelation is about to be set in train in the form of activated promises (cf. Heb. *nātan* 'put' in v. 2 as joined to Heb. *bᵉrît*, where the sense is that of 'setting the covenant in operation'). Particularly the promise relating to descendants is taken up in vv. 3b–8. The stipulations demanded of Abram in v. 1 are extended by vv. 9–14. There is a distinct parallelism between these two sections, as the prefatory introductions to both indicate (cf. 3b–4a "And God said to him, 'As for me, Behold my covenant is with you'"; v. 9 "And God said to Abraham, 'As for you, you shall keep my covenant'"). These two sections are further explicated by the detail of vv. 15–21 which expand vv. 3b–8 and vv. 22–27 which report the implementation of the demand of vv. 9–14.

The innumerability Abram's descendants, nations in multitude and kings, is attested (vv. 4–6). This reference cannot refer to general Abrahamic descent (i.e. Edomites, Midianites, Ishmaelites etc.) since this promise is repeated to Sarah (v. 16). Perhaps it has the final company of nations in view, and it is in terms of Abraham's general fatherhood of believers that the New Testament takes it (Rom. 4:16–17). Associated with this promise is the change of name (Abram to Abraham, with an intended distinction in meaning[34]), indicating the changed status of the patriarch at this time of covenant implementation. The new item in vv. 7–8 in which the familiar Abrahamic components of progeny and land appear, is the extension of the covenant to succeeding generations, and its depiction in terms familiar to us from Genesis 9, as an 'everlasting covenant'.

---

[33]. By J. A. Motyer, *The Revelation of the Divine Name*, (London: Tyndale Press, 1959), pp. 29–31.

[34]. It is often suggested that the fuller name Abraham is simply a variant of the shorter name. But N. M. Sarna, 'Abraham', *The Encyclopedia Judaica*, Vol. ii, (Jerusalem: Keter, 1972), p.112 notes that 'father of multitudes' is certainly a possible meaning of the new name.

This latter term is often suggested to be a particular hallmark of Priestly ('P') authorship, but its distribution throughout the Old Testament is too wide for such an argument to be convincing. Particularly is it associated with covenant theology, for in addition to its use in Gen. 9 and 17, it finds a place in Exod. 31:16; Lev. 24:8, as used of the Sinai covenant, in 2 Sam. 23:5; Isa. 55:3, of the Davidic covenant, in Isa. 61:8; Jer. 32:40; 50:5; Ezek. 16:60; 37:26 as referring to the new covenant, in 1 Chr. 16:17; Ps. 105:10 as relating to the Abrahamic covenant. In Isa. 24:5 it is an apparent reference to the creation covenant. Clearly the spiritual implications of this covenant are 'everlasting'. Yet there are temporal aspects which do not persevere beyond the end of the Old Testament period. It is to be noted here that Heb. $^{c}\hat{o}l\bar{a}m$, ('everlasting') has primarily continuity in mind, but the duration of that continuity is contingent upon the type of arrangement which is in view.[35]

The demand imposed is now dealt with in Gen. 17:9–14. Circumcision, an ancient rite usually suggested to have marked the entrance to manhood, is connected with the Abrahamic covenant as an outward sign in the flesh. It was available at this stage to what we should later term 'gentiles' (17:12b, 13) though their very close connection with the Abrahamic household as a condition of reception of circumcision is stressed. As a sign, circumcision is not, as the bow of Gen. 9 was, a cognition or a remembrance sign. It functions as a sign of covenant separation and thus consecration (cf. Lev. 19:23–25 where fruit trees in the initial years of growth are 'uncircumcised' and thus profane, and cf. Jer. 4:4). It is thus in the Old Testament, by its reception, an indication of claimed inclusion within the Abrahamic relationship. A refusal to accept it is the equivalent of covenant rejection and thus merits excommunication (v. 14).

Verses 15–21 narrow the promise down to the future Israel as the general tenor of Gen. 12:1–3 has led us to expect. Sarai is renamed as Sarah (there is no distinction in meaning between these two names) as an indication by a slight change of name of the dimension of the promises which are now hers. The covenant promises of multitudes are repeated to her. The lesser role of Ishmael is outlined and the covenant blessings are specifically assigned to Isaac. The chapter concludes (vv. 22–27) with the implementation of the demand of vv. 9–14.

ii. *Gen. 17 as a summary of the Abrahamic covenant. Is the notion of b^{e}rît in the chapter uniform?*

Genesis 17 has operated as a consolidation of the Abrahamic covenant and as an extension of its detail. In this connection, material contained in chapters 12 and 15 is represented and summated. In verses 1–3a there is a general recollection of Gen. 12:1–3, though the resemblances

---

[35]. Cf. James Barr, *Biblical Words for Time*, SBT 33, (London: S.C.M, 1962), p. 70.

between chapters 15 and 17:1–8 are closer.[36] Like chapter 15, Gen. 17 begins with a divine appearance to which there is an appropriate response by Abraham (cp 17:1–3a with 15:2–3). The substance of the promise of descendants and their significance is then repeated (cp 17:4–6 with 15:4–5), while the covenant is then confirmed between the parties, including Abraham's descendants, with particular reference to the land (cp 17:7–8 with 15:7–12). The stipulation of circumcision (17:9–14) is the new item, while 17:15–21 and 22–27 support, as we have noted, earlier material of the chapter.

In the whole chapter, however, the primary stress has been upon the function of the covenant. The occurrence of $b^e r\hat{\imath}t$ thirteen times in the chapter is evidence of the dominance of the concept and its use as a connective theme in Gen. 17. In our view the use of $b^e r\hat{\imath}t$ in this chapter has been consistent and logical but C. Westermann has recently argued[37] that $b^e r\hat{\imath}t$ shows under Priestly influence, the course of development that, he argues, the word underwent in Israelite theology.

Westermann would see $b^e r\hat{\imath}t$ as bearing the simple and basic meaning of 'promise' in v. 2a since 2b, he argues, which is concerned with the promise of descendants (the basic Abrahamic promise on his view), restates v. 2a. $B^e r\hat{\imath}t$ in v. 4a continues the thought of v. 2, with vv. 4b-6 adding further details which bear upon the promise. P's own use of $b^e r\hat{\imath}t$, Westermann adds, may be seen in v. 7 where $b^e r\hat{\imath}t$ refers to the permanent *institution* which the covenant became arising out of the early promises. Verse 7 is therefore for Westermann the primary theological statement of the chapter. In vv. 9–14 demand (circumcision) and penalty (exclusion from the worshipping unit, if circumcision is not carried out) are included in $b^e r\hat{\imath}t$; i.e. $b^e r\hat{\imath}t$ has now widened to include the connotation of law as gospel. The fully developed sense of $b^e r\hat{\imath}t$ is clear from vv. 19–21. It is the arrangement with Israel as it came to be experienced in Israelite history. It is no longer simply related to the earlier promise of descendants, since in these verses this promise is given to the covenantally excluded Ishmael as well as to the accepted Isaac who is about to be born (Gen. 21). The promise has now been confined to one line and limited to Israel – in short promise has hardened into the institution to which v. 7 had referred.

This view that the 'Priestly author' has made in Gen. 17 a conscious theological adjustment to an older concept is, however, really not tenable. The chapter shows the same series of interconnections as Gen. 15 exhibited and $b^e r\hat{\imath}t$ within the chapter consistently refers to the basic Abrahamic relationship which included the promises of land, fame and descendants as Gen. 15 repeating 12:1–3 had done. Verse 2a cannot be taken in contextual isolation. The meaning which we have proposed for Heb. *nātan* of that verse is to be accepted. We are therefore being told that the divine reassurance of Gen. 15, which addressed the same problem as

---

[36]. S. E. McEvenue, *Analecta Biblica* 50, p. 152 has noted the close relationship existing between Gen. 17:1–8 and Gen. 15.

[37]. 'Genesis 17 und die Bedeutung von berit', *ThLZ* 101 (1976), pp. 161–170.

that to which v. 2a speaks (namely the lack of an heir, in view of the immediately preceding subject matter of the birth of Ishmael in Gen. 16), is about to be put into effect. Not an Ishmael (nor an Eliezer), but a direct heir will be the recipient of the promises (as Gen. 17, in fact, goes on to argue). If v. 2a is taken as a purpose or a result clause (cf. the NEB 'so that I may set my covenant') as is most probably the case, then the point being made in Gen. 17:1–2 (in dependence upon the events of chapter 16) is that Abraham's fidelity to the divine word will bring with it a further development within the relationship, already designated by $b^e r\hat{\imath}t$ (15:18). We could hardly argue that Gen. 17:1 ('Walk before me, and be blameless') imposes prior conditions which must be observed by Abraham before the covenant can be activated, for the grammatical construction of the verse (Heb. imperative followed by a cohortative) is the same as Gen. 12:1, the effect of which was to summon Abraham to receive a divine gift. As at 12:1 the emphasis in Gen. 17:1 is upon what God will do, and this is specified in v. 2 for which 17:1 is preparatory.[38] The Heb. construction of v. 4 (in which the thought of v. 2 is repeated) supports the view we have already argued for. The covenant already exists and is now about to be implemented in terms of promises, for v. 4 should be rendered, 'My covenant is with you and you shall become father of a throng of nations'.[39] That is, the *realisation* of the promise is dependent upon the prior covenant. Verse 2a thus operates, not as introductory, but as the major statement of the chapter which will then be expanded.

Verses 3b–8 expand the thought of v. 2a. Verse 4a has repeated this verse while vv. 4b–6 add further detail regarding descendants, including the change of Abram's name to Abraham. Vv. 7–8 are obviously intimately connected with what precedes, since they confirm the arrangement referred to in v. 4a (v. 7) and add the promise of land (v. 8). Here the connection between vv. 7 and 8 should be carefully noted. Verse 8a essentially responds to v. 7a, whereby the covenant to be carried out (7a), is described in terms of content (descendants and land 8a). Verses 7b and 8b, each of which describes the relationship of God to Israel, are clearly parallels.[40] What this close interconnection in thought throughout vv. 2–8 means is that $b^e r\hat{\imath}t$ in 2a includes the two arms of the Abrahamic promise, i.e., descendants and land, carefully brought together in vv. 7–8.

There is a close link between $b^e r\hat{\imath}t$ and commandments in vv. 9–14, as Westermann has argued, but not an identity. Circumcision is not equated with $b^e r\hat{\imath}t$ in v. 10, it is the obligation which stems from the $b^e r\hat{\imath}t$. Likewise in v. 14 covenant and punishment for covenant breach are (contra Westermann) merely put side by side. Vv. 15–21 in separating particular promises from the covenant relationship, in divorcing covenant from any necessary connection with Abraham's general descendants (and thus

---

[38]. Cf. 'The Covenant with Abraham and its Historical Setting', BS 127 (1970), where Cleon L. Rogers Jr. makes these points. cf. p. 253.

[39]. Cf. T. O. Lambdin, *Introduction to Biblical Hebrew*, (London: Darton, Longman and Todd, 1973), p. 169, for a comment on the use in Gen. 17:4 of the Heb. *hinnēh* clause plus a converted Heb. perfect tense.

[40]. McEvenue, *Analecta Biblica* 50, p. 166 stresses the close stylistic connection between Gen. 17:7 and 8.

excluding Ishmael etc.), simply confirm what our study has yielded so far. The covenant is not to be identified with the promises or demands bound up with it. Covenant refers to the relationship from which promises and demands will flow. Thus v. 2a referred to the existence of the relationship and to what it would effect, v. 4 repeated this, v. 7 (cf. the use of *hēqîm*) pointed to its continuance, vv. 9–14 referred to the obligations which the relationship would bring. Verses 19–21 indicate its elective origins and the mystery of divine choice which underlay it.

In short, there is no theological development of the concept *bᵉrît* in Gen. 17. That chapter is merely a reaffirmation of the material of Gen. 12 and 15. In chapter the formation of the twelve-tribed Israelite confederacy is foreshadowed. They are now the covenant people, and we are standing upon the threshold of their history.

E. OPERATION OF THE ABRAHAMIC PROMISES IN THE LATER PATRIARCHAL
NARRATIVES

The Abrahamic covenant was continued with Isaac (Gen. 26:1–5) and Jacob (28:13–15). Isaac is a lesser figure, but in the Jacob accounts land and descendants are the major items (note the divine manifestation to Jacob as he leaves the land to seek descendants, 28:10–17, and note the same on his return to the land with descendants, 32:22–32, when the covenant name of Israel is added). The Joseph narratives link the Patriarchs to the Exodus account, making it clear that if the land comes to Abraham's seed, it must come by way of gift. In the providence of God, Joseph's enslavement would lead to the preservation of God's people. At a time of very great crisis in Israel's fortunes, Joseph is at the very centre of power and blessing (Gen. 42:2). Thus the notions of nationhood and posterity are preserved and Israel at the end of the book of Genesis has become a very great and populous people. The point of book of Exodus will be to add by way of redemption, the gift of the land. One great arm of the Abrahamic relationship has thus been realised, redemption will add the other.

The narratives of Gen. 12 – 50 emphasize the stamp of God's purpose on history and the enigmatic way in which that purpose is very often realised, in directions which run quite contrary to human expectations. The patriarchal narratives are artless in the way in which they make no deliberate attempt to move Israel onto the historical scene, or to have Israel in particular consideration, though that is precisely their function. They provide us with no real concept of political goals, no system of organized worship, nor even with the consciousness of a standardized form of divine address. They are clear witnesses to the willingness of these generations to wait upon divine initiatives to open up the human future, and the lofty concept of God which we encounter in these narratives is hardly equalled elsewhere in the Old Testament.

The Abrahamic covenant continues to be seen throughout the Old Testament as the framework within which all other concepts of relationships which concern the people of God would arise. We shall note the interconnections between the covenant and the Sinai covenant, and we shall note also that it will be a major purpose of the Book of Deuteronomy to present the Sinai covenant as a partial fulfilment of the Abrahamic covenant. Naturally, in the historical period the Sinai covenant dominates, as the relationship with which the nation of Israel is especially to be identified, and particularly as the Sinai covenant is expanded by the added covenant with David. There are thus only echoes of the direct Abrahamic arrangement from within the historical period (cf. Ps. 47:9; Isa. 29:22; Mic. 7:20). With the decline in nationalism that the post-exilic period brought, there is a marked revival of interest in the Abrahamic covenant in scriptures which project, or are of the period (Isa. 41:8; 51:2; 63:16; Jer. 33:26), though it must be said that within the pre-exilic period, at times of very great national calamity, when the future of the nation or a section of it may have seemed to have been imperilled, the people readily availed themselves of the wider ground of appeal which the Abrahamic covenant always provided.

In covenantal terms we have seen Gen. 12:1–3 as the divine response to Gen. 3 – 11. The Kingdom of God established in global terms is the goal of the Abrahamic covenant. Biblically, this aim has begun with a set of separations, of Abram from his world, of Isaac from the wider Abrahamic family, of Jacob from his brother, Joseph from his family etc. This has given us some sense already of Israel's vocation, for it too was to be called upon to put distance between itself and its historical scene. It was to witness by its separateness until the fulfilment of the times, when as a result of the redemption effected by Abraham's seed, the salvation which was 'of Israel' would be offered to all. Those who responded would then realise that it had been this man, Abraham, who indeed had been the spiritual father of them all (cf. Rom. 4:16).

Summary

In discussing the content of Gen. 15 we noted that the mention of $b^e r\hat{\imath}t$ in v. 18 was set within the framework of a reassurance to Abram of the validity of the Gen. 12:1–3 promises. As in Gen. 1–11, the use of $b^e r\hat{\imath}t$ at Gen. 15:18 served to confirm the relationship which the call and promises of 12:1–3 had established (12:1–3 was seen as a clear divine response to the human dilemma created by the fall of man and the consequent fall of society, narrated in Gen. 11:1–9). The syntax and content of 12:1–3 revealed a structure of two promises relating to Abram's posterity, and two promises relating to a Gentile relationship to the Abrahamic peoples. The 'great nation' of 12:2, though having

Israel immediately in view, refers finally to the end-time people of God. We noted the significance of 'blessing' in Gen. 12:1–3 as divine promise to realise the potential involved in the summons to Abram, while we also saw 'blessing' in this passage as a response to the 'curse' of Gen. 3–11. Gen. 12:3b does not appear to entertain the notion of 'mission' to the nations, though that issue is left somewhat open at this point in biblical time. Finally Gen. 17 was seen as confirmatory of the earlier arrangements adding the further general demand of circumcision. $B^e r\hat{\imath}t$ in this chapter does not, as some have argued, betray any 'development' in usage. The course of the Abrahamic promises in the remainder of the Old Testament was briefly surveyed.

3

The Sinai Covenant – Israel as a Nation within the Abrahamic Framework

A. EXODUS 19:3b–8 AND THE COVENANT INTRODUCTION OF THE DIVINE NAME
YAHWEH

i. The general setting of Exod. 19:3b–8

The question of a covenant within the framework of Israel's experience
at Sinai is raised formally for the first time at Exod. 19:5, 'Now therefore,
if you will obey my voice and keep my covenant, you shall be my own
possession among all peoples; for all the earth is mine.' Exod. 19:1–2 has
placed the Israelites at Sinai after the desert march from Egypt, and the
announcement of the nature of the covenant in which they stand
involved occurs in 19:3–6. This is followed by Moses' account of this
experience to the people (since the revelation of the content of the
covenant had been made to Moses alone, on the mountain, cf. 19:3), and
their pledge to accept the terms of the covenant in 19:7–8. That chapter
then continues with the indication of a further divine appearance about
to come, which though primarily directed at Moses, is to be heard by all
the people (v. 9). Verses 10–15 take up the question of preparation for
the theophany. Verses 16–25 describe the course of the theophany after
the three days of preparation for it. The divine presence is typically
heralded by thunders and lightnings, thick cloud and a trumpet blast,
after which Moses goes up onto the mountain. He returns with
instructions for the people who then directly hear the ten words (i.e. ten
commandments) which are recorded in Exod. 20:1–17.

Absorbing in this context for both its interest and its importance is
Exod. 19:3b–8, a passage whose interpretation is the subject of on-going
debate. A correct understanding of these verses which summon Israel,
as a result of Sinai, to its vocation, is vital. The history of Israel from this
point on is in reality merely a commentary upon the degree of fidelity
with which Israel adhered to this Sinai-given vocation. Firstly, however, we must draw attention to the phrase of Exod. 19:5, to 'keep my
covenant'. The phrase 'my covenant' contains the same unilateral

implications as are suggested by references such as Gen. 6:18; 9:9ff, hinting thus that the Sinai revelation may in fact be further specification only of an already existing relationship. The use of the word $b^er\hat{\imath}t$ (v. 5) as confirming at this point an existing relationship indicates much the same thing. With some justification we could point to the Exodus liberation as having established the relationship, but there has been no mention in the earlier Exodus material of a covenant as specifically established by the Exodus event itself. Elsewhere in the Old Testament where the relatively infrequent phrase 'to keep a covenant' refers to human responsibility within a divine initiative (Gen. 17:9, 10; 1 Kgs. 11:11; Ezek. 17:14; Ps. 78:10; 103:18; 132:12 for precise Hebrew parallels), what is referred to is fidelity to a prior covenant, not merely to a prior relationship. Since Exod. 6:4 has referred to the Exodus event as being in fulfilment of the patriarchal covenants, it seems that 19:5 also points in that direction, all the more so when the patriarchal-type address of 19:3 ('Thus you shall say to the house of Jacob, and tell the people of Israel') is borne in mind.

ii. *Yahweh and the call of Moses*

The new element associated with the Sinai covenant is the divine name Yahweh (Exod. 19:3), a name said to have been unknown earlier or not to have been asssociated with the partriarchal period (Exod. 6:3). This divine name is clearly and closely associated with the Mosaic experiences in Exodus 3, and moreover this chapter (cf. v. 1) seems to have been a personal anticipation in Moses' experience of the general Israelite encounter of chapter 19. A consideration therefore of Israel's call in Exod. 19 to which the name Yahweh has been attached cannot be made in isolation from the detail surrounding the revelation of the divine name to Moses in Exod. 3:13–15. It is interesting, but speculative, to wonder whether Moses' father-in-law had had prior connections with Sinai, and whether Sinai was already in the Mosaic period a sacred site. Interestingly, we know that the divine name Yahweh, as connected with the deep south of Palestine (and thus with the Kadesh/Sinai locations), figures in Egyptian records as a place name at about the Exodus period of 1400 B.C.[1] The point is disputed, but the inference of this occurrence may be that the name Yahweh had been long and well-known in the south and had given this name to the area so described in the Egyptian material.

For our purposes, the call of Moses in chapter 3 is of more than passing interest. There is no need for us to dwell upon the background to Moses' Horeb experience, nor upon his flight from Egypt, except to

---

[1] An evaluation of the Egyptian evidence is found in R. de Vaux, 'The Revelation of the Divine Name YHWH', in *Proclamation and Presence – Old Testament Essays in honour of G.H. Davies*, ed. J. I Durham and J. R. Porter (London: S.C.M., 1970), pp. 55–6.

remark that the details of the Exodus narratives are not only plausible but perfectly credible. Moses' name is both genuinely Hebrew (cf. Exod. 2:10), yet equally acceptably Egyptian; i.e., as given, it may have been assimilated to the Egyptian background in which he was educated.[2] He is born into a Levitical family (Exod. 6:20), a fact which provides further credence for his general Egyptian background since there is a fair sprinkling of Egyptian names among the early Levitical lists (i.e. Merari, Phinehas, Hophni and probably, Aaron). His adoption as a member of the court circle of Egypt is consistent with the access to the Egyptian court which we know that foreigners enjoyed in the period of the Egyptian New Kingdom.[3] And while there is an undoubted Egyptian colouring of the Moses' accounts, Exod. 3 is at pains to point out that the call of Moses provides continuity also with the patriarchal promises. Verse 6 states specifically that it is the God of Abraham, Isaac and Jacob who meets with Moses, and who through this encounter continues the expectations for Israel which were contained in the patriarchal promises. The intriguing point in the Exod. 3 account, however, is the fact (in view of the divine name being well-known in the region and perhaps known also to Jethro, cf. 18:12) that Moses, having been commissioned to lead Israel out of Egypt, asks for the name of the God involved in the call.

As pointed out, it is hardly likely that this name of God was new. Not only is the name of Yahweh widely attested in the Genesis narratives (deeply imbedded, cf. Gen. 4:26, and not merely appearing in editorial junctions) but the name almost certainly occurs as a compound in such early names as Jochebed (Moses' mother) and Joshua. One imagines, therefore, that what is requested by Moses is the significance of the name in this new relationship to be established. Here it is noted that the correct understanding of the name of the deity was not an unimportant matter in the ancient world. In giving his name, the deity was considered to be giving himself, for a causal connection was recognised as existing between the name which the deity bore and the nature which stood behind the name. In an atmosphere in which in the ancient world, man felt himself at the mercy of mysterious powers, there was a very great need for him to be enabled to make correct approaches to the particular deities who in given situations carried the power to help. Without the proper recognition of the deity concerned, and thus without the disclosure of the divine name, there could be no relationship established with this deity. Where the name, however, was given, there the deity had given himself to the worshippers concerned in commitment and trust.

---

[2] Support for such a view is contained in the article, 'Moses', in *The New Bible Dictionary*, (London: I.V.F., 1962), p. 843.

[3] For the relative ease with which foreigners enjoyed access to the Delta region, cf. *The World History of the Jewish People*, Vol. iii, (London: W. H. Allen, 1971), p. 71.

So it is then that biblically, Yahweh is seen to be Israel's special possession. The heathen do not know this name (cf. Ps. 79:6), and in the context of Exod. 3 the request for this name is a question regarding the precise meaning of this new revelation to Moses. Sometimes it is suggested that Exod. 6:3 is in conflict with 3:13–15 since it seems to indicate that the name of Yahweh was unknown during the patriarchal period, when the dominant divine name in use was God Almighty (El Shaddai). There is an apparent difficulty here in that between Gen. 12:1 and Exod. 3:12 the name Yahweh is found something like one hundred and sixteen times.[4] Admittedly many of these references could be editorial or anachronistic, yet in more than forty cases the name is to be found on the lips of Patriarchs, or is used in communication with them and we have already noted (Gen. 4:26) that the book of Genesis takes the name back to its very early use by Seth, the direct ancestor of the Shemites from whom Abraham had sprung. J. A. Motyer must thus be followed[5] and Exod. 6:3 must be construed to mean that it is now in the Exodus period that the significance of the name Yahweh is communicated.

iii. *Significance of the name Yahweh*

What then is this note of new significance which is now to be emphasized? What information we have on this question is to be discerned from the divine reply to Moses in Exod. 3:14–16. At first sight the divine response of verse 3:14 seems to be enigmatic and evasive. Many have taken it as the indication of a divine refusal to be any more direct at this stage of Israel's experience. Yet v. 14b appears to convey the impression that meaning had been imparted and that the name of 'I am who I am' when taken to the Israelites in Egypt is to operate by way of some reassurance. The traditional translation, 'I am who I am', enjoys wide support but cannot be more than probable. For, although there is general agreement that the divine name Yahweh is a verbal component of the Hebrew verb 'to be', there is no unanimity as to whether the form is that of the simple (Qal) theme of the Hebrew verb or that of the causative (Hiphil) theme, nor indeed whether the verbal form is to be translated as third singular present or future. Between these two themes the choice then lies between 'I am who I am' (or 'I will be who I will be') as Qal, or 'I create (i.e. cause to be) what I create' (or 'I will bring into being what I will bring into being') as Hiphil. The preference exercised for the Hiphil is usually associated with the assumption that the Exodus

---

[4] Cf. J. A. Motyer, *The Revelation of the Divine Name*, (London: Tyndale, 1949), p. 25.

[5] Motyer, op.cit., p. 16. For a comprehensive review of the point involved, which reaches, however, a different solution, cf. G. J. Wenham 'The Religion of the Patriarchs' in *Essays on the Patriarchal Narratives* ed. A. R. Millard and D. J. Wiseman (Leicester: Inter Varsity Press 1980), pp. 157–188.

represented the 'creation' of Israel, but that view seems denied by the continuity with the past to which Exod. 3 points. The technicalities of this on-going debate will not be taken further (note however, the Greek Old Testament translation of 'I am he who is', which on the grounds of Hebrew syntax is fully possible). The explanation in Exod. 3:14b continues with the use of what seems to be the simple form of the verb 'to be'. This makes it likely that the traditional interpretation of the divine name Yahweh as present or future of the simple verbal theme should prevail. Perhaps we can do no better than to adopt the suggestion of Brevard Childs at this point,[6] namely, that what is being said in 3:14–15 is that Yahweh's nature will be known from his future acts, particularly from the now imminent liberation. Moses is thus commissioned to go back to Egypt with this name which is now understood to be an indication of Yahweh's intention. The character of the name ought to be clear when the patriarchal promises are borne in mind. Israel must now recognize in Yahweh the only really existent Deity, who directs her future. The very nature of the disclosure is at once an assertion by Yahweh of his uniqueness, his exclusive right over, and his relationship with, Israel. It can be no accident therefore, that when the ten commandments are delivered, the identification of God as, 'I am Yahweh who brought you out of the land of Egypt', is followed in terms of the complete covenant claim which that statement asserts, by, 'You shall have no other gods but me'. The new name of Yahweh, we are told in Exod. 3:15, is the name by which God is hereafter in Israel to be 'remembered'. That is to say, it is the name by which the covenant relationship is to be actualized in whatever may be the nature of Israel's responses to the covenant, whether that be in the faith responses of obedience and trust or in the more formal invocation of the name in Israel's worship.

iv. *Exodus 19:3b–6*

(a) Structure of the passage

The redemption foreshadowed in Exod. 3 is then put in train, and, as we have noted, at Exod. 19 Israel has arrived at Sinai. In this chapter, the theme verses are 3b–6. That this section is somewhat self-contained seems clear by the inclusion with which it is bound, beginning and ending ('thus you shall say to the house of Jacob', v. 3; 'these are the words which you shall speak to the children of Israel', v. 6) with messenger formulas. The message opens (v. 4) with a threefold state-ment of the historical basis of the present Sinai encounter. God had rescued Israel from Egypt, in the desert situation he had borne them on eagle's wings protectively, and he had so arranged Israel's itinerary as

---

[6] B. S. Childs, *Exodus*, (London: S.C.M., 1974), p. 76.

to bring them to himself, namely, to Sinai. This threefold statement of v. 4 is then paralleled by a threefold description in vv. 5–6 of what is to be Israel's relationship to Yahweh. Israel is declared to be God's own possession among all peoples (v. 5), a kingdom of priests and a holy nation (v. 6). Verse 4 thus refers to the particular election procedures which have now resulted in the relationship to which vv. 5–6 refer. The future referred to in the 'now therefore' of v. 5a is thus dependent upon the divine activity which had preserved and promoted the patriarchal relationships to which v. 3 had referred. This redemption which is now celebrated in these verses is in fulfilment of a divine covenant commitment. It is therefore appropriate that v. 5 should begin with a reminder of the existence of this covenant relationship which must now be 'kept'.

(b) Three key terms in vv. 5–6

Of especial interest, and requiring some detailed treatment, are the three terms descriptive of Israel's vocation which follow in vv. 5–6, namely, 'my own possession', 'kingdom of priests', and 'holy nation'. The common factor in all three terms is the note of separateness of Israel from her world which they strike, a position which is made clear not only by the terms themselves as we shall see, but by the additional separate note of choice from 'among all peoples' which is referred to in v. 5. Of major significance is the elective term 'my own posession' (v. 5 – Heb. s^{e}gullāh). The Akkadian term (sikiltu) from which this Hebrew word is derived basically refers to what is owned personally or what has been carefully put aside for personal use. Interesting to note is the fact that the Akkadian word occurs in correspondence between a Hittite king and a Canaanite vassal king of the city state of Ugarit whereby the vassal is described by the Hittite king as his sikiltu.[7] It is thus a term which is used in the important sphere of suzerain/vassal relationships, and thus the field of the international treaty. We shall have occasion to see that the forms of such treaties have greatly influenced the presentation of the material of Exod. 19–24. Elsewhere in the Old Testament, the word is found in covenant contexts at Deut. 7:6; 14:2; 26:18 where it describes the worth of Israel as an object of divine choice, at Psalm 135:4 in direct dependence upon Exod. 19:5, as well as at Mal. 3:17 where it is used to describe the true Israel who shall be seen for what they are at the last judgement.

Interesting are the two occurrences of the word s^{e}gullāh in what might be termed a secular sense at 1 Chr. 29:3 and Eccles. 2:8. In the former reference, David mentions that apart from the general endowment of empire resources which might have been expected to have been committed to such a project, he will devote part of his personal treasure,

---

[7] E. Fiorenza, Priester für Gott, (Münster: Verlag Aschendorff, 1972), p. 140 refers to evidence deducible from Akkadian texts found at Ugarit.

his private property, to the building of the temple. Such a distinction between general and personal ownership is endorsed by Eccles. 2:8 where the word is used to refer to what belongs to a king personally, i.e. his royal fortune which is not to be equated generally with the royal domain. As an election term at Exod. 19:5 the note of the specialization from within what is generally available or at the divine disposal, and thus for 'private' use, cannot be missed in the word. It must be also observed that in v. 5 s^{e}gullāh, which has within itself inbuilt election connotations, is closely attached to the prepositional phrase which follows, '(from) among all peoples'. The RSV translation "among", has taken the Heb. preposition *min* (from, among) as separative. If this is correct the choice of Israel is being presented not as absolute, but it would seem (as the context continues), as a means to an end, for the basic affiliation of Israel with its world is recognized by the use in v. 5 of the kinship term 'peoples' (Heb. ^{c}ammîm). By the collective use of the word 'people' in v. 5 humanity is being viewed as a unit, the general royal domain within which Israel is to assume a special function.

More difficulty has surrounded the initial phrase of Exod. 19:6, *mamleket-kôh^{a}nîm*, 'kingdom of priests'. We shall discuss these two Hebrew nouns separately and then take them in relationship.

Heb. *mamlākāh* (of which *mamleket* is the normal form when the word stands in a genitive relationship) refers not so much to the domain which is ruled but to the office of kingship itself or to the function or worth of the office. Though it can be used of the occupant of the office, such a use is abnormal.[8] On its most probable etymology and certainly by its usage Heb. *kôhēn* ('priest') refers to installation for cultic service.[9] At Exod. 19:6 *kôh^{a}nîm* does not refer to a structured cultic priesthood, since that will be brought into being by legislation flowing from the Sinai arrangement. The use of the word here appears to be wider than merely cultic and be associated with the blessings conferred on Israel by virtue of her Abrahamic connection, to which the 'covenant' of v. 5 seems to refer.

As related in the verse the two terms stand in a genitive relationship. Normally in such a relationship the second Hebrew word functions as a modifier of the first. 'Priests' would thus be the expected qualifier in an adjectival sense, of 'kingdom'. We should therefore seek some such translation as 'priestly kingdom', 'priestly royalty' or the like. Yet it is possible that in such a relationship the second word may stand in apposition to the first. In this case the sense conveyed would be 'a kingdom, namely priests' i.e. the exercise of royal office by those who are in fact priests. These two suggestions are not in fact unrelated and the one

---

[8] The normal Heb. word for king is *melek*. W. L. Moran, 'A Kingdom of Priests', in *The Bible in Current Catholic Thought*, ed. J. L. McKenzie, (New York, 1962), pp. 11–12 argues strongly that *mamlākāh* can be used for the occupant of the office in the Old Testament. This is, however, a matter of dispute and the word is more properly restricted to the function of kingship, cf. Fiorenza, op.cit. p. 114.

[9] Fiorenza, op.cit., pp. 114–116.

does not really exclude the other, though in absolute terms the first ('priestly royalty') is to be preferred because of the clear parallelism existing between the phrase and the following 'holy nation'. One imagines that there is a clear correspondence between the political terms 'kingdom' and 'nation' as there is between the characterizing adjectives 'priestly' and 'holy'.

The application to Israel of the phrase 'holy nation' and not the expected 'holy people' demands some reference here to what has been previously remarked upon in regard to the use of *gôy* at Gen. 12:2, though the use of the word here is narrower. There may be some force in the customary argument that *gôy* is employed here as the expected correlate of the prior mention of 'kingdom'.[10] But we cannot miss the very clear reference to Gen.12:2 offered by the use of *gôy*, nor the fact the Sinai in a very obvious sense marks an advance in the Abrahamic promises but now particularizes them to operate through Israel. Israel's national distinctiveness, and thus her national role, is also in mind. No longer does she belong merely to a general community of peoples from whom she can only with difficulty be differentiated. She has now been elevated into a distinct entity and endowed with special privileges. Probably then we are here, as we noted in connection with Gen. 12:2, thinking of Israel as offering in her constitution a societary model for the world. She will provide, under the direct divine rule which the covenant contemplates, the paradigm of the theocratic rule which is to be the biblical aim for the whole world.

As a nation, Israel is to be a 'holy' nation. In the Old Testament, holiness is properly ascribed, as a characteristic, to Yahweh alone. Yet as the 'holy one of Israel' his separation *to* Israel is often stressed. Reciprocally, Israel is thus withdrawn from the sphere of common international contact and finds her point of contact as a nation in her relationship to Yahweh. It is the function in Exod. 19:6 of the prepositional phase 'to me' to emphasize this. Since holiness in the Old Testament regularly refers to what has been withdrawn from general use and made special to the Deity, the point of the term in this context may lie in a reference to the nature of the national relationship established at Sinai, and thus the allegiance that *Israel* owes from this point to God. Whether or not more may be being said, will depend upon our decision as to the direction that the overall context of Exod. 19:3b–6 appears to assume.

(c) Israel as a 'priestly royalty'/'holy nation'

We proceed now to a further discussion of the relationship of the two phrases 'priestly royalty' and 'holy nation' to each other. Recently there

---

[10] As previously noted (p. 82) Heb. *gôy* is rarely used of Israel in the Old Testament. For a discussion of the point involved cf. A. Cody, 'When is the Chosen People Called a GOY?', *VT* 14 (1964), pp. 1–6.

has been a revival of an older view which had argued that by the two terms two different entities were being referred to.[11] The nation in general is headed, or is to be headed, by a priestly elite. The reference to a 'priestly royalty' thus refers to a governing class, the reference to a 'holy nation' to that which is governed. In this suggestion the notion is contained that the governmental structure of Israel was meant from the beginning to be hierocratic or priestly. Such a priestly rule would endorse, and by its leadership provide the example for the view in Exod. 19:6 of Israel as a 'holy nation'. This would mean that in these verses we are thinking of Israel's internal constitution rather than her supposed national influence on her world, i.e., the stress is domestic rather than more generally functional. The weakness in such a view is that the facts do not accord with the theory, for we cannot point to priestly leadership as having played a significant governmental role in the early development of Israel. When called into being, the priesthood in the early period was very much subordinated to the more major figure of Moses, whose own role was much more analogous to that of the later Judges (and Prophets) than it was priestly in its emphasis. As has been pointed out, in the ancient world kings enjoyed priestly status. The converse of this cannot generally, however, be argued. Moreover as J. H. Elliott[12] has pointed out, what we should be looking for in this covenant context in view of the contact with the international treaty arrangements which Exod. 19 – 24 exhibits, is the proclamation of the kingship of Yahweh and not that of the kingship of the vassal. We are therefore best served by adopting the parallelism between the two phrases and suggest that what is being said here by 'priestly royalty' is restated by 'holy nation' from a slightly different point of view, but that in each case total Israel is involved.

Do these two phrases refer to Israel's worth or to her function? On the face of it the context appears to endorse an argument that it is Israel's *function* which is proclaimed. Verse 4 had referred to Yahweh's action redemptively, v. 5 to Israel's resulting relationship, and then v. 6 to Israel's designated role and thus to her function. Verse 4 begins with Heb. 'and you' while v. 5 continues this with Heb. 'and now'. Verse 4 describes the redemptive events, v. 5 the state resulting. Verse 6 with its introductory 'and now' appears to provide a direct response to v. 4, Israel's status of v. 5 being presupposed.

Important here is the closing statement of v. 5, "for all the earth is mine". Usually the Heb. *kî* ('for') is said to introduce a clause here which provides support for Yahweh's arbitrary choice. He may fairly do as he pleases for his is the whole world! Such a view, however, makes the phrase an apology for the divine choice rather than acting as a justification for it. In

---

[11] W. L. Moran. op.cit. pp. 10–13.

[12] J. H. Elliott, *The Elect and the Holy*, (Leiden: E. J. Brill, 1966), p. 54. note i.

conformity with this, in most English translations the phrase is dealt with
seemingly as an apologetic parenthesis. But no attempt is ever made in
the Old Testament to justify the divine choice of Israel other than in
circular terms of divine love which is expressed in terms of choice. As we
have noted, such an elective concept comes out strongly by the use of
s^egullāh in v. 5. This is all the more so if Heb. min ('among') in that phrase
is taken comparatively, (i.e. 'rather than') with election being thus seen in
the usual Old Testament terms as a very deliberate process of *selection*.
The alternative is that Heb. min should operate as separative, merely to
emphasize the fact of separation of Israel from her environment. A
comparative sense, however, given to min would make for a more
significant understanding of the context, especially as the *separative* notes
which election necessarily confers are, as we shall see, bound up with the
choice of phrases in v. 6.

(d) Israel's function with the Abrahamic covenant

To return to the major point taken up in the last paragraph, the phrase,
'for all the earth is mine', seems to come somewhat too late in the
argument, in any case, to function as a *reason* for choice. It is better seen
either as the conclusion of an argument which ends with v. 5 or as a
bridge which joins v. 5 to v. 6. Of these alternatives the former seems
more satisfactory. The introduction to v. 6, 'and now', (Heb. w^{e'}attem)
appears to balance the beginning of v. 4 and thus to begin a new phase
in the argument. Heb. kî ('for') thus acts in this context to resume the
thought of the whole and thus to summarize it by way of conclusion.[13]
If this line of thought can stand, then 'for all the earth is mine' assumes
the character of the major statement of vv. 4–5 since it conveys the
purpose for which Israel has been chosen. Such a concept would draw
us back to the intent of the Abrahamic covenant which this section
restates, namely that Israel is the agent used by God to achieve the
wider purposes which the Abrahamic covenant entails, purposes which
involve the redemption of the whole world. On this view, in vv. 4–5 we
have a virtual restatement of Gen. 12:1–3. Moreover, clear analogies
between the choice of Abraham and Israel may be drawn. Both are
chosen outside of the land of promise, the choice of both is meant to
serve the wider purposes of divine intention expressed through the
intial act of creation, and both Israel and Abraham are the points of
contact through whom this wider scope of divine purpose will be
achieved.

To carry this line of argument further, the continuation of the thought
in v. 6 is probably to explain the way in which Israel as s^egullāh is to
function. Indeed in a context which majors on the fact of divine choice it

---

[13] For the use of Hebrew kî in this sense, cf. R. Mosis, 'Exod. 19, 5b, 6a: Syntaktischer
Aufbau und lexikalische Semantik', *BZ* 22 (1978), p. 16.

would appear strange if Israel's *worth*, either present or prospective, were on view in v. 6. In short, the terms 'priestly royalty' and 'holy nation' are designed to throw into relief the way in which Israel will continue to exercise her Abrahamic role, and thus to provide a commentary on the way in which the promises of Gen. 12:1–3 will find their fulfilment.

Undoubtedly the designation 'priestly' implies ministry. But in what sense and how will this ministry be exercised? Are we meant to gather from the use of the term that Israel's world role will be mediatorial? If we are referring to Israel's contact with her world whereby she would offer positively to the nations the blessings of the covenant relationship, then the answer must be that Israel's role in the Old Testament was not mediatorial. If by mediatorial we mean that Israel was meant to be a passive intermediary between God and her world then there is more to be said from the Old Testament for such a view. Indeed one could well argue that in the Old Testament the priesthood performed a passive role. It kept alive within Israel by a type of dedicated service, what the kingdom of God concept demanded from Israel in terms of both separation from her environment and purity within it. Primarily the Old Testament priesthood seems to have been intended to demonstrate the separation which covenant allegiance demanded. This is not to deny that the priesthood was meant to display the reality of divine forgiveness and to communicate it, but the possibility of this being the case really depended upon the degree of separateness from its society which the Israelite priesthood observed. Thus, in defining Israel's role in v. 6 as a 'priestly royalty', the nature of Israel as a *separated* divine possession is being underscored. The same notion is virtually conveyed by 'holy nation', for the analogy which is being constructed by these two phrases seems basically a simple one. Just as a priest is separated from an ancient society in order to serve it and serves it by his distinctiveness, so Israel serves her world by maintaining her distance and her difference from it. Of course election also conferred worth and as a holy nation Israel was committed to the policies of national and personal sanctity, a point to which the later prophets would continually draw attention. But the major point which v. 6 makes is in expansion of the argument of v. 5, namely that Israel will affect her world by being the vehicle through whom the divine will is displayed. Thus the notion of v. 6 is basically passive rather than missionary, though the ontological consequences for Israel which her new state entailed cannot be left out of consideration.

The further point which Exod. 19:3b–6 makes is that behind the note of Israel's priestly royalty, there clearly stands the concept of Israel as the domain over which God rules. The theology of the kingship of God is here prominently displayed. But kingship and covenant are, as we have already noted, co-ordinates since the presupposition of covenant is divine rule, while covenant in and through Israel is the implementation of divine kingship in national polity.

B. RELATIONSHIP OF 'COVENANT' AND 'LAW'

i. *Exod. 20 and the meaning of Heb. Tôrāh*

The remainder of chapter 19 is given over to the special preparations required for the theophany in the course of which the covenant codes were to be delivered. Only when the dimensions of the divine holiness which are to be met in the commandment are fully expounded in this theophany are the commandments themselves given in Exod. 20 – 23. When given, the ten commandments are an elaboration of what is involved in the keeping of the relationship to which 19:4 has referred. The point here is that the giving of the law presupposes the framework of grace in which it can be received. This much is clear from 20:2-3 where appeal is made firstly to the fact of redemption before the demands to which the relationship points are advanced. Thus the law cannot be received by Israel unless Israelites are first addressed and are reminded of the state of grace in which they stand. Covenant loyalty is now specified in the ten commandments (the Decalogue) in terms of the life goals which must be implemented if covenant experience is to be enjoyed and maintained. The divine commitment to Israel will be unvaried and unvariable, but Israel's experience of divine blessing within her national life will depend upon the measure by which the divine will expressed through law is realised in her national experience. The call of the Decalogue is thus to translate faith into action, and the ten commandments will have no force unless they serve always to point back to the redemption which is their presupposition.

At this stage, though the word does not appear in Exod. 20, some account should be taken of the general Old Testament word for law, Heb. *tôrāh*, used frequently in the Old Testament to refer to the complete covenant obligation (cf. Deut. 4:44). It is unfortunate that this term, the most generalized Old Testament concept for the covenant demand, should be translated by 'law', for undoubtedly such a translation has led to views of the Old Testament dispensation which do not correspond to the reality of the revelation progressively delivered. What is primarily involved in this Hebrew term is direction for life within the framework of the presupposed relationship. The connotation conveyed by the English word law (as is the notion conveyed by the customary Greek word for law, *nomos*) is unfortunate. It is a connotation of regulations imposed by a competent authority, to which have been attached the backing of some sanctions or other, so that the subject upon whom law is imposed will incur a penalty if the law code concerned is breached. While Heb. *tôrāh* does contain the concept of categorical imposition, this cannot be divorced, however, from the notion of guidance or instruction for life that the term also conveys. In the Old Testament, adherence to law is thus not so much a matter of fulfilling a legal demand as demonstrating by way of national or personal life that a sphere of divine blessing has been entered. Biblical law, especially the Decalogue, though prescriptive, provides only outlines for conduct. It offers, thus, no more than general principles by which life's way within the parameters of the covenant relationship can be regulated. Such general principles invited the individual Israelite to make particular moral decisions in any given context in which he might find himself. To put this otherwise, Old Testament 'law' is never absolute but always relative to the context in which the demand is expressed. In the final analysis (and this point will be important for an understanding of the 'demand' framework of the book of Deuteronomy) biblical law is thus relational. What is good and thus to be adopted is known from God's endorsement of it; what is evil is correspondingly to be avoided because God forbids it. To conclude this slight digression and to lay the basis for what will be said when the covenant materials of the book of Deuteronomy are being discussed: a concept of the law's relativity does not, however, preclude its absoluteness, since the ultimate relationship in which the demand is to be set is the covenant relationship arising from creation. Within that relationship the particular Sinai covenant functions as a sub-set.

ii. 'Commandments' (Exod. 20) and 'Ordinances' (Exod. 21 – 23)

In coming to the substance of Exod. 20–23 we are required to notice the distinction in the type of biblical law which these chapters contain. The Decalogue comes to Israel totally, by way of direct command, and not through the mediation of Moses.[14] God speaks to all Israel and thus by the intimate nature of the second person singular address lays the Decalogue upon the conscience of each Israelite. But there is a clear distinction made between the Decalogue of Exod. 20 and the further legal material in chapters 21–23. This is a distinction which is observable firstly in name, since the Decalogue, perhaps to heighten the intimacy of the nature of the divine address and to underscore its personal nature, is styled in Hebrew as the 'ten words'. The social, economic and agricultural commands of chapters 21–23, however, are termed 'judgements', and the most customary sense which the Heb. term *mishpāṭ* (judgement) conveys is that of a case decision which rests upon some prior precedent established. The implications contained in the use of these two differing terms as applied to Exod. 20 on the one hand and 21–23 on the other are validated by further differences between the two types of law. In the case of the Decalogue no fixed social context in which they are to apply is in mind. The very generality in fact of the ten commandments suggests therefore that they are not to be tied to a specific social situation. In the main, no punishments are suggested by the Decalogue and no fines are imposed. The laws of Exod. 21 – 23 impose both fines and punishments upon offenders for particular social breaches. While the Decalogue is prescriptive, the

---

[14] One might conclude from Deut. 5:5 that the ten commandments were mediated by Moses. Noting the difficulty, M. Kline, *Treaty of the Great King*, (Grand Rapids: Eerdmans, 1963), p. 63 suggests Deut. 5:5 might refer to Moses' developed covenantal role.

so-called 'covenant code' (21 – 23) is descriptive of laws which have been contextually tailored to fit the particular needs of an emerging society. If the Decalogue embodies principles which have then to be applied to particular situations, the covenant code appears to be such a particular application of principles to a specific social context. The uniqueness of the Decalogue in Israel's world, or at least the uniqueness of the material in its Israelite form, is admitted. On the other hand the laws of the covenant code contain many detailed parallels to custom law well known from a more general Ancient Near Eastern context. It would seem then that Exod. 21 – 23 is contextual exposition based upon the general social demands of the Decalogue. Put otherwise, the Decalogue is primary and permanent, the covenant code derivative and valid only for its age. This important distinction is reinforced, not only by the differences in terminology ('words' v. 'judgements') as between Exod. 20 and Exod. 21 – 23, but also by the fact that the Decalogue came to all Israel directly and personally, while the covenant code came to Israel intermediately (21:1), through the person of Moses.

C. ISRAEL'S UNDERSTANDING OF THE SINAI COVENANT

i. *The ratification of the covenant (Exod. 24)*

The formal ratification of the covenant by all the people took place as described in Exod. 24. Moses rehearsed to the people all the words and the ordinances (v. 3), i.e. both types of law so far encountered in chapters 20 – 23. The 'words' at least were then reduced to writing and Moses built at the foot of the mountain an altar comprised of twelve pillars, one for each of the associated tribes. Burnt offerings and peace offerings were sacrificed, and half of the blood of the slain victims was dashed against the altar. Then the 'book of the covenant' (presumably the covenant document reduced to writing) was read in the hearing of all the people who then indicated their assent to its contents. The remaining blood was then dashed upon the people with the reminder to them that the blood so dealt with was the blood of the covenant which Yahweh had made with them on the basis of the 'word' transmitted.

The use of the blood in this context is virtually without parallel in the Old Testament and is thus difficult to evaluate. Since it is not the manner in which later sacrificial blood is dealt with, the antiquity of the narrative and the authenticity of the detail can hardly be doubted. Some remote parallels for the use of blood in this way can be drawn from Arab analogies of the first millennium A.D. whereby blood somewhat similarly used sealed a covenant between Arabic clans.[15] The evidence

---

[15] cf. W. Eichrodt, *Theology of the Old Testament*, Vol. i (London: S.C.M., 1961), p. 157 who refers to such practices.

is tenuous but such parallels would argue for the use of blood in the
Exodus passage as effecting a family union between God and Israel. The
later prophetic evidence whereby the covenant is regularly described in
kinship or marriage terms (and indeed evidence in this direction from
within the book of Exodus itself) lends plausibility to such a view.
Support for it is lent also by the fact that the sacrificial terminology used
for the offerings (Heb. *zebaḥ* and *shᵉlāmîm*) is used in the later developed
system for offerings which are shared between Deity and worshipper.

More to the point, perhaps, for the elucidation of the symbolism
involved in this use of blood is the account of the consecration of Aaron
and his sons (Lev. 8) where the blood of the ram of the investiture was
sprinkled upon the person of the priests. Since a covenant between
Yahweh and what is virtually the house of Aaron (Num. 25:12–13) came
into existence with the high-priesthood in view (cf. Mal. 2:4 which
perhaps on the basis of Deut. 33:8–11 knows of a general covenant with
the house of Levi), perhaps Exod. 24:8–11 bears some relationship to
Lev. 8 in regard to the use of blood within a covenant arrangement.
Such a use has as its aim the consecration of the human agent.
Admittedly, in the New Testament, Jesus takes up Exod. 24:8–11 in a
much more personally sacrificial sense during the course of the Last
Supper, yet in this case the element of consecration within a covenant
arrangement cannot be ruled out and is most probably strongly implied.

In Exod. 24:9–11, an associated ceremony of ratification in the shape
of a covenant meal proceeds. Seventy elders are now summoned to
come up to the mountain where they conclude a meal in God's
presence. Fellowship thus follows upon consecration. We can hardly see
this meal as covenant ratification since that has already occurred. Yet
the association in the ancient world of a meal with covenant conclusion
was fairly common, presumably as an indication of the close nature of
the resulting new relationship. But more capital should probably be
made of the extraordinary character of this meeting. This vision of God
received by the representative seventy elders is unique in the earlier
part of the Old Testament and this meal on the mountain seems clearly
an anticipation of such projected eschatological meals in the later Old
Testament (cf. Isa. 25:6–8), meals which are also so much a part of the
New Testament end-time expectation (cf. Rev. 19:7–9).

ii. *The Hittite treaty analogies*

(a) The form of the treaties

We have touched upon the extra-biblical parallels to the form of the
Sinai covenant which existed in the contemporary world. These parallels were in the shape of the international treaty forms of the day, best
exhibited in the materials available from Hittite empire sources. The

Hittites, located in central Asia Minor, controlled at the height of their power (c. 1400 B.C.) a vast Asiatic empire and regulated the relationships between themselves and their vassals by a treaty arrangement. This took a precise form of six fairly fixed components, and served virtually as a statement of imposition from the Hittite suzerain to the respective vassal. Since the early 1950s careful attention has been paid by successive scholars to the implications of this treaty form for Old Testament covenant studies. In the ancient world generally, it was the practice (which the Hittites adopted) to regulate the affairs of competing powers much in the way that is done in our own day, that is, by legal compact or treaty. The Hittite state treaties, remarkably preserved and covering the period of major influence of that power (c. 1400–1200 B.C.), are thus prime examples of a practice which at that time had long since been current. It is to be noted that the form of treaty remained basically intact with only minor changes for at least a further seven hundred years.

The details of the vassal treaty form (there were, of course, other treaty forms, i.e. parity forms between major powers such as the Hittites and Egypt) are given here, briefly, and for the sake of completeness. The parallels which are often drawn between them and the Sinai covenant are in our judgment convincing, though admittedly the equation between the treaty form and the Sinai covenant is not precise. The point of this parallelism is not merely a support for the early dating of the Sinai materials (since the treaty forms preserved from the later Assyrian period retained the same basic structure and differed only in emphasis attached to certain components), but rather as illustrative of Israel's understanding of the nature of the relationship which was involved in the Sinai compact.

Six elements normally comprised the treaty structure and the presentation below follows that of a fairly recent analysis:[16]

> 1. Firstly came the preamble to the treaty, in which the principal party identified himself. In this section therefore, the name of the Hittite king concerned would have been found together with his titles, something of his ancestry, an appeal to his position and to the basis of his authority.
> 2. The second section contained a review of the preceding history of relationships between Hittite king and vassal. This was intended to act as an encouragement to the vassal to continue his stance of fidelity for here the benefactions of the Hittite king were emphasized and particular attention was paid also to the relationship demonstrated by the vassal.
> 3. Thirdly, there was a statement in very general terms as to how the relationship forged was to continue. Here the question of the friendship

---

[16] cf D. J. McCarthy, *Treaty and Covenant*, 2nd ed. (Rome: Pontifical Biblical Institute, 1978), pp. 51–81. McCarthy himself does not see the Sinai narratives as exhibiting treaty parallels. Much would depend, however, as we have argued, on how the general treaty form has been used by the biblical author.

to operate between overlord and vassal was paramount. In very general terms this section called for mutual faithfulness to the conditions agreed upon.

4. Fourthly, the treaty moved into the area of specific stipulations. The principal demand here was that the vassal should have no independent foreign policy. Whatever internal difficulties arose, if they were of such a character as to disturb the relationship, were to be reported to the suzerain. For the most part, however, unlike the ten commandments, the stipulations were conditional and related to particular circumstances.

5. As a fifth item in every treaty, the gods of both parties were involved as witnesses, a normal procedure in contractual arrangements in the ancient world. This point is, however, an important one for the history of the Old Testament covenant relationship and there are echoes of it, as we shall see, in the later prophetic indictments of Israel for covenant breach. Interestingly, natural phenomena such as mountains, seas, rivers, springs, heaven and earth etc., were also appealed to.

6. Finally, blessings and curses followed fairly naturally as a sixth item. This was an indication that the invocation of the respective gods was not to be taken lightly. The blessings usually took the form of a guarantee of the protection of the gods, which would assure the stability of the vassal's political situation and the fertility of his land. Conversely the curses took the form of every conceivable calamity.

Apart from the above fixed items, there was often a provision for the vassal to appear before the king once a year and usually the amount and the nature of the tribute were fixed. The treaty gave the vassal the right to expect protection by the Hittite king against external threats and domestic enemies. A treaty was required to be committed to writing and indeed came into force only at that stage. The conditions were recited by the suzerain to the vassal, the vassal confirmed them with an oath. The permanent record thus obtained could not be altered since the words of the 'great king' could be neither repudiated nor broken. At times, public reading of the text was prescribed though this does not seem to have been a constituent element of the agreement. The parties to such treaties could be a nation, the people of a land or even individual rulers. Finally, the treaty was deposited in the sanctuaries of the principal deities of the lands concerned.

(b) The application of the model to Exod. 19 – 24

This treaty model has been seen by commentators to be reflected in such contexts as Exod. 19:3b–8, Exod. 20, or throughout the entire course of chapters 19 – 24.[17] Fittingly, however, in view of the sequence of thought in these chapters, the model should be seen to apply primarily to Exod. 19 – 24. Chapter 19 thereby would act as preparation for the main covenant exposition which occurs from 20:1ff. Exod. 20:1 is usually held to operate as 'preamble', where the 'I am Yahweh'

---

[17] cf. K. Baltzer, *The Covenant Formulary*, (Oxford: Blackwells, 1971), pp. 28–31.

identifies the suzerain, Ex. 20:2, (in the light of the background which chapter 19 has already supplied) 'who brought you up out of the land of Egypt', as a review of antecedent history. Exod. 20:3–17 (the ten commandments) functions as stipulations (of which chapters 21 – 23 are explication or application). Nothing in the Exodus material offers any real parallel to the invocation of the deities of both parties which is found in the secular arrangements, but such an absence is understandable by the very nature of the biblical materials. Perhaps we may cite Exod. 24:4 (the erection of twelve pillars) as in some sense a replacement for the witness element, though many have pointed to the blood ritual of 24:4 –8 as imprecatory in the double sense of people and God being involved. Though again, the notions of blessing and curse do not appear as formal items, a dominant note of blessing which stems from obedience permeates the entire arrangement. In this connection some have noted the emphasis in the commandments upon Yahweh's jealousy, and have pointed out that though such a notion is basically elective and thus explanatory of the choice of Israel, it does carry with it a certain measure of implied threat for disobedience. Certainly, and in great detail in the more major expositions of the Sinai covenant in the book of Deuteronomy, blessing and curse elements are found in profusion (cf. Deut. 28).

The absence of a treaty oath has often been remarked upon but here again the function of Exod. 24:4–8 (with consecration through imprecation still the theme of these verses) may be oath-like in character. Certainly the conditions of the Sinai covenant were committed to writing and ratified by Israel within the same general context of 24:1–11. The deposit of the tablets within the ark of the covenant (cf. Exod. 25:16) could well have provided the analogy to sanctuary preservation in the secular sphere of treaty. The later Old Testament evidence (cf. Deut. 31:9–13) firmly requires regular public reading. We have already pointed to Exod. 19 as preparation for the actual covenant ceremony. This is correct, though it is possible to argue also that this chapter contains the actual covenant arrangement in condensed form. The following chapters would then explicate such an arrangement before the ratification is effected before the people in Exod. 24.

Assuredly, as many have pointed out, there are real differences between the Hittite model and the Sinai covenant, But equally, the similarities cannot be ignored. Perhaps the social, political and religious factors which operated in Israel would have produced the changes in the biblical form which then became a free variation of what were current treaty forms. Both in terms of content and form the Old Testament always borrowed freely from its environment. Such borrowing was never unreflective and transmutation in both areas regularly occurred by way of some theological rearrangement or emphasis. Certainly also the Hittite treaties were bilateral, and parties were bound together on the basis of mutual concession. The connections to which Exod. 19 point show us that the Sinai covenant was unilateral. Yet, the borrowed treaty form points not so much to the type of covenant as to the implication of vassalage which the use of the form implied. Again, it has been pointed out that the Hittite stipulations were conditional as opposed to the ten commandments which were prescriptive and categorical. This is also true but it must be countered that the ten commandments are categorical only in the sense that they define carefully the notion of life within a relationship and are thus in that sense descriptive. That is to say they are prescriptive in the absolute sense only if we separate them from the relationship in which they are embedded, which is ultimately a set of relationships arising from creation itself. In short, the use of the treaty analogy refers us to the domain within which the covenant relationship is operating. At the same time it points also to the monarchical (suzerain/vassal) structure, the overlord model which the treaty framework provides. It is to be observed also that the treaty form yokes covenant and law together, elements between which a wedge has often been driven by Old Testament theologians.

(c) Israel as Yahweh's vassal

From all of this we are meant to deduce that Israel's covenant under-standing was that of a subjection to Yahweh's kingship in a vassal situation, by which she was bound to him and yet living in a state of particular privilege. By the Sinai covenant impetus was thus given to the theocratic nature of Israel's emerging constitution. She was an entity over which God ruled, a fact which she must not forget whatever subsequent course her political forms took. The Hittite treaties in their links between antecedent relationships and demand, provided also, as we have pointed out, the link between covenant and law (if that was ever in doubt). Israel's keeping of the law was thus an expression of a relationship which had been called into being prior to the demand; it was not a prerequisite which established the relationship. The notion of a law to be kept did not thus stem from the abstract concept of a duty to be performed, nor from a theory of social contract which sought a balance between freedom and responsibility. As the book of Deuter-onomy particularly later expounded it, it sprang from the depths of a grateful heart in whose experience the blessings of redemption were vitally real. The commandments came from the Lord of the relationship and were productive, as they were kept, of harmony within the community existing under the relationship.

The differences which characterized Israel's law from codes in the Ancient Near East, were not simply that Israel's law expressed a heightened moral awareness, nor were they simply in the imperatival character of the basic ten commandments. The law in Israel referred to an ethical base on which her moral life was now to rest. This base was rooted in the nature of the God who stood behind the relationship. As

W. Eichrodt has noted,[18] the commandments recalled a liberating event
and they led in turn to a reciprocity between the liberator and his
chosen people. The liberated would in their turn bear witness to the
covenant by their exclusive worship of Yahweh. For his part, he would
guarantee the continuance of the state of blessing in which they now
stood, and since these blessings were seen to include the occupancy of a
promised land, this guarantee would relate also to the protection of
Israel from her enemies. Of the continuance of the covenant there could
be no uncertainty. It was a covenant with Abraham's descendants and
as such it would stand forever. Since, however, Sinai tied political
forms, which would produce a national state, to the theological concept
of Israel, a new factor had emerged. While the future of the Israel of God
could be unequivocally guaranteed it would be a different question
whether the notion of the territorial state which Sinai would call into
being would survive. The stability of the political arrangements resulting from Sinai would depend entirely, as the book of Deuteronomy
makes plain, upon the national response to the blessings of nationhood
and land conferred. These blessings would be retained if their source
was gratefully remembered and if the national life gave expression to
this. They would be lost if the political or national goals became an end
in themselves and Israel were to forget the ultimate authority to whom
she owed allegiance. As we know, this in fact happened in the Old
Testament era. That is why the Old Testament becomes a history of
Israel's national failure.

iii. *The Covenant and family relationships*

The treaty parallels provide analogies which refer us to the important
political imagery resulting from the Sinai covenant. But when delineat-
ing the Sinai relationship we cannot overlook the very important use of
kinship terminology and family terms which also abound in the Exodus
narratives. More especially so as the prophets later take up such
language to provide a progressive understanding for Israel of the
significance in terms of relationships of the Sinai covenant. The major
prophetic image of covenant which is taken up is that of marriage and
we shall have occasion to examine this more closely at a later stage.
Correspondingly covenant breach is described in terms of adulterous
conduct, offering thus a negative comment upon the degree of intimacy
between Israel and Yahweh that the prophets saw the Sinai covenant as
involving. While therefore the treaty models pointed to distance and
transcendence, the family language of the Exodus directs us to presence
and immanence.

Important among the family metaphors which the book of Exodus
takes up is that of sonship by adoption (Exod. 4:22). This is a notion

---

[18] W. Eichrodt, 'Covenant and Law', *Interpr.* 20 (1966), pp. 302–321.

which is expanded in the later Old Testament both in terms of Israel and in terms of Israel's king as representative. Following logically upon this is the description of Yahweh's redemptive act of the Exodus as that of Israel's next of kin who steps into the breach and redeems an enslaved relative. Entering thus the vocabulary of salvation at the Exodus period is the significant term *gô'ēl* (kinsman-redeemer). The verb occurs in the major statement of Exod. 6:6 where what is planned for Israel is broached, and again when the redemptive act is being credally reviewed at Exod. 15:13. Since the participle ('redeemer') as well as the verb is very prominent in Isaiah 40 – 55 when the redemption from the Babylonian exile is being viewed as a 'second Exodus', the use of the verb in these two Exodus contexts must be given due weight. The Hebrew verb 'redeem' appears to contain the basic meaning of recovering what had once belonged either to an original owner or a family but which for some reason beyond the power of the owner etc. had become alienated. It thus suggests the return of things to what had been their normal position. In the social legislation of the Old Testament the *gô'ēl* or kinsman acted to redeem an enslaved relative, to buy back a family property which had fallen into the hands of others, to ensure family continuity in the case of a childless widow who was a relative. In the secular realm, then, the term is used to ensure the restitution of basic family solidarities where they have been disrupted or threatened, since every such disruption is viewed by the Old Testament as intolerable and as in need of correction. So in the credal statement which the poem of Exod. 15:1–18 assumes, it is Yahweh who has bound himself to Israel as a self-designated relative, and thus the Exodus there is commemorated as God's redemptive act.

Thus, as next of kin God intervenes as father to demand the return of his son from a tyrant who has enslaved him. As such he is a redeemer. Under the social regime of the Old Testament the enslaved son or relative thus delivered came under the complete power of the redeemer. In the same way land which had once belonged to a family member but which had been bought back by the *gô'ēl* was not thought of as generally restored to the family but as now belonging to the *gô'ēl* who had purchased it as a family member. The understanding of the nature of Israel's Exodus redemption and thus of her covenant state is thus highlighted by the application of the redeemer concept. Israel had once been bond slaves in the land of Egypt. Now by redemption she had passed into the service of one whose service (slavery) was perfect freedom. Here again by an easy transition family metaphors pass readily over into the sphere of master/servant, king/subject relationships.

iv. *Exodus 15 – The goal of the Sinai Covenant*

A reference to imagery of this character leads to a consideration from Israel's point of view of the goals which the Sinai covenant had in view, of what Sinai meant as Israel came to reflect on it. Here we can do no better than to turn to the old poem of Exod. 15, which assumes all the forms of a credal statement. This ancient hymn, which celebrates the Exodus victory, falls into two major divisions, that which deals with the significance of Yahweh's victory over Pharaoh (15:1–12) and that which deals with Yahweh's leading of Israel through the desert on the march to the promised land (15:13–18). In the first part of the poem the prosaic and more functional account of Exod. 14 is translated into the language of somewhat more abstruse theological reflection. In this section of the poem an image is developed in the depiction of Yahweh which is to assume considerable biblical importance. We refer to the presentation of Yahweh as a warrior who fights Israel's battles and subjugates her enemies (cf. Exod. 15:3). In the battle terminology of the late Bronze Age Yahweh is depicted as warrior with uplifted right hand (v. 6) in which presumably the traditional mace which 'shatters' (v. 6) is held. Yahweh's instrument with which the hosts of Pharaoh are defeated is paradoxically the traditional chaos factor which is ever opposed to created order—the sea. The sea, usually so recalcitrant and the subject of much biblical emphasis as the source from which all pagan opposition springs, is a passive force in Yahweh's hands. Through its unruly waters, piled high in towering banks, Israel safely passes. Pharaoh, who often represents personified paganism, attempting to do the same, is drowned with his hosts.

This victory of Yahweh over the sea and his use of it has basic points of reference to the Ancient Near Eastern creation myths, current in Babylon and Canaan, whereby creation is viewed as the imposition of order upon chaos, represented by the unruly sea. Order results in these myths from a victory achieved by the warrior deity (Marduk in the Babylonian epic, Baal in the Canaanite creation epic).[19] In Exodus 15 the language of these old myths has been transmuted, nevertheless the underlying allusions are clear. The redemption which the Exodus victory has achieved is being presented in terms of a 'New Creation', with the assertion being made in this way that through the Exodus the creation intention for the world is being furthered. The second half of the poem makes it clear that Israel, now newly constituted, is invited to realise in the promised land the rest intended for mankind generally as a result of creation. In the promised land, as in Eden, the direct presence of God will be encountered in a way which would parallel the condition of man in Eden. The mythic allusions to which we have pointed had as their theme the assertion of divine rule over the cosmos. They are thus appealed to as an explanation of the meaning of God's victory over

---

[19] More than probably both the Baal/Yaam and Enuma Elish myths are common ancient Near Eastern cosmologies. That the Baal myths perform this function at Ugarit is sometimes disputed, though unreasonably so since it is clear that the victory of Baal over Yamm imposes order upon chaos. On the whole question cf. J. J. Collins, *The Apocalyptic Vision of the Book of Daniel*, (Missoula: Scholars Press, 1977), p. 99.

Pharaoh and his hosts who are personified in the poem in terms of a threat to creation. They are intended also as an explanation of the nature of the relationship, the covenant bond, into which Israel has been called. The very close relationship of creation and kingship which is a feature of the mythic presentation is added to here by the further close association of both of those elements with covenant. Moreover, in the Ancient Near Eastern mythic cosmologies, the victory of the warrior deity led not only to the acceptance of his kingship by all, but also to the provision of a suitable dwelling place or palace for the deity upon the proclamation of his kingship.

Thus the second half of the poem expands upon the significance of Yahweh's victory in these terms, namely kingship and sanctuary. The victorious march of Israel to the promised land, about to occur, is portrayed as taking place as a passage through petrified peoples, who in the manner of the unruly waters of the first half of the poem, make ready a way for Israel to pass through their midst (vv. 14–16). Shepherd language, familiar of kingship in the Ancient Near East, is used of Yahweh's guidance in Exod. 15:13ff, a guidance which is compassionately concerned for the welfare of his people. The easy passage of Israel through groups of people who range themselves in serried ranks, is the language of faith. We know the difficulties which Israel will need to undergo in what will be an extended desert pilgrimage, but what is underscored at this point in the poem is the certainty of the fulfilment of the divine promise of entry into the promised land and the overcoming of all obstacles which will be met. Yahweh's intention is made explicit in v. 17. He will plant Israel in the promised land, the land which he has chosen for his own abode, and his sanctuary shall be established in their midst. The reference in v. 17 to God's own mountain which is the sanctuary which God himself has established has often been supposed to be an anticipation of the establishment of the Jerusalem temple (or on the view that the poem is later than the foundation of the temple, a direct reference to it). Alternatively the march described in the poem has been thought to have Sinai itself in mind as the sanctuary of v. 17, a view which is less likely when the clear implication and precise references of the poem are borne in mind. Both of these views are rendered unnecessary when we recognize that in v. 17 under the imagery of the mountain sanctuary we are dealing with another very familiar Ancient Near Eastern point of contact. In the ancient world the dwelling place of the deity was thought to be on some inaccessible mountain (cf. the Mt. Olympus of Greek mythology), which then served as a point of cosmic contact between the heavens and the earth. Such inaccessibility and remoteness characterized the abodes of El and Baal in the Ugaritic literature, and we are reminded that the Babylonian temple towers (the ziggurats) embodied the same concept whereby the sanctuary was thought to be the point of contact between the two spheres. Even in Egypt, though geographically featureless, the notion of a 'cosmic hillock' which served as the point of contact for the Egyptian deity Atum, is found.[20]

In the Old Testament this concept finally finds its centre in the choice of Jerusalem as the temple site and, as we shall note, Jerusalem becomes, in the later prophetic eschatology, the place to which, as the divine sanctuary, all the world must come in pilgrimage. In Exod. 15:17, however, the reference to the mountain sanctuary is a clear reference to the entire land of Palestine. This is evident from within the verse itself by the mention of Israel as 'planted' on the mountain, and then its description as 'the place' (Heb. $m\bar{a}k\hat{o}n$). A similar term is found elsewhere in the book of Exodus (23:20, Heb. $m\bar{a}q\hat{o}m$) and in the Old Testament generally and is applied to Canaan. But it is evident also from the clear interpretation of Exod. 15:17 by Ps. 78:54 where the Psalmist as he reviews the Exodus period notes, 'He brought them to his holy land, to the mountain which his right hand had won.'

Under this symbolism Palestine is being presented as the special place where revelation will occur, with the whole of the promised land thus being singled out as the divine sanctuary, the special place with which the presence of Yahweh is associated and where he will sit as enthroned. If we may anticipate a point which the book of Deuteronomy will labour, under this imagery the promised land is being viewed as Eden recaptured. The association of Eden both as the garden of God and yet as the sanctuary 'mountain' with which God is to be identified is an underlying Old Testament connection to which Ezekiel in the post-exilic period gives open expression (cf. Ezek. 28:13–14). In Exod. 15 the linkage of this sanctuary concept of the land as the divine abode moves logically and clearly on in verse 18 to a statement of divine kingship to be exercised by royal presence over Israel. The order of that poem had ranged from a supremacy exerted over foes to the recognition of a need for a divine abode to express the kingship imposed and acknowledged. Underlying this was the appeal, previously noted, to mythic materials whose details the chapter appears to presuppose. The association of divine kingship and 'temple' was an assumed Ancient Near Eastern one. The point which is therefore being made in Exod. 15:18 is that kingship of this character exercised at this stage over Israel is, within the terms of such a passage as Exod. 19:3b–6 which presupposes divine kingship over Israel, simply an historical demonstration of the realities of divine cosmic rule through redemption. To sum up, in the hymn of Exod. 15 the basic covenantal themes of a redeemed people, a New Creation, the promised land, divine kingship are all confes-

---

[20] On the general subject of the 'cosmic mountain' in the Ancient Near East on which the deity was enthroned, cf. R. J. Clifford, *The Cosmic Mountain in Canaan and the Old Testament*, (Cambridge Mass.: Harvard Univ. Press, 1971), who treats Ex. 15 at pp. 137–139. Reference must also be made to the helpful discussion of Exod. 15:1–18 by N. Lohfink in "The Song of Victory at the Red Sea", in his *The Christian Meaning of the Old Testament* (London: Burns and Oates, 1969) pp. 67–68.

sionally rehearsed in this credal-type presentation which seeks poeti-
cally and imaginatively to explore for Israel the implications of the
Exodus redemption.

v. *Worship as the recognition of divine kingship (Exod. 25 – 31)*

Exodus 25–31—to follow now the course of the Exodus narrative
again—deals with the blue-print for the erection of the tabernacle. At
first sight it seems to be a digression and thus to interrupt the covenant
narrative sequence of chapters 19 – 34. The intent is, however, to
provide a portable expression of divine kingship for Yahweh's rule
before Israel leaves Sinai. On the march to the promised land the
tabernacle was to be located at the very centre of Israel's camp
formation, a representation in this way of the exercised rule of Yahweh,
to which Ezekiel in the post-exilic period will return as an ideal in his
new temple vision (cf. Ezek. 47 – 48). The actual construction of the
tabernacle is reported in Exod. 35 – 40 after Exod. 32 – 34 has dealt with
the necessary renewal of the covenant arising from apostasy. It is to be
noted that the directions given to Moses close the account with an
instruction to keep the sabbath (Exod. 31:12ff) and that the account of
the actual erection of the tabernacle in Exod. 35:1ff commences with a
repetition of the sabbath command. It would thus seem inferential that
the connection between tabernacle and sabbath is close and that in
some sense the building of the tabernacle and the observance of the
sabbath are simply two sides of the same reality. The reason for this
must be sought in the total symbolism which the tabernacle conveys of
the visible representation within Israel of divine rule. The tabernacling
presence of God in Israel was intended to ensure for her the enjoyment
of the very great covenant blessing, namely that of 'rest' in the promised
land. Correspondingly, the sabbath which is strongly linked to creation
by the third commandment (Exod. 20:11) is to function as a weekly
symbol of creation intention for men. Both tabernacle and sabbath thus
witness to God's rule over creation. The book of Exodus ends on the
note of the tabernacle having been built and this is clearly the point to
which the author has been progressing in his account of the Exodus
redemption. Redemption has involved a redemption *from*, and this has
been from the slavery with which the book of Exodus commenced. But
redemption also involves a redemption *for*, and this equally clearly
means for a worship which is the acknowledgement of the covenant
presence and importantly of divine kingship expressed through the
tabernacle symbolism.

D. COVENANT FRACTURE AND RENEWAL (EXOD. 32 – 34)

i. *Apostasy and covenant renewal (Exod. 32 – 34)*

Between the projection of the tabernacle and its erection there occur the great national apostasy of the golden calf (Exod. 32) and the consequent renewal of the covenant (chapters 33 – 34). At the end of chapter 24 Moses is called up onto the mountain where he is to remain for a period of forty days, to receive two tables, the ten commandments reduced to written form. When he returned to the camp he found that an act of gross apostasy had been committed. A golden calf, a common deity symbol in the ancient world, had been made, and worship had been offered to it. God is deterred from action which will blot out the apostates only by the appeal of Moses both to the divine character and to the patriarchal promises (Exod. 32:13). Moses broke the tablets, rallied the Levites to him, conducted a purge of the idolaters and then returned to the mountain to intercede. As a result the divine promises are renewed, the people are to be led to the promised land (33:1-3) because of divine fidelity to the promises given to the patriarchs. Attention now switches to the manner in which the Deity will now be present among Israel on the march and thus to the mediatorial role of Moses. Here the Mosaic tent of meeting in which Moses, outside the camp, communed with the Deity, whose presence was manifested in terms of the pillar of cloud which descended, is discussed (Exod. 33:7-11). This tent, though often associated with the tabernacle, has no connection with the worship tent, nor has it any connection with the ark, as some have again supposed. The function of this tent seems to have been oracular and revelatory, and to continue the Sinai immediacy in Moses' own experience.[21] In the continuing narrative of Exod. 33:12-17, the revelation given to Israel through Moses in 3:14 is virtually transferred to Moses personally (note the tenor of 33:12 where Moses now has 'the name'). The presence is guaranteed to Moses only, as is the promise of rest (note the singular pronoun in v. 14). Moses at once identifies himself with his people and mediates for them, an action which achieves the continuance of the divine support. The presence will go with Israel (vv. 16–17) and confirmation of this comes to Moses in chapter 33:18–23 in a theophany which forms a personal parallel to the general parallel of the theophany given to Israel after the covenant specification of Exod. 19.

In chapter 34 the covenant with Israel is renewed. This is not, as Deut. 10:1-5 makes clear, a repetition, as some have supposed, of earlier

---

[21] The relationship between the tabernacle and the tent of meeting and their distinction, one from the other, is carefully reviewed by M. Haran, *Temples and Temple Service in Ancient Israel*, (Oxford: Clarendon, 1978), pp. 260–271. Additionally, on the relationship between tabernacle and sabbath note B. S. Childs, *Exodus*, p. 542.

material, for there are important differences between the endorsement of the covenant in Exod. 34 and the earlier delivery in chapters 19 – 20. Exod. 34:1–9 is the preparatory theophany for covenant renewal (paralleling in this way the latter half of chapter 19), and the actual covenant renewal occurs in Exod. 34:10–27. Important in this chapter is the declaration of the divine nature which is a concomitant of the theophany in vv. 1–7. Here, there is brought into direct connection with the Sinai covenant the significant descriptive term *hesed* (v. 6), normally translated as 'steadfast love', 'covenant fidelity' or the like. This becomes the word which from this point onwards summarizes the divine commitment to the relationship. The significance of this word as connected with Sinai thus requires explanation. In a human context[22] *hesed* refers to a specific action taken by one party on behalf of another where a close personal relationship has provided the basis for action. Such action designated as motivated by *hesed* is designed to meet a need other than a casual one and is undertaken in a spirit of faithfulness to a prior arrangement. The recipient of such a kindness is in the Old Testament always the contextual inferior of the actor, with the further implication arising that the actor feels free to make the decision as to whether he will or will not respond to the need. If he chooses to act, the act does not arise from a sense of obligation, i.e. merely from a legally binding commitment, but from a sense of personal loyalty which the relationship involves. The point has been made that the word *hesed* is not applicable to the establishment of a relationship, but reflects rather fidelity and loyalty to an existing relationship. The aim of the *hesed* exhibited is to preserve the tenor of the relationship which already exists. There is thus a sense of fitness about the use of this word in the important context of Exod. 15:13 where it denotes the leading of Israel by God to the promised land. This was the act whereby God bore witness to the continuance and the fulfilment of the obligation in which he had freely involved himself.

In the context of Exod. 34:1–7 God is described as one who is 'great in *hesed*' (v. 6). This description implies that God's *hesed* was qualitatively different from the similar exercise of obligation freely undertaken which would have devolved upon a normal covenant partner. The display of faithfulness after chapter 32, when by that incident Israel had forfeited all claims to be the people of God and had thus severed by rebellion any right to hope for divine mercy, was more than Israel either deserved or could have expected. By the use of this word the extraordinary kindness of God in remaining faithful to his original commitment is conveyed. Thus *hesed* in this context is analogous to the 'grace' of the New Testament. In itself *hesed* was not synonymous with forgiveness, yet within the covenant relationship the word tended to develop that

---

[22] K. D. Sakenfeld's article, 'The Problem of Divine Forgiveness in Numbers 14', *CBQ* 37 (1975), pp. 317–330, helpfully surveys the covenantal use of *hesed*.

connotation. Only continued divine forgiveness could sustain the covenant, given the continual infidelity of Israel throughout the historical period. The association therefore of 'faithfulness' and 'forgiveness' in Exod. 34:7 becomes a natural one. If the covenant was to endure, only divine faithfulness would sustain it. In the long run it would be maintained only because God was concerned to preserve it. Its continuance, therefore, would depend upon the unchangeability of the divine nature and not upon the indifferent quality of human performance.

Only on the basis of such a forgiveness could the covenant be renewed in the terms which Exod. 34:10–27 display. The tense of v. 10, though a Hebrew past tense, must with the RSV be taken with a future reference, for the actual re-endorsement of the covenant is connected in v. 27 with the reduction of the commandments to writing. Emphasis in the intervening verses is upon the conduct for which Israel is to be responsible in the promised land. There are strong warnings against idolatry (v. 14) and the need for separation is emphasized (vv. 15–16), and there are detailed stipulations in vv. 18–26 concerning life in a new, agricultural setting, with particular emphasis being placed upon the keeping of the passover, the maintenance of the sabbath, and thanksgiving for the gift of the land.

ii. *The Veil of Moses (Exod. 34:29–35)*

Particular attention must be paid to Exod. 34:29–35 which conclude the whole covenant episode of chapters 19 – 34 and these verses are thus critical by virtue of their position. Some of the interpretations offered concerning them are fanciful, but the basic facts are clear. The veil (or mask – the translation of the Heb. word in v. 33 is uncertain) is put on by Moses whenever (vv. 33–35) he is not acting as a mediator or divine spokesman to Israel. Before the Lord, in the tent of meeting, or in the actual conveyance of the message of the covenant, Moses is unveiled. The glory which Moses acquired in the presence of the Lord is clearly perceived whenever he came out of the tent into the camp and acted mediatorially. Drawn thus into the atmosphere of the divine presence in the tent, Moses' face glowed and this glory was visible to the Israelites whenever revelation was being delivered to them, perhaps in order to authenticate the nature of the message. While this Old Testament section is allusively difficult, by position it seems to operate as interpretative of the whole covenant narrative which began at Exod. 19. In its progression this narrative was interrupted by the very real failure of Exod. 32, which then cast a doubt upon the continuance of the covenant.

We are virtually dependent upon St. Paul for the exegesis of this important Exodus material because of the cryptic nature of the original. When the details are taken up by St. Paul in 2 Corinthians 3 it is in the course of St. Paul's argument at the point at which he is defending his ministration of the New Covenant. In 2 Cor. 3 St. Paul clearly has in mind a comparison of his own with the Mosaic office. He reminds the Corinthians at the outset of that chapter that letters of recommendation, which they sought, were not able to be produced visibly in the way in which Moses had produced the two tables of stone on which the requirement of the Old Covenant had been engraved. They were to be seen in the evidence of the changed lives (i.e. as the argument of the chapter proceeds, in the divine glory thus demonstrated) of the Corinthians themselves. In these terms the argument of 2 Cor. 3:7ff is concerned to expose the difference between the 'letter' and the 'spirit' and the point which St. Paul underscores is that the full effect of the Sinai covenant in terms of its renewal in Exod. 34 could not be seen by the waiting Israelites, but only in the glowing face of Moses. There is no thought in St. Paul's mind, however, that the glory of Moses was transitory.[23] The intent of the veil was that the Israelites might not continue to look upon the high point of the Old Covenant revelation (cf. Greek *telos*, v. 13). The reason given for this in the general context of 2 Cor. 3 was that their hearts were then hardened (since Exod. 32 had intervened – this is apparently the presupposition in thought from which St. Paul proceeds), and thus contact with the divine glory in that situation would have been dangerous. In short the Mosaic experience could not be shared by all Israel in the Exod. 34 situation. But all Christians, St. Paul continues, are now in the Mosaic situation, for the righteousness which Christ gives is that which was potentially available under the Mosaic dispensation. At least this was the original intention (as we shall note when we return to Exod. 19–34) and thus the aim of the Old Covenant. For Israel to recover this original position, or what had been originally contemplated, a twofold operation is required. The veil must first be removed from the national heart (v. 14), but also from the Mosaic narrative when read (v. 15). The hardening of the heart which had produced the inability to receive the direct revelation communicated through Moses in the general context of Exod. 19 – 34, had been inbuilt into the revelation reduced to writing, and thus had been 'canonized' (cf. 2 Cor. 3:15). Perhaps, at this point Paul is saying that the apostasy of Exod. 32 was typical of Israel's continued and recorded reaction to the divine word throughout the Old Testament period. In 2 Cor. 3:16 St. Paul contemplates the Mosaic position in the tent. When Moses turned to the Lord the veil had been removed, i.e. he had been placed in a position in which he was able to receive direct revelation. The generality of 2 Cor. 3:16 makes the Mosaic position

---

[23] The notion that in 2 Cor. 3 Moses' glory is described as 'fading' is bound up with the unwarranted translation of the Greek verb *katargeo* (annul) at v. 7, 11, 13, 14 as in the middle voice. But D. W. Oostendorp, *Another Jesus*, (Kampen: J. H. Kok, 1967), argues cogently that it should be passive, cf. p. 37, note 24.

possible, St. Paul seems to be arguing, for any Christian. The veil on the natural heart is able to be removed as a man 'turns to the Lord'.

The general analogy from this Old Testament episode is made even more specific by St. Paul in v. 17 ('Now the Lord is the Spirit, and where the Spirit of the Lord is, there is freedom'). St. Paul's intent by the use of v. 17 seems to be to compare the revelation by Yahweh (the 'Lord' of v. 17 – 'Lord' is the customary Greek translation for Heb. Yahweh in the Greek Old Testament) to Moses with the potential available through the Spirit to Christians. Just as Moses had been the receptor of the Old Covenant, given directly to him by Yahweh, so Christians may directly receive the blessings of the New Covenant, which is the fulfilment of the Old, by the operation of the Spirit on their hearts. It is this immediacy of the revelation, St. Paul argues here, this ability to know the mind of God, which characterizes the new era. In the Old Covenant dispensation revelation was indirect, in the new it is direct. That is why St. Paul is able to remind us in 2 Cor. 3:18 that we are all now in the Mosaic position, the recipients of direct revelation, beholding the glory of the Lord with unveiled face and being changed into his likeness from one degree of glory unto another.

iii. *Moses' mediatorial role*

With the above in mind we may return to the function of Exod. 34:29–35 within chapters 19–34. In chapter 19 the commandments are given to a united people who personally hear them. This is the clear meaning of Exod. 20:18 and it is supported by Deut. 5:4, 22–24, where in the latter references the personalized contact between God and Israel is especially stressed. The commandments thus came without the aid of any intermediary, a fact which stresses not only their importance, but also their need of personal apprehension. Admittedly, Exod. 20:19ff suggests that subsequent legal material will be given only through Moses. We are left somewhat in the dark by the context, however, as to whether this was a concession to the fear of the people expressed as a reaction to the divine presence or whether, perhaps more probably in this context, the material is so presented as to underscore the importance of the ten commandments. Admittedly Moses is thrown into prominence by Exod. 20:19ff and Exod. 24:1–2, but the fact is that at the ratification of the covenant in 24:1–11 seventy elders with Aaron, Nadab and Abihu accompany Moses up to the mountain and eat in the divine presence. This indicates that still no real prohibition was being placed upon direct encounter between Israel or her representatives and the Deity. When at the end of Exod. 24 Moses goes up onto the mountain into the more immediate divine presence to reduce the ten commandments to writing, whatever mediatorial role he possessed to that point has only very reservedly been exercised. All Israel individually has heard the covenant requirements and all Israel has ratified them.

But when Moses again renews the covenant for Israel after the golden calf episode, his mediatorial role is dominant. For between the first encounter of chapter 19 and that of chapter 33 a breach of so heinous a character had occurred that Yahweh's presence could no longer directly accompany Israel, lest Israel be consumed (33:3). It is made clear in the course of this chapter by the appearance at that point of the tent of meeting that it is with Moses alone that God will commune in future. The position of the openness of Israel to the divine word which she had assumed in Exod. 19 has now disappeared, and indeed there is a hardness of national heart against which Israel is from this time constantly warned, which displays itself nationally. The unveiled face of Moses in communication with Israel in Exod. 34:29–35 suggests the still essential openness of divine revelation. On the other hand the normally veiled face of Moses, when not engaged mediatorially or when not in the divine presence, vividly suggests the enjoyment by Moses of a spiritual experience which could not be shared at that time by the remainder of Israel. The conjecture is that as a result of the national apostasy of Exod. 32, an apostasy of the kind which continued to trouble Israel right to the end of its history, the full significance of the Sinai covenant is now veiled in her experience. This situation would continue for Israel until the veil would be removed in Christ and through the Spirit Israel would be placed in the Mosaic position (and indeed in the Exod. 19 position). Never again in the Old Testament does Israel return to its original Sinai position or realise its Sinai potential. As a summary of lost opportunities and as an indication of the unfortunate state into which the Sinai covenant had lapsed, Exod. 34:29–35 appositely concludes the Sinai covenant account.

E. SIN WITHIN THE COVENANT FRAMEWORK – SACRIFICE

i. *The efficacy of the sacrificial system*

Exod. 35 – 40 is taken up with the implementation of the blueprint offered to Moses for the building of the tabernacle and thus the book concludes, as we have had occasion already to note, with Israel potentially at worship. Since this is so, we can hardly conclude any account of the Sinai covenant without taking into consideration the way in which the covenant was protected by the means of approach and forgiveness that the sacrificial system provided.

We turn therefore, to consider somewhat summarily the evidence for the conduct of covenant sacrifice which the book of Leviticus provides and to discuss the efficacy of sacrifice within the covenant framework. The view is usually held that the covenant sacrifices were typical, looking forward to a removal of sin to be brought about by some later divine intervention of which the sacrificial system and its components were proleptic. Support for such a view is often drawn from the New Testament, particularly from the Epistle to the Hebrews where the Old Testament sacrifices are thought to be dismissed summarily as simply the window dressing of what was an ineffective period. It is thus stressed, we are reminded by commentators, that the blood of bulls and goats could not take away sins (Heb. 10:4). It is further pointed out that within the Old Testament the prophetic movement was very critical of and indeed saw no use for the cult. Yet strong claims can be advanced for the view that, for the pious Israelite, sacrifice was considered to be an effective means of actual forgiveness for sins committed within the covenant relationship. The clear understanding of the book of Leviticus is that sacrifice did effect atonement (Lev. 4:35), that is to say that by it the worshipper was cleansed or purified from sin.[24] Of course, as the book of Hebrews does point out, the Old Testament offers no permanent solution for the problem of sin. Only the blood of Christ sacrificially shed could do that. No Old Testament believer would have believed, however, that the blood of bulls and goats did remove sin. Animal sacrifices were simply part of the general mechanism by which the reality of sin was underscored. Such sacrifices took place within the covenant, not as a means of approach whereby a relationship might be established. The aim of covenant sacrifices was to preserve what had been established, not to initiate new relationships. When the worshipper drew near with his offering and laid his hand upon it by way of personal identification, then killed the beast etc. at the sanctuary, it was a personal recognition that a breach in covenant relationships had occurred, whether vertically between the Deity and the worshipper or horizontally between worshipper and worshipper. This breach must be dealt with and sacrifice was the appointed means. Forgiveness of sins was so achieved and to suggest that forgiveness was only symbolic or typical would have been to compare the system to a vague and meaningless ritual.[25] Here the common view that the Old Testament sacrifices were sufficient for unpremeditated sins only is in need of re-examination. The book of Leviticus makes it perfectly clear that both 'unwitting' sins and sins committed with a 'high hand' were forgiven (cf. Lev. 4 for 'unwitting sins' and 6:1–7 for premeditated sin). Of course what the sacrificial system did, as the 'high hand' context of Num. 15:30ff suggests, was to deny the effects of the system to the unrepentant sinner. In the Old as in the New, there was no experience of forgiveness for unconfessed sins.[26] Of course the Old Testament sac-

---

[24] The background of the common Levitical phrase 'to make atonement' lies most probably in a notion of purification rather than in a notion of the covering of sin. Cf. B. Levine, *In the Presence of the Lord* (Leiden: E. J. Brill, 1974), pp. 56–137.

[25] On the efficacy of Old Testament sacrifices note the article of H. E. Freeman, 'The Problem of the Efficacy of the Old Testament Sacrifices', *Bulletin of the Evangelical Theological Society* 5 (1962), pp. 73–79.

[26] As J. Milgrom, 'The Priestly Doctrine of Repentance'. *RB* 82 (1975), pp. 195–6 argues. 'Unwitting' sins apparently did not require confession.

rifices were finally validated by the sacrifice of Christ, a point which the epistle to the Hebrews makes generally and St. Paul at Romans 3:25 specifically. But that must not lead us to suppose that for the Old Testament believer the system was recognized as inadequate or temporary. Forgiveness by sacrifice, then, was the divinely appointed means of approach which normally obtained. But it did not operate mechanically and as the need for confession indicates, it was ultimately dependent upon the divine willingness to forgive. To point to the exceptions which occur in the Old Testament where pardon is extended other than on the basis of sacrifice (cf. 2 Sam. 12:13 in the case of forgiveness offered by Nathan to David after his adultery with Bathsheba) is only to remind ourselves that sacrifice was the customary means of approach, but that forgivness was God-given and not mechanically distributed.

ii. *The meaning of the system*

We are not told in the Old Testament how the system as a whole operated, though forgiveness is brought into connection with blood sacrifices. Yet there are some indications that the whole system (burnt offering, peace offerings, sin offering, guilt offering) when taken together, offered some comment upon the function of the sacrificial system within the sphere of covenant relationships. Here we refer to the observations of Anson Rainey[27], who has drawn our attention to the manner in which, in varying orders, the sacrificial system in its parts is detailed in the book of Leviticus.

> Three defined orders of operation are, in fact, to be seen in Leviticus. In Lev. 1–6:7 we have the order of burnt offering (1:3–17), the associated cereal offering (2:1–16), the peace offerings (3:1–17), then the propitiatory offerings,i.e. sin (4:1 – 5:13), and guilt (5:14 – 6:7). This grouping in this initial presentation in the book appears to have been that of association, with sacrifices which were either performed together or which were related in type being presented together. A second, long, descriptive section then follows (6:8 – 7:38) and the offerings are presented in a slightly different order, i.e. burnt, cereal, sin, guilt and finally, peace. The content of this whole passage is detailed as 'torah' or instruction and its concern is with the administrative procedures associated with the offerings, i.e. the manner in which the offerings were to be presented, the need to maintain the altar fire, the attention which was to be paid to priestly dress regulations. Especial attention is paid to the blood offerings, particularly to the matter of how the carcases of victims were to be disposed of, i.e. either eaten by priests or burnt outside the camp.

---

[27] A. F. Rainey, 'The Order of Sacrifices in the Old Testament Ritual Texts', *Bib* 51 (1970), pp. 485–498.

After the consecration of Aaron and his sons to the priesthood the system is actually seen to be operating in Lev. 9 and yet another order of operation occurs. The order here is significant, namely first a sin offering and a burnt offering is made for Aaron and the priesthood (Lev. 9:7–14) and then a sin offering and burnt offering is made for the people (9:15–17), followed then by a peace offering for the people (9:18–21). Here is an order of sin, burnt and peace offerings and where in the Old Testament the actual operation of the system is on view[28] this is the order which obtains.

The conclusions which Rainey draws from this order when the system is in force are worthy of note. In the actual working of the system emphasis has been placed upon sin which needs to be forgiven, and thus upon a breach of relationships which must be healed. If we may take, as is normally done with some plausibility, the whole burnt offering as a symbol of dedication and thus of commitment, propitiation for sin is followed by what may be termed personal consecration. In its turn this evidence of renewed commitment issues finally into shared peace offerings, that sacrifice which brought worshipper and Deity together and which was thus emblematic of fellowship established. Seen this way, the sacrificial system offers the progressive rationale of propitiation, consecration and fellowship. The sacrificial system finds its ultimate rationale in the forgiving love of God which is finally free and sovereign. This is not to say, however, that in its period a sacrificial system which was not able to be explained in its final rationale was depreciated or under-valued by Israelites in the Old Testament epoch. Like any system or any attempt to systematize grace, the imperfection of its human factors quickly became clear, but the frequent prophetic rebukes of sacrifice are not to be seen as demands for the abolition of the system. Rather they operate as emphatic appeals for its reform and thus as an endorsement of its rightful place in the Israelite economy of worship. In the sense that it pointed beyond itself and yet emphasized the barriers to fellowship which sin had set up, the Old Testament system exercised an educative function which would cause a worshipper to ponder on the fitting connection between the shedding of blood and the remission of sins. As such, it pointed, of course, to the Lamb of God who would take away the sin of the world, and whose death would provide the satisfactory basis upon which forgiveness for all sin could be offered. For the believing, repentant Old Testament Israelite, therefore, the system was a means of forgiveness which God, whose nature is always to have mercy, had given to maintain the covenant which he himself had initiated.

---

[28] Cf. Lev. 14:12, 20; Num. 6:16–17; Ezek. 43:18–27; Ezek. 45:17b; 2 Chr. 29:20–36.

F. DEUTERONOMY AS COVENANT ADDRESS

i. *Structure of the book and the use of b^erît*

The remainder of the Pentateuch is concerned with Israel's passage through the wilderness (Numbers) and covenant renewal in the plains of Moab (Deuteronomy). In the plains of Moab and thus recorded in the book of Deuteronomy, the covenant was not only renewed but expounded in the interests of the expression of a total national commitment in a promised land shortly to be entered. The book of Deuteronomy is structured around three major addresses of Moses, (1:6 – 4:43; 5 – 28; 29), all of which are covenant based and all of which have as their aim the commendation and the explanation of the Sinai covenant in terms of fulfilment of what had been promised to the patriarchs as well as admonition to Israel to maintain a life-style appropriate to an elected people. The first of these three addresses recalls the historical circumstances in which the covenant was concluded, and rehearses in particular the march of Israel from Horeb to the plains of Moab, but reminds Israel at the same time (Deut. 4) of the circumstances of the actual delivery of the covenant and thus of its essential nature. The concern of Deut. 5 – 28 is to detail various statutes which were attached to the covenant, chapters 5 – 11 with decalogue obligations and their implication, 12 – 26 with ancillary statutes of social legislation very similar to (or sometimes identical with) Exod. 21 – 23. Deut. 27 – 28 is concerned with the blessings and curses which are attached to the keeping of the covenant. Chapter 29 (and perhaps 30) is a final appeal by Moses to Israel to accept the Sinai covenant as the basis upon which life may proceed with good success in the promised land.

In the book of Deuteronomy the occurrence of *b^erît* is both frequent and multiform. At its first mention in chapter 4:13 it is virtually identical with the ten commandments and thus exhibits the very close relationship between covenant and law which is a characteristic feature of the book. Since the decalogue summarizes in effect the nature of the new people of God which the covenant has called into being in the national sense, such a close connection between covenant and law could only be regarded as natural. At Deut. 4:23 *b^erît* occurs in conjunction with a peculiar and dominant notion of Deuteronomy, that the covenant is not to be 'forgotten', that is to say, it is to be actualized by constant performance of its requirements. In this particular case the specific requirement, and one to which the book devotes considerable attention in view of the religious challenges to which Israel would be exposed in Canaan, is the call to refrain from apostasy by which the covenant would be denied in its essence. In Deut. 4:31 *b^erît* emphasizes the fidelity of God to the covenant concluded with the 'fathers', who can hardly (as the reference is by Moses) be any other than the patriarchs. Here again, as we shall note further, 'covenant' brings into play a further major theme of the book, namely its insistence that Abraham and Sinai are bound in close connection, the Sinai covenant being the theological fulfilment of the earlier arrangement.

'Covenant' occurs next when the ten commandments are about to be expounded and Israel is about to be reminded by Moses in Deut. 5:2–3 that the covenant which stands behind them and which calls them to definite standards of conduct is not simply something which is historical and 'back there'. It is something which must be contemporized and contextualized by every generation. Other uses of *bᵉrît* in Deuteronomy may be dealt with somewhat summarily and briefly. Chapter 7:2 refers to a prohibition which is placed upon any covenant arrangement with Canaanites. Verses 6 – 8 place that reference to *bᵉrît* in the important context of Israel as *sᵉgullāh* and as the fulfilment of the oath sworn to the fathers (note also 'covenant' in general association with the oath sworn to the Patriarchs at Deut. 7:12; 8:18; 29:14). General references to the Horeb/Sinai occurrences are made by the use of 'covenant' at Deut. 8:18; 9:9, 11, 15; 10:8 (to the ark); 29:1, 9, 12, 14, 21, 25 (the notion is freely scattered in this final appeal of Moses). Deut. 17:2 is a typical warning not to transgress the covenant statutes.

ii. *Deuteronomy and the treaties*

In regard to the form of the book of Deuteronomy, it is almost universally held that the book betrays clear evidences of contact with the Ancient Near Eastern treaties. Before analogies of this kind were drawn in the early fifties, it was argued that the form of Deuteronomy was that of a typical Old Testament farewell address (and thus, similar to Josh. 23; 1 Sam. 12; 1 Chr. 22, 29), with four clear divisions visible within the book. These were the historical presentation of the actual conclusion of the covenant at Sinai, the direct exhortation based on that event, i.e. Deut. 1–11, the reading of associated law, 12 – 26:15, an actual covenant renewal ceremony, seen clearly at Deut. 26:16–19 (with which was to be taken 27:9–10), and then the actual blessings and curses associated with covenant obedience or disobedience, Deut. 27 – 28.

More precise parallels are, however, offered by the treaty analogies. Thus M. Kline[29] has comprehensively included all of Deuteronomy in comparisons with the treaty from which he has drawn.

On his view we have chapter 1:1–5 as preamble in which Moses as mediator is introduced, chapters 1:6 – 4:49 as the historical prologue in which the history of relationships between Yahweh and Israel is the theme, 5:1 – 26:19 in which stipulations as to the way in which life within the covenant is to proceed, 27:1 – 30:20 where wide-ranging covenant sanctions are offered, and 31:1 – 34:12 which is concerned to provide what is in effect dynastic succession for Moses in the shape of Joshua.

---

[29] Kline, *Treaty*, p. 28.

Kline's view, however, seems a little contrived. Deuteronomy is covenant *renewal* and we have no parallel in the Ancient Near East for a
similar use of treaty form to renew the same arrangement. There is no
reason, of course, why a general form current in Moses' day could not
have been adapted to the particular circumstances of its Deuteronomic
use. Thus in regard to the specific Old Testament use of current
material, G. J. Wenham, while pointing to the correspondences between
the Old Testament material and its formal background, has at the same
time argued recently for a distinctive Old Testament use of law form
which Deuteronomy particularly exhibits.[30] In practice, the adducing of
possible parallels for the form has led to little resolution of the
controversy surrounding the problem of dating the book of Deuteronomy, the more so since the treaty form varied so surprisingly little
over the course of nearly a millenium, up to the end of the Assyrian
period. Again, as in Exodus, the use of the formal features establishes
purpose and intention, and is thus theologically valuable if it is not, in
dating terms, apologetically convincing.

G. DEUTERONOMY – LIFE IN THE LAND

i. *Deuteronomy 26*

Within the clear purposes of covenant renewal, what are the major
issues which the book of Deuteronomy takes up? A useful starting
point for a covenant survey of the book might be the material of Deut.
26, which reflects the attitude of the grateful pilgrim who comes before
Yahweh on the occasion of the Feast of the Weeks (Pentecost), with a
gift of produce as a return for the gift of the land. Since Deuteronomy is
commonly seen as conveying a concept of how life in the land is to be
lived, this kind of response, which represents the ideal response which
the worshipper is to make, provides a helpful commentary, highlight-
ing many of the facets of the theology of obedience on which Deuteronomy majors. Deut. 26:1–11[31], which is to be taken as a unit, is
concerned to emphasize the nature of the land as gift. Deut. 26 comes at
the end of a very detailed exposition of the demands which stem from
the covenant, and it is appropriate that such an exposition should end
with such a sustained outburst of praise as the chapter displays.

In it the individual worshipper is placed prospectively in the situation of Pentecost, a pilgrimage feast at which he will give thanks for the
harvest now finally reaped. The basic declaration which the worshipper
will make occurs in v. 3 in which acknowledgement is made that the
good land into which the people have come has fallen into their
posession as a result of Yahweh's fidelity to partriarchal promises. The
response continues in v. 5 with the recognition by the worshipper of
the non-Palestinian origins of the patriarchal father of Israel, Jacob, and

the fact that in Egypt he had become a populous nation. There God had heard their cries and had brought them into the promised land where this appropriate response is now offered.

ii. *Canaan as Israel's 'inheritance'*

Inasmuch as Deut. 26:1 commences with the assertion that Palestine is God's gift to Israel, we remind ourselves that we are here dealing with what is a major covenant theme in Deuteronomy, the basic theological aim of which is to unite the Sinai and Abrahamic covenants, to marry nation and land. Here we may recall that the immediate aim of Moses' first speech in Deuteronomy (1:6 – 4:40) was to delimit the geographical borders of the land. The boundaries to which Moses refers in Deut. 1:7 are substantially those which had been referred to in the promises made to Abraham in Gen. 15:18–20. Verse 8 states specifically that the land about to be described is that which had been promised to the forefathers. Verse 9 continues by explaining that one of the patriarchal preconditions that Israel should become a great multitude as it occupies the land has now been met (cf. v. 10). Israel is this day as the stars of the heaven for multitude, a great and populous nation. Thus the theme of an expectant people about to be united to land promised is that which immediately confronts the reader in Deut. 1. Yet, if chapter 26 lays heavy stress on the land as a gift, it also maintains that it is now Israel's, because in some sense Israel has had legal rights to it which have now been met. It is a land which God had given them for an inheritance and they are to move in and to 'disinherit' (RSV 26:1, 'possess') the present occupants. In this terminology we thus have the paradox of a land which is given yet which has to be taken. Two closely related biblical themes are therefore bound together in Deut. 26:1, namely that Israel has received by way of gift the land which she will occupy, and yet it is the fact of conquest which will make that gift an actuality. Such notions of 'gift' and 'inheritance' stress divine ownership of the land. In such a favoured relationship Israel might have been expected to have enjoyed the blessings which would have surely been associated with the notion of the divine presence in what has been defined in Exodus terms as a sanctuary. In short, we may see good reason, as we shall note later, for the book of Deuteronomy to dwell extensively upon a theology of rest, relating to the life of faith in the promised land. Since the concept of the land is much an important one and since it is taken up in detail for the first time in the book of Deuteronomy, it should come as no surprise to

---

[30] Wenham's view is quoted by J. A. Thompson, *Deuteronomy* (London: Tyndale, 1974), p. 18.

[31] For the unity of Dt. 26:1–11 (as opposed to a widely held view that 26:5b–11 within this unit constitutes an ancient 'credal statement') note the arguments of C. H. Brekelmans cited by J. P. Hyatt in *Translating and Understanding the Old Testament, Essays in Honor of Herbert G. May*, ed. H. T. Frank and W. L. Reed, (Nashville: Abingdon, 1970), p. 160.

us that the dimensions of the land are so carefully defined in the book. We have noted the patriarchal boundaries which have been referred to and we simply need to add that the land is always defined in West Jordan terms. For this reason a great deal of weight is placed in the book of Deuteronomy upon the crossing of the Jordan, so much so that the Hebrew verb to cross (Heb. *ᶜābar*) can be used to describe the actual conquest of the land (cf. Deut. 6:1). The description which is offered within the book of how possession is to proceed is also strikingly similar to the divine injunctions given to the patriarchs whereby the land is to be possessed. Israel is told (11:24) that every place upon which the sole of their feet shall tread (cf. the somewhat similar Gen. 13:17) shall be theirs, and this phrase seems legally similar to the Genesis concepts of taking active possession of territory by entering upon it. Perhaps it was for this reason that the Heb. verb 'to inherit' was chosen to convey the note of possession, for Heb. *yārash* ('inherit') has a basic meaning of walking or treading,[32] with similar legal connotations about it.

That the deity was the owner of the land which his devotees possessed was a common enough notion in the Ancient Near East. In Egypt the only landowners were Pharaoh and the Egyptian priests on his behalf, Pharaoh because he was a deity and the priests because they were his ministrants. In Mesopotamia, within the city state system, the deity of the state was the legal owner of the city and its environs. If we may make judgements from the Canaanite epic materials from Ugarit in which the deities El and Baal are responsible for the life forces which attached to the land (productivity, fertility, etc.) then the notion of divine ownership of the land was well known in Palestine also. In Canaanite religion, the direct association of the deity with the land, being responsible for its fertility etc., made for the doctrine of the total dependency of the worshippers upon the capriciousness of the deity. It explained the differences in productivity as a result of fluctuating seasonal conditions resulting from the arbitrary exercise of power by the controlling deity. In Israel, however, blessings and curses associated with the land were tied to covenant response by Israel. The assertion of divine ownership of the land made with such clarity in contexts such as Lev. 25:23 ('The land shall not be sold in perpetuity, for the land is mine; for you are strangers and sojourners with me'), while strongly within the Ancient Near Eastern stream of thought, underwent, therefore, customary theological modifications to which all contemporary notions absorbed into Israel's faith were subjected. The Israelites were placed in the position of Abraham who had left his place of origin and had taken residence elsewhere at the cost of the forfeiture of all rights of full citizenship. In Israel, land was inalienable and the laws of Sabbath

---

[32] Cf. J. Wijngaards, *The Dramatization of Salvific History in the Deuteronomic Schools*, (Leiden: Brill, 1969), p. 84.

and Jubilee were designed to promote the understanding that the land belonged to Yahweh. Any attempt to sell land in Israel or to transfer it out of ancestral spheres met with fierce opposition (cf. Elijah and Naboth's vineyard, 1 Kings 21).

Some have argued that Israel, when entering Palestine, simply took over Canaanite feudal structure and practice in another form. Like the Canaanite peasants who were subject to their overlords, the Canaanite city state 'kings', Israel was the vassal of the 'Great King' in whose land they dwelt and whose gifts they enjoyed as a result of his royal beneficence. The Israelite farmer thus saw himself as farming Yahweh's fief, within the feudal system in which they were set, not dependent upon some internal power structure to which they were finally responsible, but finally dependent upon a connection with Yahweh, upon whose grace they were continually thrown. There is some force in this argument and certainly the general acceptance by Israel of the land as Yahweh's naturally gave rise to the image of Palestine as a 'holy' land and to the view of the natural blessings arising from the land as a sort of 'holy materialism'.

The perils of the common Ancient Near Eastern concepts of divine land ownership are echoed in the book of Deuteronomy, since we have a consistent reference to the reality of apostasy as bound up with Canaanite fertility practices which in Canaanite religion were designed to ensure productivity. For Israel the divine ownership of Palestine arose not by the localization of the Deity of by the recognition of his peculiar rights to that territory as opposed to those of other deities over other geographical areas. The concept arose by virtue of Israel's commitment to the divine lordship over all creation. Canaan was Israel's inheritance and thus the gift of Yahweh who owned all lands (Deut. 32:8). The term 'inheritance' applied to Israel's posession of the land (Heb. *nah̬ᵃlāh*) had a firm meaning of landed property which had been apportioned to an individual from a larger whole.[33] Thus the lordship of land which in Canaanite religion was predicated of Baal was freed in Israelite theology from any particular fertility limitations.

iii. *Canaan as Eden recaptured*

The fertility of the land is the subject of comment in Deut. 26 (v. 9) and thus the gift of the first fruits in that chapter is linked not only with Yahweh's ownership, but also with the fact of historical redemption. We note that the references to the land in chapter 26 in terms of its

[33] As H.E. von Waldow, 'Israel and her Land. Some Theological Considerations' notes, in *A Light unto My Path: Old Testament Studies in Honor of J. M. Myers*, ed. H. N. Bream et. al., (Philadelphia: Temple Univ. Press, 1974), p. 494. Our indebtedness to his perceptive article and to that of P. D. Miller, "The Gift of God: The Deuteronomic Theology of the Lord" *Intepr.* 23 (1969) pp. 451–65 is acknowledged.

potential yield are similar in type to those reported by the scouts who
had been sent out (cf. Num. 13:27) to evaluate the future homeland. In
Deuteronomy the promised land is extravagantly idealized. It is the
very quintessence of fertility and fruitfulness. There is nothing lacking
in it of what may be fervently desired. Not only will it give forth
heavenly fare (milk and honey were traditionally the food offered to a
deity, cf. Isa. 7:15), but it is actually watered from heaven (Deut. 11:11).
It is a land of brooks and water, fountains and springs, which flow forth
into soft valleys and hills (cf. Deut. 8:7). Moreover, it is not merely
potentially rich, but it is supplied with cisterns which Israel did not dig,
houses which she did not build, olive trees which she did not plant
(6:10ff). In such a land the fullness of life will be enjoyed, for Israel will
be blessed above all peoples (7:14), all sickness will be removed (7:15),
as well as every threat to Israel's security (7:15). God's particular care is
cast upon the land, for his eyes are always on it and his concern for it is
continual (Deut. 11:11–12).

From a covenant point of view, the implications of all this are as
important as they are obvious. One can hardly escape the impression
that what is being depicted through such references is Eden recaptured,
paradise recovered. Since it had been anticipated that the promised
land would be a sanctuary for Yahweh, such a picture is a consistent
one. In keeping with its sanctuary status and equally consistent with
such high expectation surrounding the use of the land, everything
which was unclean or which threatened to pollute Israel was required to
be removed. As in the Eden situation, the occupants of this projected
sanctuary would enjoy the blessing of God's special presence, and as in
the Eden situation, there would be continued occupancy of this divine
space by Israel if the prerequisites for life in the land were observed.
There are thus real parallels which can be drawn between Adam's and
Israel's position. Like Adam, Israel was formed outside of the land (cf.
Gen. 2:8); like Adam Israel was then put into a sanctuary which God
had created; as in the case of Adam life in the land was to be regulated
by covenant; and finally, like Adam Israel was to be expelled from the
land because the understanding upon which the land was possessed
and the divine presence was enjoyed, the covenant relationship which
bound Israel and Yahweh together, was from a national point of view
irretrievably breached.

iv. 'Given' and yet 'to be taken'

In connection with the land, there is a further point to be made.
Deuteronomy stresses in chapter 26:1 that the land was a divine gift,
given at the expense of the original occupants who were dispossessed.
What the confession of 26:5–11 underscores, however, is that as Yahweh
had led Israel out of Egypt, so he had been responsible for leading her
into Canaan. Here we recall that when Israel had tried to possess the

land without divine backing, she had been quickly repulsed in an abortive attempt to enter from the south (Num. 14:39ff, Deut. 1:41ff.). As the confessional statement in chapter 26 (cf. v. 9) makes clear, the land will be Israel's only because Yahweh will put it at her disposal. He will add the land to a people which he had made multitudinous. Thus Yahweh will be made responsible for the victories which will achieve posession of the land. This will not, however, be a created theological fiction, but will correspond to Israel's experience of the divine intervention into the affairs of history relating to her conquest of Palestine. A theology of conquest thus arises, a notion of 'holy war' came into being whereby it is concluded that behind Israel's armies stand Yahweh's hosts. In this way the tension which could have existed between the land as gift and the land as conquered is resolved. The book of Deuteronomy assumes, as has often been noted, a particularly martial character, anticipating in this way the battles of the conquest which are about to be fought (cf. Deut. 20 for a schematic presentation of what is to be practically involved in Israel's campaigns under divine leadership). This is an expression of the conviction that the conquest would achieve the virtually impossible, that a mixed multitude from the desert would dispossess an entrenched civilization. Against insuperable odds Israel would enter the land in such a way that it would be clear to her that only divine intention could have accounted for the conquest successes of the book of Joshua.

v. 'Rest' in the land

Arising also from Deut. 26 (v. 3) is the fact that with the possession of the land there is completed, in outline at least, the promises given to the patriarchs. The Abrahamic theology of the land is thus brought within the context of promise and fulfilment. Thus the book of Deuteronomy indicates in this way how the Sinai covenant fits into the broader Abrahamic framework. Yet it does more. The full significance of the Deuteronomic conception of the occupation of the land is summed up in the particularly Deuteronomic theology of 'rest'. Admittedly this notion of 'rest' does not occur in the otherwise embracive Deut. 26. It is worthwhile to note, however, that the ceremony of thanksgiving with which this chapter commences follows upon the charge of Deut. 25:17–19 which declares that when enemies round about have been dealt with, rest in the land will follow. An appropriate response to that rest will be the celebration of the gift which made it possible (Deut. 26:1ff).

The notion of 'rest' to which the book of Deuteronomy makes frequent reference (3:20; 12:9; 25:19; 28:65) is admittedly bound up with the concept of a pleasant life in the land, secure and blessed (15:4; 23:20; 28:8; 30:16). This means no more, however, than that Israel will enjoy the gifts of creation in the way in which they had been meant to be

used. In this theology of rest we are clearly returning to the purposes of
creation set forth in Gen. 1:1 – 2:4a and typified by the Eden narrative,
namely that mankind was created to rejoice before the deity and to
enjoy the blessings of creation in the divine presence. The notion of rest
in both Gen. 2:2 and the book of Deuteronomy implies this, while
Deuteronomy is very conscious of the need to underscore the fact that
'rest' can be a secure doctrine only if it is tied to the correct notion of
how the presence of Yahweh in the land is to be understood and
appreciated.

For this reason, in a somewhat extensive argument in Deut. 12 the
concept of the divine presence in the land is seen to be bound up with
the place which Yahweh will choose. This will be the place at which
Yahweh 'will cause his name to dwell' (cf. v. 11). Whether or not
Deuteronomy contemplates one covenant sanctuary as a pilgrimage
resort is still a disputed question. In our judgement the verse usually in
dispute (Deut. 12:5) is to be taken distributively and thus as pointing to
a number of possible sanctuaries, each of which could have served as a
central pilgrimage shrine for the time being. Such a view is not only
exegetically permissible but is also consistent with 2 Sam. 7:6 where
God refers to the fact that up to the choice of Jerusalem as the central
sanctuary, mobility has characterized the doctrine of the divine presence. If a series of sites is on view in Deut. 12, then such a mobility of
the divine presence endorses the idea of the whole land as a sanctuary.
The particular phrase, 'to cause his name to dwell', has often been
argued to mean that not Yahweh himself, but a personification of his
presence only will be resident at the sanctuary, with the further
suggestion offered that such a view was intended to be a corrective for
older immanistic views which were held about the nature of the divine
presence in Israel. So far, however, from being this sort of introduced
sophistication, the phrase is a biblical retention of a much older idiom
which in general use extra-biblically meant to 'assert ownership over
something' or the like.[34] Occuring thus within a theology of the
promised land as a divine possession, and bound up in Deut. 12 with
the doctrine of rest there adverted to (cf. v. 10), the phrase seems to
reinforce the sanctuary significance of the doctrine of the promised
land.

Important also not only for the doctrine of rest but for the wider
creation covenantal notions with which it is associated, is the notion of
the Sabbath in the book of Deuteronomy. It is to involve (5:12–15) every
stratum of Israelite society as well as non-citizens, i.e. all humankind
(and even domesticated animals), and it is brought into close connection with the Exodus redemption. In the parallel presentation of the ten

---

[34] Evidence gathered on this interesting Old Testament phrase by Dean McBride is
referred to by G. J. Wenham in 'Deuteronomy and the Central Sanctuary', *Tyn. B.* 22
(1971), p. 114.

commandments in Exod. 20:8–11 the Sabbath was understood to prefigure the rest which the completion of creation had foreshadowed for mankind. Two such different applications of the fourth commandment have often been thought to be contradictory. They are in fact complementary, since it is the Exodus redemption which makes the new life in the land, and thus the Edenic values recaptured, possible. Israel in Canaan is a microcosm of mankind as blessed, an illustration of what is intended for the whole world. Of course, we know that the expectation of 'rest' was not realised in Israel's experience and that finally she was driven from the land. The Epistle to the Hebrews in the New Testament makes much of this Old Testament failure, reminding us that while Israel failed to enter this rest, (Heb. 4:8–10) there still remains for the believers a Sabbath rest as the fulfilment of creation's purpose.

vi. Israel's response – 'Law' and 'love'

The acknowledgement which Deut. 26:1ff thus makes of the land which is Yahweh's and the gratitude which it expresses for the manner in which it was received by Israel are not isolated in that chapter from the response which was required of Israel. The mention in Deut. 26:11 of the Levite and the sojourner who are also, though underprivileged in the society of the time, to give thanks, leads the text of 26:12–15 to take up the question of provision for the Levitical tithe. When direct covenant exposition is taken up again in vv. 16ff Israel's response to the covenant statutes is at issue. In the context of Deut. 26, as in the book as a whole, such a response is a rejoinder to prior grace (cf. 26:1–11). At this point the question of the role of law in Deuteronomy may be raised, since one of the major catechetical functions of the book is the explanation of the significance of law and the role of torah as a teaching medium. Of force here is the typical instructional pattern which Deut. 6:20–25 displays. There, when the son in time to come asks a father the meaning of the commandments, i.e. asks their significance and relevance, the father is to answer that the commandments really express a transition from slavery to freedom, from bondage in Egypt to life in the land which Yahweh had sworn to give to their forefathers. That is, the very existence of the commandments as demand, points to a relationship in which the demand is to be expressed, and endorses the proposition that true freedom is to be found in perfect service. The point which is being made at Deut. 6:20–25 is made constantly throughout the book of Deuteronomy, namely that the law has significance only within the framework of relationships already established by covenant. In the previous context of Deut. 6:4ff, the inwardness of the law as being laid upon the heart has been stressed and appeals of this character in the book prevent us from limiting torah to codified ordinances which can be absolutely objectified.

For these reasons law and love are closely related in the book of Deuteronomy. Love is treated by the book neither as a mere emotion nor as an intellectual exercise but as an active commitment arising out of God's prior choice. God's love is presented in fact as synonymous with God's choice (Deut. 4:37, 10:15), a reminder that election in the Old Testament is presented to us as a deliberate choice between possible alternatives (cf. Exod. 19:5). Since, however, the love bestowed on Israel has been of such a gracious character, the response can be considered almost so automatic as to be viewed as having hardened into an obligation which must lead to displayed conduct. For it has been noted that love in the book of Deuteronomy is invariably associated with prescribed activities, such as 'keeping the commandments', 'walking in his ways', 'obeying his voice' etc.[35] The contents of the great summarizing passage bearing upon Israel's responsibility in Deut. 10:12–22 are instructive in this regard. The initial demand is for Israel to 'fear' God. The reference is to the Sinai experience which has imported an element of distance into the relationship. An attitude of awe before the revelation of the divine character, a proper cognizance of the nature of the Deity who stands behind the demand which follows in this passage, are both implied in the term 'fear'. 'Fear' is thus the appropriate response to the holy jealousy of God revealed in the Sinai encounter, the required interior response to the God of the covenant. On the other hand 'love' is the attitude which expresses itself in outward conformity to what God requires of Israel. At Sinai God had expressed the wish that Israel should hear him and fear him (Deut. 4:10) and should teach their children to do so. That is to say, obedience is the proper response to awe. Deuteronomy reminds us that it is a fearful thing to fall into the hands of the living God, that privilege brings with it responsibility, for if Israel forgets Yahweh, he will destroy her from off the face of the earth (Deut. 6:12ff). Thus the generation of the Exodus and their descendants are to fear God and keep his commandments (6:24–25), that they might be preserved alive. Love is thus the outworking of the faith response which is fear.

The point has often made that biblical love, as we have noted in the book of Deuteronomy, is not merely an emotional response. Here, we must not let the free use of kinship terms in Deuteronomy detract from the force of this observation. Israel is spoken of in sonship terms (cf. Deut. 8:5, 14:1), and while elements of emotional response are obviously very much present in the use of such relational terms, we must also remember that the family structure of the Old Testament was tightly

---

[35] V. H. Kooy, 'Fear and Love in Deuteronomy', in Grace Upon Grace, Essays in Honor of L. J. Kuyper, ed. J. I. Cook, (Grand Rapids: Eerdmans, 1975), p. 114, notes this connection. Kooy's helpful treatment has, in the main, been followed in this section and mention should be made also of general reference to L. E. Toombs, "Love and Justice in Deuteronomy", Interpr. 19 (1965), pp.399–411 on the question of tôrah in Deuteronomy.

authoritarian. Family life was very carefully regulated by the family head who disciplined his son as a sign of ultimate concern (Deut. 8:5). Moreover, Deuteronomy insists that love may be inculcated. Through instruction the path of duty may be made plain (cf. 6:4–8; 11:18–21; 31:12). To love God is to keep his commandments, not only from the sense of duty which the inferior owes to the superior, but also in order that there might be personal participation in the whole political constitution which God has established for Israel at Sinai. We would do a disservice to Deuteronomy, however, if we were to suggest that the preservation of the link between God and his people was based upon a joyless response. In the last analysis the display of conduct, for which the book looked on all levels, was impelled by a set of deep and inward convictions which had seized the heart. Deuteronomy never fails to draw attention to the interiority of the covenant which has lodged in the national heart (Deut. 6:5; 10:12; 26:16; 30:14). No co-erced obedience to a formal prescription of conduct is thus finally involved, but actual behaviour which finds its motive in the rightly aligned heart.

The requirement of obedience is the note therefore on which the summarizing chapter Deut. 26 concludes. The ability of Israel to make a response is a consequence, verse 18 reminds us, of Israel's election. It has been Israel's special honour to be singled out above all the nations and to be distinguished as a holy people, as a special possession. Israel, as we know, did not continue in this high condition of privilege. The book of Deuteronomy with its themes of covenant renewal sets Israel in the plains of Moab between the choices of blessing or curse (cf. Deut. 27 – 28). Moses calls on Israel to choose life (cf. 30:15ff). Life is life in the land which God is to give them, the full realisation of Abrahamic nationhood. The history of Old Testament covenant relationships reveals that paradoxically, Israel chose death, with the gospel of the book of Deuteronomy ringing hollowly in their ears as, exiled, they finally left the land.

Summary

The aim of the chapter was to review the Sinai covenant from its inception to the provisions made for its enactment in the land, in the book of Deuteronomy. The setting of Exod. 19:3b–8 in which the first mention of covenant in connection with Sinai takes place sees the Sinai covenant as confirmation. This and the introduction of the name Yahweh as associated now with the Sinai covenant directed us back to the significance of the call of Moses with whom the divine name Yahweh was particularly to be associated. We noted the function of the divine name as assuring continuity of the older promises. The structure of Exod. 18:3b–6 was then reviewed. The three key terms, s^egullāh, mamleket kôh^{a}nîm and gôy qādôsh were examined. The latter two were considered to be an explanation of the function inherent in the first

term, while the key phrase in the section was shown to be the
concluding phrase of 19:5, 'for all the earth is mine'. Exod. 19:6, in
which v. 5 was more narrowly explicated, was seen to operate as
defining Israel's role within the Abrahamic structure to which this verse
more generally referred.

Since the addition of the law occurred within the Sinai covenant, the
role of law was then considered. It was argued that by the use of *tôrāh*,
general and specific direction was given to Israel for life within the
covenant relationship. Account was then taken of Israel's understanding of the significance of the covenant, as demonstrating Yahweh's
kingship and yet Yahweh's elective care (family terms). Note was taken
of the role of Exod. 25 – 31 in which worship appeared to be a response
to Yahweh's kingship. A theological understanding of the covenant is
presented in Exod. 15 whereby the aim of the redemption was seen to
be the restoration of the Eden conditions. We should expect that
Deuteronomy, which deals with life in the land, would take this
explanation further.

In very general terms, worship (Leviticus) as a covenant response was
then dealt with. The efficacy of the sacrificial system as a real means of
dealing with sin was argued for and the meaning of the system as
leading to renewed fellowship through propitiation was elaborated.
Finally Deuteronomy was considered as containing a theology of life in
the land. The land of Canaan viewed as Israel's inheritance was noted as
underscoring God's dominion over Israel and his final ownership of
Israel and her land. Israel in Canaan is presented in terms analogous to
Adam in Eden – created outside the land, placed in the land, placed
under obligations by which the land was to be kept, and yet finally to
forfeit the land. The important concept of 'rest' of which the book makes
so much was seen to refer us back to the divine intention for man and
his world, with Israel in Canaan acting as a model. Finally Israel's
response in the land was reviewed in terms of 'law' and 'love' with no
incompatibility being seen between the two, but also with the strong
implication in these concepts in the book of Deuteronomy that the lack
of such responses would result in dismissal from the land. The
remaining chapters of this work will trace the consequences of Israel's
rebellion, but yet with the continued divine fidelity to covenant
intentions which eventually leads to the Jeremianic New Covenant.

4

The Covenant with David:
The Covenant and Messiahship

i. *The conquest*

The purpose of the covenant with David, the details of which are contained in 2 Sam. 7, was to engraft the developing monarchy into the existing Israelite covenantal structure. To this extent the Davidic covenant is a slight modification of the Sinai covenant, and is, as we shall see, presented as being within the process of the fulfilment of the Abrahamic covenant. We shall need, however, to set the emergence of the Israelite monarchy within the historical developments which led to its rise from the conquest onwards.

At the time of the conquest (c. 1400 B.C.) Egyptian influence was still being nominally exercised over Palestine, but was in decline. The Tell El Amarna letters (correspondence between Canaanite city-state kings and Egyptian court, named after the site in Egypt, where in the late 19th century the material was found) indicate the social disruption and general disarray which prevailed in the Palestine of the day. Particularly troublesome were a group whom the correspondence frequently mentions, the Habiru (or, on the preferred spelling, the Hapiru). As a group, these people were known throughout the Ancient Near East from about 2000 B.C. onwards, usually as strangers and outsiders to any society with which they were related. It is now agreed that the Habiru constituted a social class and not an ethnic group, a fact which makes their relationship to the Hebrews of the conquest period interesting (since the term Habiru is almost certainly philologically related to the term Hebrew), but difficult to assess. This is all the more so since the Habiru were particularly active in certain areas which the incoming Hebrews made initially their own (the Shechem area, for instance, which, incidentally, is not mentioned as having been conquered by Joshua, and the Jerusalem region as well). The Tell El Amarna letters stamp the Habiru as political renegades, disrupters of the status quo, though not necessarily underprivileged. Perhaps the term may have been applied to the incoming Israelites because of a basic similarity in social type to the entrenched disruptive elements already in Palestine, and it is worth noting that invariably in the Old Testament, the term Hebrew is used by foreigners of Israelites, or by Israelites as a means of identification to foreigners.

Certainly the prevailing disruption and the weakened Egyptian position made the Israelite task all the easier. We leave to one side the details of the conquest, though the basic soundness of the strategy by which the centre was first penetrated, and then attention paid to the south and then to the north, has often been commented on as conveying historical credibility. The concern of the book of Joshua which reports the conquest is, however, to see the irruption into Palestine as the implementation of the Mosaic programme sketched in the book of Deuteronomy, with the process of conquest culminating in the covenant renewal ceremony which Joshua 24 reports. Covenant renewal within Israel's history occurs at significant moments and there is force in the reminder that Joshua gives to Israel at Joshua 23 – 24 in his closing charge. The success of the Israelite campaigns which had resulted in land distribution among the tribes, was on the one hand in fulfilment of what the book of Deuteronomy had prefigured, and would, on the other hand, lead Israel to a further stage of commitment.

In Joshua 23, a summary of the achievements of the period in the shape of conquest and land distribution (both of which tasks Joshua had been charged by Moses to perform, cf. Deut. 31:7) is presented. Joshua 1 – 12 had narrated the fact of conquest, Joshua 13 – 22 the allotment of the land. In chapter 23 Joshua's appeal is to the nature of the entry into the land as a divine operation. This had resulted in the very great Deuteronomic blessing of 'rest … from all their enemies round about' having been given to Israel. However, much still remains to be done – a point made in this chapter (cf vv. 1, 5), and one which will assume growing importance up to David's time. The formula for Israel's continued success to which v. 6 refers is a virtual resumption of the Mosaic charge to Joshua to which Joshua 1:7–8 had alluded. What will guarantee the future is adherence to the covenant formularies (cf. the mention in v. 7 of the need for steadfast adherence to what was required by the Mosaic book of the law).

Joshua 23 prepares the way for the covenant renewal ceremony of Joshua 24. That chapter is divided into a survey of Israel's history from Abraham to the conquest (vv. 1–13), and covenant renewal proper (vv. 14–28 plus concluding verses). In terms of the treaty analogies to which we have previously referred, a preamble occurs at v. 2a; vv. 2b–13 represent the historical prologue; Israel's response to the covenant stipulations is in vv. 14–25 (in the course of which the people offer self-witness as to the extent of their obligation, vv. 19–22, and are required to put away foreign gods, v. 23). There is provision at v. 26 for the deposit of the 'treaty'. This ceremony of covenant renewal is presented as the high moment of Joshua's career and the narration of his death then follows (vv. 29–33).

ii. *The period of the Judges*

When we move to the book of Judges we are undoubtedly presented with a period of very great internal dissension, and at the same time with the exposure of Israel to extensive external pressures. The summary judgement which the author of the book offers in conclusion at Judges 21:25 reviews the lawlessness of the age. Whether that reference goes further and endorses (as is customarily argued) the monarchy as the needed alternative to the anarchy of the period, is a debatable point. It is clear however, that the excessive individualism of the times had led to the sorry record of the tribal fragmentations and internecine disputes which the writer has compiled.

The editorial theme of the book of Judges has plainly in mind the exhibition of constant covenant breach as occurring within the era. The framework of the first sixteen chapters is set within a recurring cycle of the sin of Israel, the foreign aggression which follows, the call to repentance, the appointment of a deliverer hero, the deliverance which is then effected and the rule of the deliverer which then takes place. Such a schematic presentation has led the majority of interpreters to place little credence in the details of the book and in particular to question the nature of the 'Israel' which the editor has in mind. Certainly, theological interpretation of material has very patently occurred. It is further possible that the narratives are not presented in strict chronological order, since in terms of the geographical location of the incidents, we commence with the deep south, (Judges 3 and Othniel) and conclude with the Samson incidents (Judges 13 – 16) which concern the tribe of Dan whose geographical location is finally in the far north (though the incidents themselves had taken place in the south).[1]

There is no doubt, moreover, that the type of rule which characterized the period (the hero figures of chapter 3 – 16) is curious, and extraordinary in the sense that it ran counter to the natural progression from a patriarchal to a monarchical state which was occuring elsewhere. This fact in itself invites some comment upon the age and particularly upon the leadership roles of the period which are without parallel elsewhere in the Ancient Near East. Consequently it is often asserted that theological presentation has again supplanted history at this point by endowing local figures with an all-Israelite authority. There are two issues here to be considered. The first is the authority of the 'Judge' of

---

[1]. Cf. A. Malamat, 'Charismatic Leadership in the Book of Judges', in *Magnalia Dei: The Mighty Acts of God: Essays on the Bible and Archaeology in memory of G. Ernest Wright*, ed. F. M. Cross, W. E. Lemke and P. D. Miller (New York: Doubleday, 1976), p. 154.

the times and the second concerns the nature of the 'Israel' of the era. In regard to the first issue, it cannot be demonstrated from the book of Judges that the authority of any particular judge was ever limited or local. Any attack upon a local area always had geographical repercussions beyond the area in question, and the expulsion of the enemy for the time being was achieved only by constant tribal co-operation. In a small country like Palestine, a local incident would in any case very quickly have assumed the significance of a national threat. Moreover, while it is the case that the twelve tribes are never engaged in concerted action in the first sixteen chapters of the book, it is equally to be borne in mind that, with the possible exception of the incident recorded in Judges 4, there was never really an occasion when they should have been.

The most detailed presentation of any Judge of the period is offered of the last of them, namely Samuel, and we gain some insight into the nature of the office by noting how Samuel functioned. His activities are described in fair detail in 1 Sam. 7, where in typical deliverer fashion he appeals to Israel (v. 3) to put away foreign gods, to turn to Yahweh who will then, Israel is assured, respond by removing Philistine oppression. 1 Sam. 7:5–14 continues with a parade example of how divine intervention on Israel's behalf happened. The Philistines are routed without Israel having been physically involved. But the architect of this victory is Samuel who as Judge has played the instrumental covenant role of connecting Israel and Yahweh again. Following upon this success, Samuel judges Israel for the remainder of his life (cf. vv. 15–17) and moves in circuit progression around the land, arbitrating in disputes at what may have been the principal sanctuaries of the period. Since Shiloh is not mentioned, we may assume that it had already been destroyed in the Philistine campaigns.

The concept of Judge in Samuel's case is that of a divinely endowed person who maintains Israel's covenant relationship by calling for inward reformation and by providing for defence against external aggression. This is, in fact, the nature of the office which the hero figures of Judges 3 – 16 exercise. They are raised up by Yahweh, they are men of the Spirit (cf. Judg. 6:34, 11:29, 15:14 etc.,) and they are said in each case to exercise authority over all Israel. But they are, we might note, surrogates only for Yahweh himself who is *the* Judge of Israel (cf. Judg. 11:27). That the term Judge can be (and is probably primarily) applied in this way should make us reluctant to interpret it in a merely narrow judicial sense, and here we should note that the Hebrew verb 'to judge' (Heb. *shāpaṭ*) in early Semitic conveyed a basic meaning of 'rule' or 'administer'. The role of the Judge would thus have been an extremely wide one, and being episodic, non-transferable, and non-predictable, is antithetical to dynastic kingship. We note that political models of dynastic kingship were freely available to Israel from its neighbours during the era. Kingship of this character (or of any character) however came relatively late in Israel's history and was firmly rejected as a possibility by probably the most successful Israelite figure of that period (cf. Judg. 8:23).

The second issue to which we now turn is the nature of the 'Israel' of the period. The concluding comment of Judges 21:25 presumes an entity which can be styled Israel, which survived the period, and indeed was the twelve tribe confederation politically united by the Sinaitic covenant in the Mosaic period. The prevailing consensus of opinion on this question, however, would deny the historicity of the Judges accounts and regard Israel as a political entity as not achieved until David's time. The consensus opinion would be that during the Judges period Israel was a loose religious confederation of an undetermined number of tribes, operating with virtually no political unity. Some of the points normally taken in support of this view have already been considered. Others need some brief discussion. It is asserted that the book looks forward to the emergence of the monarchy by which political integration would replace the anarchy which prevailed. It is noted that there is no mention in the book of Judges of the later important concept— political as well as religious—of a central sanctuary to which Israel resorted in worship.

So far as the question of a central sanctuary around which Israel was united is concerned, we have already referred to the position on this matter that we judge the book of Deuteronomy takes. We can see real merit in the position normally adopted by those who contend that the concept of a central pilgrimage sanctuary had been built into the Sinai worship responses expected from Israel. This position is, that while there was no defined central sanctuary in the early period, the temporary centrality of any one of a number of shrines was bound up with the presence of the ark at one of the many early possible sites (Gilgal, Shechem, Bethel etc. – it is also conceivable that certain feasts were associated with specific shrines).

In regard to the composition of Israel during the Judges period, we would recognize that attitudes to this question are finally a matter of presupposition and probabilities. But the book of Judges presupposes the unity of all Israel, with the twelve tribes united in holy war, virtually in the campaigns of Judges 1 and certainly in the inter-tribal dispute of Judges 20 – 21 (an account which seems on the face of it to be ancient). We are confronted with a transparently united Israel in the early chapters of 1 Samuel when the providential choice of Saul from the tribe of Benjamin (a tribe which had been all but eliminated at the close of the Judges period) was made. Moreover, there is continuity in the matter of the sanctuary of Shiloh between the books of Judges and Samuel. It is with the somewhat unusual rise to prominence of this shrine that the book of Judges closes, while the early chapters of 1 Samuel give us further details of what is expectedly (in view of the Judges presentation) a debased Shiloh. We would not deny that the book of Judges ends with a condemnation of the fragmented Israel of the times and the blatant individualism and apostasy which characterized the period. But granted that, the note which the book strikes in conclusion does not seem so much an anticipation of the helpful changes that monarchy would bring. Rather, notwithstanding the absence of the tight administrative controls which would characterize later bureaucratic Israel of the monarchical period, it is recognized that the Judges period had ended as it had begun, with twelve tribes in association.

By the final comment of Judges 21:25 the author is really referring to the nature of Israel and how the ideal would always be preserved. He is saying that despite the lack of human support which might have preserved a religious or a political ideal, in spite of the fact that there was no king in Israel and every man did what was right in his own eyes, Yahweh, by direct intervention through the saviour figures of the age, had preserved the covenant with Israel. It may be argued therefore, that the purpose of the book of Judges is to invite us to reflect upon the fact that Israel at any age would not owe its existence to political constitutions of its own devising (certainly not to monarchy which as an institution is later roundly condemned for what it came to be). It would owe it to the fidelity of its covenant partner who would never defect from his contractual obligation. Such a presentation reminds us also that Israel in the Old Testament was never primarily a geographical or a political concept, even though it best came to be known in those terms. The notion of Israel could never thus be exhausted by pointing to common ethnic, linguistic or social features by which a political unit would normally be identifiable. Judges reminds us that the Israel of the Old Testament was a covenant entity, the people of God, given some political coverage at Sinai, but owing its existence to an elective call rooted in the experience of her 'fathers' who had served other gods on the 'other side of the river'.

B. SAMUEL AND THE RISE OF THE MONARCHY

i. *The Crisis.* (1 Sam. 1 – 6)

The social pressures operating at the end of the period of the Judges eventually led to kingship and to the transition from a basically patriarchal type of society to the emergence of a monarchical state. Thus the two books of Samuel bring us to a time of great political and social change in Israel, in the course of which the covenant relationship was to be modified by the addition of kingship. The books commence with a detailed account in the first three chapters of the nature of the debased worship in Shiloh. This was a situation for which Eli, the High Priest, was primarily responsible by his inability to control his two sons Hophni and Phinehas. We have, as we have already remarked, been prepared for this by the way in which the shrine of Shiloh had been introduced in the closing chapters of the book of Judges. The nature of the Shiloh shrine at the beginning of the books of Samuel appears to have been imposing. A semi-permanent establishment, which falls short, however, of actual temple status, is there and in the shrine the ark of the covenant is lodged. The loss of this shrine and also of the ark which it housed, as a result of the Philistine attack in 1 Samuel 4, posed a very serious crisis for Israel. In particular, the resulting loss of the ark is seen as an appropriate punishment meted out on the corrupt leadership which had reduced Israel to such sorry straits.

In these circumstances, Samuel, for whose ministry chapters 1 – 3 had prepared us, became the man to rescue Israel from the crisis which had developed, and thus the deliverance of 1 Sam. 7 of which Samuel was the architect, followed the oppression of 1 Sam. 4 – 6. Those chapters had been concerned to emphasize that *the* covenant symbol of Israel, the ark of the covenant, had 'gone into exile' (cf. 4:22) with the implication drawn at the end of 1 Samuel 4 that we had come to the end of an era in the history of Israel. Had Yahweh indeed forsaken his people and was the covenant therefore now at an end? But a new beginning ensues in 1 Sam. 5 when the battle of the deities (Yahweh and Dagon) is joined and Philistine presumption rebuked, indicating that perhaps Yahweh had not fractured the covenant but had only disciplined Israel. In 1 Samuel 4 – 6 there is a very heavy use of Exodus imagery (cf. the explicit allusions to the Egyptians at 1 Sam. 4:8, the plagues which befell the Philistines, their reaction, which when they were confronted with the power of Yahweh, was similar to that of the Egyptians.[2]). Such a use of Exodus language and parallels implies that in a similarly desperate historical situation to that of the Exodus, Yahweh will begin again with Israel. That appears to happen in 1 Sam. 6 when a decision is made by the Philistines to send the ark back. Yet the fact that the ark remains for some twenty years on what was at that time the outer limits of Israelite occupation of the hill country (cf. 1 Sam. 7:1), until it is fully returned under David in 2 Sam. 6, makes the divine intention for Israel's future at that time difficult to gauge. Not until David conducts the ark into Jerusalem does the political history of Israel seem secure and this thoroughly accords with the transition from the era of the Judges to that of fully-fledged monarchy which was taking place in those years.

ii. *The request for a king and the choice of Saul*

In this period of uncertainty the approach of the Israelite elders for kingship is made to Samuel in 1 Sam. 8. The request is made because of

---

[2]. Full Exodus parallels are drawn by A. F. Campbell, *The Ark Narrative*, (Missoula, Montana: Scholars Press, 1975), pp. 203–5. Campbell has clearly noted the theological function of the ark in these early chapter of q som.

dissatisfaction with Samuel's sons and the belief that Samuel's office would pass on to them. There is no thought in verses 1–5 of denying the worth of Samuel's office, though the paradox of what may have been Samuel's attempt to institutionalize his charisma may underlie the content of these verses. 'Behold,' the elders say (1 Sam. 8:5), 'you are old and your sons do not walk in your ways; now appoint for us a king to govern (Heb. "judge") us like all the nations.' Of course, such a request was anticipated in Deut. 17:14 and was, as that context indicates, to be carefully reviewed. The request, here, however, is deemed (in view of its repetition after Samuel's resumé of the difficulties it will provoke, cf. 1 Sam. 8:19–20) to have a number of inbuilt incompatibilities.

In the first place there is confusion in the minds of the elders in regard to the character of the leadership over Israel which Samuel had exercised. In the office of Judge there had been no element of continuity, one did not appoint a successor who would 'judge' in sequence, for what appointments were needed were made by Yahweh as a crisis in Israel occurred. Moreover, the office of Judge had ascribed the final governmental decisions to Yahweh alone. Not only could no successor be predicted from a human point of view, but even the centre from which a consequent rule would be exercised was not known in advance. Kingship, on the other hand, was predictable in most or all of these respects. After the model of the Canaanite city state, which Samuel appears to refer to in the ensuing speech in 1 Sam. 8:10–18, kingship was dynastic (i.e. father/son succession), centralized, absolute and contained the potential abuse of power to which Samuel refers as the chapter proceeds. The inbuilt danger in the importation of a system of this character into Israel was the possibility for arbitrary conduct that the monarchical office contained. This was the oppressive direction, by a royal figure, of internal Israelite politics through alliances, treaties and compacts. All of this could (and did in fact) prove inimical to the concept of covenant since further members of a dynasty would come to the throne without direct divine intervention. This would further loosen the bonds of theocratic rule which the era of the Judges had so plainly seen at work.

The request for a 'king' who would 'judge' was thus an uncomfortable and imprudent combination of potential absolutism in the shape of kingship, with a simultaneous recognition of divine control, and thus theocracy as the ultimate form of government, on the other hand. The further point of contradiction in 1 Sam. 8:5 comes in the request for a kingship which would make Israel like the other nations. In the final analysis this is a request which seeks to undo Israel's special world position established by Exod. 19:3b–6. There it is the measure by which she is able to establish a separation from her world (a separation which is paradoxically attractive), which will be the yardstick of her political success. On any view, to ask for kingship is an implicit denial of divine rule; to ask for a kingship which will identify Israel more with her world is, in effect, to ask for the abrogation of the basis (Exod. 19:3b–6) on which covenant rule over Israel had rested.

In 1 Sam. 9 – 12 the question of the nature of Israel's kingship is taken further. The choice of Saul gives expression to a form of government which was a compromise between what had been the rule of the Judges period and that of the later monarchy. Saul's acceptance by all Israel was in large measure based upon his feats against the Ammonites recorded in 1 Sam. 11, where he acts precisely as a Judge of the earlier period might have acted. Prior to that he had been singled out by Yahweh and anointed by Samuel. But it seems clear from the type of public endorsement that follows Saul's victory in 1 Samuel 11 that the emerging monarchy had to that point produced few changes within Israel. After his victory the people proceeded with him to Gilgal. The order of what happens there is interesting. First the 'kingdom is renewed' (v. 14 at Samuel's suggestion, we note), then, Saul's kingship is generally accepted (cf. v. 15). What may be meant by the 'renewal of the kingdom' may be not the renewal of Saul's mandate to reign so much as the renewal of the kingdom structure within Israel, i.e. the recognition at Gilgal again of divine kingship over Israel,[3] since the word 'kingdom' at 1 Sam. 10:16, 25, as well as at 11:14, seems to be used in the wider sense of the administration of Israel as the domain of Yahweh. When, however, Saul's personal authority had been taken up in 1 Sam. 10, it was in a much more low-keyed way. It is true, as J. R. has noted, that he is publicly acclaimed as 'king' (v. 24), but earlier in the chapter when the question of his authority to act is being taken up, the descriptive term used by Samuel of him is simply Heb. nāgîd, or 'leader'. Saul's appointment had been to reign over the Lord's people (1 Sam. 10:1) and thus the derivative nature of his office had been made clear from the outset. The rights and duties of the 'kingdom' (RSV 'kingship' is less precise) at v. 25, to which the attention of the people is drawn, may well have been their responsibilities within the kingdom of God framework now that political changes are about to occur. What kingship, i.e. the occupant of the office, could or could not do within the kingdom, had in any case been explained by Samuel to all Israel within 1 Sam. 8. Already, morever, the rights and duties of kingship had been taken up in some detail in Deut. 17:14–20. What was now additionally needed, however, was instruction as to how Israel was to behave under kingship, the point to which Samuel would return in chapter 12.

It is likely therefore that the renewal of the kingdom at Gilgal was in fact covenant renewal and logically the appointment of Saul formally as king, as Vannoy has seen, (only public recognition had so far been offered, cf. 1 Sam. 10:24) took place within the reconstitution of the

---

[3]. This point is carefully argued for by J. R. Vannoy, *Covenant Renewal at Gilgal*. A Study of 1 Sa. 11:14–12:25 (Cherry Hill, N.J.: Mack Publishing Co, 1978), pp. 61–91. We agree with, and have incorporated his major conclusions.

kingdom, and thus covenant, relationship. In these circumstances the farewell speech of Samuel in chapter twelve provides for the continuation of the covenant by the formal renewal of the kingdom to which 11:14 has obliquely referred. 1 Sam. 12 is not given a geographical location but we may surmise that it took place at Gilgal, and although the word *bᵉrît* does not occur in the context, the chapter is patently covenant renewal in form.[4] After the apologia of Samuel in defence of his own ministry (vv. 1–5), the history of Israel is traced from the Exodus down to the present, though it is noted (v. 8) that the origins of Israel lay back in the patriarchal epoch. In vv. 6–13, as the rule of Yahweh is being recommended by Samuel, great weight is attached to Yahweh's steadfastness during the period of the Judges. The folly of a request for a king within the framework of such divine leadership is then raised (vv. 14–15) and threats implicit in disobedience by Israel or her king are also referred to. After the divine sign is given there is a confession (v. 19) by the people of their folly. This confession is responded to by Samuel with a demand for loyalty (vv. 20–21) and with the assurance that God will, in effect, keep his covenant, though the chapter ends on the ominous note that nation and king will be undone through infidelity.

iii. *The emergence of the prophetic office*

By the renewal ceremony of 1 Sam. 12, Israelite kingship seems to have been engrafted into the administration of the 'kingdom' and thus into the covenant. At this time of great historical change for Israel the shape of the future is anticipated in this speech (as it had been in the covenant speeches of Moses in Deuteronomy and Joshua in Joshua 24). The covenant has been secured again and the nation now stands before the threshold of a new era of political advance. An advance of this character was bound to bring with it significant religious changes and adaptations and we now turn to the emergence of the new movement which we see arising in the first book of Samuel. This would prove to be of decisive importance, not only for the history of Israel's kingship, but for the history of Israel itself.

We speak of course of the rise of the prophetic movement to public importance. The office of prophet within Israel was Mosaic in origins and character, though the function of prophecy is traced by the Old Testament back to Abraham (Gen. 20:7). The emphasis in the narratives concerning Samuel's call (1 Sam. 1 – 3) had finally fallen upon the prophetic role that he did and was to exercise (cf. 1 Sam. 3:20), but it is not until 1 Sam. 9 that our attention is directed to what will be the specifics of the prophetic task as expressed by Samuel. It had already

---

4. As K. Baltzer, *The Covenant Formulary*, pp. 66–68, argues.

been made clear within the book of Deuteronomy that the office of Israelite prophecy was directly related to, and owed its rationale to, the Sinai covenant. The evidence for this is presented in some detail at Deut. 18:15ff where to Israelite prophecy and to its Mosaic succession is committed the task of interpreting the implications of the Sinai covenant to subsequent generations. The Deuteronomy text suggests that we shall see a continuity of the Mosaic office, and we have seen the function, if not the office, during the era of the Judges, whereby the role of the Judge in recalling Israel to its covenant obligations was virtually a prophetic one. Only Deborah, of the Judge-figures, it is true, is styled as a prophet(ess). Perhaps this was done in her case to underline her basic authority as Judge, since it is through Barak that physical deliverance comes to Israel at the time.

In the book of Samuel prophecy hardens into an office and from that point on becomes institutionalized in the sense that prophecy thereafter is always part of the Israelite political scene. This change which occurred at that time is noted by 1 Sam. 9:9 where the remark is offered by the author that 'he who is now called a prophet was formerly called a seer.' The significance of this remark has often been pondered but the simplest explanation which recognizes that the roots of prophecy lie in the Mosaic period, and that prophecy does not emerge *de novo* in Samuel's time, is to assume that the author's remark is directed to the change in style of Samuel's personal ministry which occurs at this time. We cannot escape the connection between this change and the beginning of Israelite kingship. The emergence of the prophet as a major political figure is directly related to the choice (in 1 Sam. 9) of Saul. It would therefore seem that one new political office is being counterbalanced by a new emphasis upon another.

Within the book there is mention also of Samuel as the apparent leader of the prophetic guilds (1 Sam. 19:19–24), so prominent later, but of whose existence we hear for the first time in the references cited. In regard to the role of the prophet we must work by inference as to its significance in this early period, particularly by inferences which can be drawn from the clashes between Samuel and Saul, on matters of policy. In all of these there is clearly no diminution of the spiritual influence that Samuel had exercised as Judge. In other political areas, however, his former powers are truncated or challenged. Leadership in war, formerly the role of the Judge, certainly passes to the king (cf. 1 Sam. 8), as does general responsibility for the day-to-day political decisions by which the nation is to be administered (also chapter 8, cf. v. 20, and note the king as the final point of judicial appeal at the later 2 Sam. 15:2). Thus a major division of responsibilities has occurred and the total Mosaic leadership role (continued through the Judges) has been split into distinct components, with kingship being responsible for what we might call the 'temporalities', prophecy remaining charged with final spiritual direction of the nation's affairs. Since the prophet is preeminently a man of the Spirit, while kingship remains by nature an administrative office, prophecy in Israel will, and must claim to, take precedence over kingship.

Prophecy was a covenant office in the sense that its rationale lay in the need for the construction of such an office because of Israel's potential infidelity. The fact that kingship came upon the scene and awakened and gave precision to the prophetic movement suggests that in kingship lay the real threat to the continuance of the Israelite covenant relationship.[5] How this threat was translated into actuality becomes clear as the subsequent course of Israelite history is pursued. The dangers inherent in kingship were perhaps the reverse of those which had appeared in the Judges period, where individualism had been rampant. That is, the danger that kingship presented was that of a construction of a centralized, personalized, bureaucratic office, which would tend to solve problems by seeking to apply judicious political solutions. The further point is that a major source of Old Testament difficulty during the prophetic period was the natural tendency for kingship to solve external difficulties by the construction of a web of foreign relationships. This invariably led to religious compromises, but it was also in direct violation of the first commandment that Israel was to have no independent foreign policy.

For all these reasons kingship and prophecy were bound to clash and the prophetic movement became (as it was intended to by its rise to prominence at this time) an integral part in the series of checks and balances which were progressively erected against kingship. Prophecy was not content to accept the division of responsibilities between politics and religion which actually took place, for it saw itself as ultimately a political office. It acted under a system of final divine kingship and as a sort of first minister. Therefore, it constantly made the demand on kingship to submit in all areas and continually rebuked the naked and unbridled use of royal authority. We cannot refer to the way in which the offices of prophecy and kingship interacted throughout the royal period, but in the light of the differences between the two offices to which we have referred, clashes between Saul and Samuel became inevitable. Light is particularly thrown upon the otherwise difficult encounter between Samuel and Saul in 1 Samuel 13 where the demand of Samuel to initiate sacrifice, even though Saul had waited the period that Samuel had specified, seems otherwise arbitrary. For what was really involved in such clashes was the absolute insistence by prophecy that its voice must prevail in ultimate decisions by which Israel's future would be decided (in 1 Sam. 13 the issue is the beginning of the holy war against Amalek). Saul, Samuel insisted, must exercise

---

[5]. On the general relationship of prophecy to kingship and the correlation of the offies, c.f. F.M. Cross, *Consonite Myth and Hebrew Epic*, (Cambridge, Mass: Harvard Univ. Press, 1973) pp. 223–9. His convincing analysis has been adopted.

authority only derivatively and within a structure ultimately presided over by the prophet, as the divine messenger.

iv. *Messianism – a theology of kingship*

The advent of kingship raised other than political issues. The need had arisen for the construction of a theology of kingship whereby it could take its place within the Sinai framework. When other covenant offices had been erected (namely priesthood and prophecy) they had been provided at the time with a theological explanation for their existence. Moreover kingship (like priesthood, particularly) was a well-known international movement bringing with it into Israel particular connotations in the public mind, not all of which could be acceptable within Israel's covenant relationship. It is therefore to be expected that with 1 Samuel a theology of kingship will arise and we find this to be the case. The elements within this theology are clear.

Firstly, kingship within Israel operated, as it began, by divine choice. In the case of both Saul and David, it is made plain that each has been the subject of careful divine election, exercised through Samuel. Perhaps something of the relative importance of the two figures might be gauged from the fact that Saul is brought to Samuel, but Samuel must seek out David, though this point is merely mentioned in passing.

Secondly, both Saul and David are anointed by Samuel. In each case the act is private, not public and performed by the prophet who has been directly commissioned for this service. The private nature of the act seems to indicate that it has something to say to both David and Saul, rather than to Israel as a whole. One therefore imagines that anointing has served to give an assurance of the election which has already been conferred. It does not therefore seem to establish a relationship between king and people, but to confirm a relationship which already exists by election, between king and God. As a result the king can be recognized as Yahweh's anointed, and when this phrase is used publicly as it is in 1 Samuel, it is a recognition that the office of kingship is ultimately a religious and not a political one. Since the phrase points back to the initial choice it can be used of Saul after he has been rejected. Its continued use in his case suggests that in itself the phrase does not indicate that the relationship initially created has been maintained.

So far as anointing is concerned, to take his point up at this juncture, its purpose is difficult to establish in absolute terms. It has been recently maintained that by it a contractual relationship was set up between the parties.[6] This may well be so, but such a view does not exclude the customary function of anointing as it can be gleaned from the comparative materials of the Ancient Near East, which was, so far as

---

6. T.D. Mettinger, *King and Messiah* (Gleerup: CWK, 1976), pp. 210–211 suggests this.

we can gather, to confer authority to execute an office. In Egypt, the king was not anointed since he was divine and thus in no need of authority beyond his own, though high officials whose authority was derivative from the Pharaoh were anointed by the king. In the Hittite realm, nobles conferred on one of their peers by anointing, authority to act as king (as *primus inter pares*). In the case of David there is a double anointing. Considerable space is devoted in 1 Sam. 16 to the careful manner in which his choice and anointing took place. He is again anointed by the people in 2 Sam. 5:3 without a reference to what was actually involved in the act, though v. 2 seems to make it clear that public anointing was simply public recognition of prior divine choice (cf. also 2 Sam. 2:4).

Thirdly, in the case of both Saul and David, there is an interesting connection developed between choice, anointing and the subsequent gift of the Spirit. Earlier, we have drawn attention to the function which the Spirit played in the leadership of Israel in the epoch of the Judges. Such a connection between the gift of the Spirit and the exercise of a leadership role within the kingdom of God framework is a common biblical one, and one to which we shall later draw attention. When Saul and David receive the Spirit (Saul, 1 Sam. 10:6; David, 1 Sam. 16:13) divine empowerment is added to authorization. The content of 1 Sam. 16:13–14 makes it plain that the reception of the Spirit by David is paralleled immediately by the withdrawal of the Spirit from Saul. Put in other terms, when David is chosen for leadership within the people of God, Saul then stands dismissed.

Fourthly,[7] the chosen king is further commended to Israel by a public display of his prowess. In the case of Saul, this takes the form of the victory over the Ammonites in 1 Sam. 11. In the case of David, the successful encounter with Goliath the Philistine (1 Sam. 17) completes the sequence of election, anointing, reception of the Spirit and the demonstration of power that we have seen also in the case of Saul. Admittedly, this pattern is not repeated with subsequent royal figures in Israel, but with the inauguration of kingship we are dealing with the establishment of an ideal, by which the political office of kingship, as later exercised by individuals, may be measured. Save in the Messianic projections of Isaiah 11 (and in features attaching to the servant in Isa. 42:1–4), the Old Testament does not return to the ideal, yet all four components to which we have referred are present at the beginning of the ministry of Jesus of Nazareth, a ministry which was intended to point to the fact that by him the Kingdom of God is ushered in.

The nature of such Israelite kingship made it clear that in the figure of

---

[7]. I am indebted to R. Knierim, 'The Messianic Concept in the First Book of Samuel', in *Jesus and the Historian: Written in honor of E. C. Colwell*, ed. F. T. Trotter (Philadelphia: Westminster Press, 1968), pp. 32ff for this and previous observations made here on the subject of messianism in 1 Samuel.

the king, the ideal features of the covenant, to which Exod. 19:3b–6 had drawn Israel's attention, had been expressed. Kingship and covenant in the office of Israel's king had representatively been linked. We shall see that this link is the more carefully forged and explained by 2 Samuel 6 – 7 when a further movement in the theology of kingship occurs as a counter to the difficulties which the tentative beginning of the office experienced in the person of Saul. Saul himself seems to have been very much a transition figure, a bridge between the Judge and the King, an attempt to accommodate the demands of a new office to the patterns of an old one. This was an experiment which inevitably led to tensions and misunderstandings and to the final rejection of Saul who had been unable to perceive the inbuilt limitations which his own office had contained.

The breach between Samuel and Saul appeared in 1 Sam. 13 and had become final by 1 Samuel 15. Here one must agree with Knierim that the differences between Saul's failure and David's success can hardly be said to have been rooted in personality disposition or charisma.[8] In fact we see nothing in the reign of Saul quite like the extraordinary failures and personal excesses which characterized the court and the person of David and which rendered the second half of his reign so disastrous. The essential difference between Saul and David was theological, not personal, for the sacral backing which Saul had lacked would be added to David's reign in the shape of an impressive divine guarantee of the eternal continuance of his royal office.

C. DAVID AND THE KINGDOM OF GOD

i. *The order of 2 Sam. 6—7: sanctuary and kingship*

We may pass over the historical details of David's rise to power and the public endorsement of his ministry by all Israel. What is next of interest for our study are the narratives of 2 Sam. 6—7, chapters which are respectively concerned with the choice of Jerusalem as the temple site and the establishment of the Davidic dynasty. Before turning to the details of these chapters, the question of their order must be raised. That is to say, the first matter to be dealt with is the choice of the site of the future temple and the city of Jerusalem from which Yahweh will rule. While the temple site is more precisely located by the purchase of Araunah's threshing floor by David, as 2 Samuel concludes (2 Sam. 24:18–25), the more general choice of the temple site has in fact been made in chapter 6. Rightly understood then, chapter 7 is not concerned with the provision of a temple, since that has virtually been anticipated by the narrative of chapter 6, but with the erection of a dynasty for

---

8. Knierim, *Messianic Concept*, pp. 36–37.

David and thus a new turn is given to the theology of Israelite kingship. What is thus being said by the sequence of these two chapters, is that Yahweh's kingship must be first provided for before the question of Israel's can be taken up. Only when such an acknowledgement of Yahweh's rule has been made may the possibility of a firmly established Israelite royal line be discussed.

Since the recognition of Yahweh's kingship over Israel will eventually involve the building of the temple upon the chosen site, some discussion is needed at this stage of the relationship of earthly kingship to the temple of the protecting deity of the state concerned. In the early Mesopotamian city-state development of kingship, the government of the city state was recognized to be merely the reflection of the cosmic reality of divine government which stood behind the city state. Thus the state with its hierarchies, culminating in kingship at its apex, corresponded to the cosmic setting with its own particular series of gradations whereby the major deity headed a pantheon of lesser figures. The ultimate kingship of the protecting city deity was thus expressed through, and paralleled by, empirical kingship exercised by the city state ruler. Such an analogy was given concrete expression in the relationship which obtained between the city state temple and the king's palace. The temple was regarded as the earthly residence of the city state deity, with the king's palace being regarded as the residence of the deity's earthly steward. In this parallelism the place of the temple was paramount, for it was the point of contact between the two worlds, the city state on the one hand, and the cosmic state which was thought to stand behind it, on the other.

In the Mesopotamian situation which paralleled the Israelite one the most closely, the city state (or later empire etc.) was recognized to be under the control of (in the case of the city state at least), or to be the property of, the controlling deity. In such circumstances the choice of the temple site was not incidental. On the contrary, the erection of a temple was thought to have been preceded by a divine disclosure of an intention by the deity to reside at a spot which had been marked out by some divine manifestation or epiphany. It was thus natural that the erection of a temple was viewed as an assertion of divine control over the political and the religious life of the state concerned. That such a view was a central theological conception in the ancient world is clear enough from the tenor of the early creation epics (cf. the Babylonian, 'Enuma Elish', or the Baal epics in the Ugarit collection). In these the establishment of order and harmony over chaos was followed by the proclamation of the divine kingship of the establisher, and thereafter the erection for him of a temple as a residence. Thus in the Baal epics, Baal, having become victor over the chaos forces personified as sea (Yamm), demanded from the royal council and obtained a palace (i.e. temple – the word is the same in many Semitic cognates, including Hebrew) as a residence which would befit his kingship. The building of such a temple was thus the endorsement of Baal's newly won place within the cosmic order.

ii. 2 Sam. 6 and the function of the ark

The relationship between 2 Sam. 6 & 7 should now be clear. In chapter 6, Yahweh, the divine king, has indicated that he will thereafter take up residence in Jerusalem, the new Davidic capital, the capture of which from the Jebusites in 2 Sam. 5 was followed by sweeping and final victory by David over the Philistines. The manner in which the ark is returned to Jerusalem leaves us in no doubt as to the divine designation of the city. Here again we need to recall that the contents of the ark were the two tables of the covenant, to contain which the ark had been expressly constructed (Exod. 25:10–22; 37:1–9; Deut. 10:1–5). Since the ark was *the* visible symbol of the Sinai covenant relationship, its presence quickly came to be identified with the fact of divine rule over Israel. The golden lid of the ark, together with the outstretched wings of the cherubim which touched above the lid, formed a place of special divine manifestation (1 Sam. 4:4). Not unnaturally, the ark came to be brought into connection with the concept of God as enthroned and God was conceived to be seated as King upon the cherubim which overshadowed the ark (cf. Ps.18:10; 1 Sam. 4:4). The connection between the divine presence and the ark is made apparent by the frequent mention of the ark as the footstool of the divine throne (cf. Ps. 99:5; 132:7–8; 1 Chr. 28:2). In covenant terms this notion is understandable in the light of evidence from Egypt and the Hittite kingdom which indicated that documents, written oaths, political agreements etc. which were of importance, were to be deposited at the feet of the god, or were to be buried under the images of the god(s) in the temple.[9]

While a connection was made between the ark and Yahweh's kingship, the ark and its contents provided an indication of how that kingship would be exercised. That is to say, the recognition of divine rule over Israel was to take the form of conformity to the divine word pronounced. Here the revelation of the Decalogue was always considered by Israel to be definitive and primary, and as offering essential guidance as to the mode in which Israel's national life (and consequently the personal response of individual Israelites) was to be regulated. Where God's word was, there was the divine presence, and as we well know in other connections, the Old Testament gave great prominence to the power of God expressed through his word as well as to his presence mediated by the word. Thus a close association between ark and sanctuary (i.e. between the demands which kingship made, and the symbol of divine rule itself), was always maintained. This had been fractured by the capture of the ark in 1 Sam. 4 but the return of the ark (2

---

9. Cf. M. Haran, 'The Ark and the Cherubim', *IEJ* 9 (1959), p. 89.

Sam. 6), indicated that once again Yahweh would place himself at the centre of Israelite life. The theological interlude in the history of the nation which the absence of the ark had suggested (cf. 1 Sam. 7:1 with 2 Sam. 6:1) was now over. Yahweh was once again willing to be associated with the national life of Israel. The capture of Jerusalem served therefore to begin a new era in the history of Israel.

The return of the ark in chapter 6 was plainly a divine initiative, as the course of the narrative serves to underline. Only Yahweh can bring the ark back, we are virtually told, just as only Yahweh could have been responsible for its capture (1 Sam. 4). David's initial attempt to bring it back was abortive and resulted in the untimely death of an attendant (Uzzah, 2 Sam. 6:7), an incident which had formed a fairly precise parallel to the way in which presumption in the handling of the ark by the men of Beth-Shemesh after it had been returned to the borders of Israel by the Philistines (1 Sam. 6:19) had been severely punished. Only after the assurance of divine favour had been given (after David's first attempt the ark remained for three months in the house of Obed Edom of Gath whose house as a result was blessed, 2 Sam. 6:11–12), did David make a further attempt. The reference at this time in 2 Sam. 6:12 to the kingship of David (for the first time in the chapter) seems an indication in itself that success will attend this second endeavour.

The joyful reception which the ark received on its return as *the* Israelite cult object (v. 15) was in recognition of what was clearly regarded as God's permissive return. That the return heralds a new beginning in the fortunes of David and his house is made clear from the closing narrative of chapter 6 in which the house of Saul in the person of Saul's daughter (and David's wife), Michal, is rejected from participation in Davidic succession. The tenuous kingship of the house of Saul, with which the ark had not been associated, was thus formally brought to an end. This in itself was sufficient indication of the absence of sacral support for Saul and we note how he was represented in 1 Samuel as bent upon the destruction of Israel's religious past (cf. 1 Sam. 22:11ff), a move which attests his own awareness of his religious isolation. There had always been indications that the kingship of David would be of a different order. Apart from the Goliath victory, his anointing was not followed by massive displays of public support. In the pursuit narratives of the second half of 1 Samuel, which show Saul in conflict with David, despite Saul's firm political base and ostensible public support, it is clearly David who enjoys divine backing. Since David's rise to power was of a different order from that of Saul we might expect that his kingship would develop in a different way. We are helped to understand that this will be so by the prophetic discernment of Abigail (1 Sam. 25:23–35), who sees kingship as associated with David's posterity also. Such narratives make it plain that when David finally comes to power it will not be because of his political astuteness or his military acumen, his reliance upon mercenary troops or his ability to manipulate the circumstances of his time. Israel will simply recognize in David the fact of divine choice.

iii. 2 Sam. 7:1–16: a charter for the Davidic dynasty

(a) The theme of the chapter

In 2 Sam. 7 we find expression given to the character of Davidic kingship and the question taken up of the perpetuation of David's line. The chapter operates as a charter for the Davidic dynasty, for by the promises of the chapter an eternal throne for David and for his house is established. Capitalizing upon chapter 6 and the return of the ark, David now raises in the first two verses of chapter 7 the question of a suitable dwelling place for the ark, i.e., whether at this stage of his monarchy a temple should be built. In doing so he points to the disparity which exists between the way in which the ark is housed and the extent of his own establishment. In 2 Sam. 7:1 two key words which control at least the first half of the chapter occur, namely 'dwell' and 'house', for the theme of the first half of the chapter is the perpetuation of the Davidic throne in Jerusalem as it will be backed by the assurance of the divine presence. The recognition by David in v. 1 is fundamental, namely that his own kingdom will not be established, nor his own line endure, unless divine rule is acknowledged appropriately within Israel. It is all the more remarkable that such an acknowledgement should come from him after the very great range of successes which he had enjoyed. Verse 1 is thus an indication that forgetfulness of divine favours, a sin against which the book of Deuteronomy continually warns, will not be an attitude which Israel, will display when led by ideal kingship.

(b) David as the architect of 'rest'

The impulse for the new movement by David derived from the fact that Yahweh had given David 'rest from all his enemies around about' (v. 1). The immediate military antecedent which had posed a final threat to David's complete occupancy of Palestine had been the Philistines who had been defeated in a campaign which had been divinely controlled (cf. 2 Sam. 5:17–25). This had enabled David to centralize all the religious traditions of Israel upon the new capital of Jerusalem. This familiar phrase, 'rest', in 2 Sam. 7:1 takes us back to the platform of the book of Deuteronomy where the greatest material blessing which would flow from the conquest and which would characterize Israel's ideal situation in the promised land was to be 'rest from all her enemies around about'. (Cf. Deut. 12:10 – we cannot overlook the fact that this verse refers to the promise of rest to be fulfilled, in a key chapter which is devoted to the establishment of a central sanctuary in Israel, and thus to circumstances remarkably parallel to the sequence of 2 Sam. 6 and 7.) This notion of rest is actively bound up with the conquest narratives. Therefore when the tent of meeting had been erected at Shiloh (Josh. 18:1) and thus the tribal sanctuary for which Deut. 12 had sought is established,[10] 'rest' is one of the fruits of victory which Joshua has achieved, since such a move had proved possible only after 'the land lay subdued before them'. The book of Joshua virtually closes with a reference to this rest which has now been achieved (note Joshua's recognition that the Lord had given Israel rest from all its enemies around about, Josh. 23:1) and thus with a charge by Joshua to Israel to pursue that faithfulness to Yahweh which will ensure that rest was retained (Josh. 23 – 24). In 2 Sam. 7:1, therefore, with rest of a more permanent character now having been granted, David, as Carlson noted, is fulfilling the charge of Deut. 8:12–14 to Israel that when she 'had built goodly houses and lived in them, and when her herds and flocks had been multiplied' she was not to forget the 'Lord her God who had brought her out of the land of Egypt'. 2 Sam. 7:1 thus indicates, and verse 11 confirms, that the defeat of the Philistines had meant that the occupation of Palestine and therefore the conquest had been completed. What Joshua's successors in the Judges period had been unable to effect because of the infidelity of the age (2 Sam. 7:11), namely to fill in the framework that Joshua's conquests had provided, David had now done. We cannot miss the idealization of David which is being undertaken by the author at this point, nor, by the further language of 2 Sam. 7, the exalted position which he occupies within Israel at this time.

Already at 2 Sam. 5:2 he had been styled Israel's ideal shepherd, and thus in the matter of Israel's leadership the surrogate for Yahweh (cf. the frequent ascription of shepherd testimony to Yahweh in the Old Testament, Ps. 80:1 etc.). In chapter 7, as the figure associated with the blessing of rest, he achieves what the Judges had failed to do (i.e. what the previous history of Israel had not experienced). It is to be noted also that the intimacy that Yahweh had had with his 'servant' Moses is now shared with 'my servant David' (v. 5), in whom the physical promises to Israel of the Mosaic period are brought to consummation.

(c) The refusal of permission to build a 'house'

Deferentially, and operating within the understood framework of reference, David conveys to Nathan the prophet his request to build (v. 2). Nathan's reply of v. 3 seems at first prophetic endorsement (to which, some suggest, later reservations were added), but in view of the

[10]. R. A. Carlson, *David the Chosen King* (Uppsala: Almqvist and Wiksell, 1964), notes the connection of 'rest' with the Deuteronomic demand for the centralization of the sanctuary, pp. 100–102. Our general indebtness to Carlson's perceptive treatment of a Som. 7 is acknowledged.

divine refusal to build which is given to David, we may perhaps construe v. 3 as merely a conventional court rejoinder.[11] The matter is taken forward in v. 5 when the substance of the oracle to be delivered is given to Nathan. 2 Sam. 7:5 summarizes the divine reply under the three notes of reference to the person who has made the request—'my servant David', the nature of the request which has been made—the building of a 'house' and the purpose which the project has in view—that it is to be a house for Yahweh 'to dwell in'. These three points then form the substance of what is conveyed in vv. 6–17.

Verse 5 is clearly a refusal to permit David to build, but opinion is divided as to the reasons which underlay the refusal. For some, the refusal is a prophetic affirmation of Israel's conquest faith. The older nomadic faith could not entertain the proposal of a fixed residence for the Deity. Yahweh had always wandered about with his people (v. 6), for by the mobility of the ark the whole of Palestine had served as a sanctuary. Pilgrimage sites had been determined by the position of the ark for the time being. Such a mobility of the divine presence had been an indication moreover that it could not predictably be located in a defined sanctuary. Indeed, when Israel had gone so far as to set up a semi-permanent shrine at Shiloh (cf. 1 Sam. 1 – 3), a corrupt priesthood and a debased institutionalism had resulted. This, in fact, had led to the withdrawal of the ark from Israel for a period of twenty years! Yahweh, further, had never requested a fixed habitation, no initiatives – as they must do – had come from him. Though a connection between dynastic kingship and temple prevailed in surrounding states, this in itself provided no real grounds for the assumptions which underlay David's request. The building of a temple would mark a major theological change for which Israel must gradually be prepared; kingship must become more firmly entrenched and its benefits seen, and prophetic opposition be overborne.

There is force in such arguments, though they finally founder on the contents of this chapter. The transcendent character of God is certainly referred to here and no doubt (in the question of v. 5) the impossibility of enshrining him. The notion could not be entertained that Yahweh should 'dwell' (i.e. sit enthroned) in a temple! It is also true that the building of a temple would bring a major theological change. But the point of chapter 7 is that these factors are recognized by the provision of a further revelation which adds Davidic kingship to the Sinai covenant. The real point of difficulty came later. One cannot help feeling that many of the misinterpretations of verse 5 have arisen from the later historical fact that Solomon did reverse the order of chapters 6 and 7, constructing an oriental type kingship and turning the Jerusalem temple into a royal chapel.

---

[11]. As M. Noth, *The Laws in the Pentateuch and Other Studies*, (London: Oliver and Boyd, 1967), p. 257, suggests.

(d) Reasons for the choice of Solomon as builder

It must be emphasized that Nathan's oracle accepts in principle the building of a temple. Only the person of David is rejected. Those who see the rejection of David's request as absolute and view chapter 7 as a later composition endorsing Solomonic kingship (i.e., a re-working of a basic oracle delivered by Nathan to David) regard 7:11 as the divine counter to what is the Davidic request of verse 5. David will not build Yahweh a temple but Yahweh will build David a 'house' (i.e. a dynasty – throughout this chapter there is a play upon the word 'house' which is alternatively used with temple and dynasty in mind).

But, as has been noted,[12] 2 Sam. 7:13a forms the real parallel to v. 5. In v. 11 what is prominent is the noun 'house' and Yahweh will 'make' (not 'build' as in v. 5) David a house. Both v. 5 and v. 13 emphasize by position the personal pronoun ('thou' in v. 5, 'he' in v. 13) and share the same verb, 'build'. The contrast is thus between 'thou' (David) who may not build, and 'he' (Solomon) to whom permission is granted. The question of v. 5 is not, therefore, a reference to the presumption of David as a mere mortal offering the request. The pronoun is emphasized in order to provide for the later contrast between the two eras, David's and Solomon's. Of course in some sense a rebuke is being administered in v. 5, if only mildly. Within Israel initiatives of such a nature come from the Deity alone, especially initiatives of this character (cf. v. 6). At the same time v. 5 may well be conveying a corrective to the notion that whatever is built will be 'indwelt'. That Yahweh must initiate the move might have been discernible from the fact that David had had to await the divine pleasure before the ark could be brought to Jerusalem, as well as from the fact that Jerusalem itself had been put into David's hands by Yahweh. Thus the marking off of the site and the movement of the ark had both of them been divine decisions. The timing of building and the person of the builder must also be.

All this, however, is not a display of divine arbitrariness. Good reasons for the choice of Solomon existed and these are given in the later books. David prepared the site, acquired the materials, but did not build. 1 Chronicles 22:8 ascribes the reason to David's preoccupation with conquest (cf. 1 Chr. 28:3). 1 Kings 5:3 indicates that David was compelled to put off the building of the temple because he lacked opportunity. These two statements are reconcileable with the continuing tenor of 1 Kings 5 in which Solomon makes it clear to Hiram of Tyre, that David had been fully engaged in the business of building an empire by the subjugation of enemies. Suggestively, to return to 2 Sam. 7, the account of David's wars by which the limits of the empire were established, follows in chapters 8 – 10 and are narratives which at that time seem to have been theologically rather than chronologically

---

12. Noth, *Laws*, p. 251 emphasizes this.

grouped. They are thus placed to point us to David as the empire builder, a fact to which 1 Chr. 28 and 1 Kgs. 5:3 refer.

Yet, while the chronological reasons for delay are advanced in the later books, the theology which necessitates the delay is contained in 2 Sam. 7. On the one hand rest had been given to David, 7:1, on the other hand, rest is yet to come, 7:11. As Carlson notes, there is a definite schema uniting vv. 9b–11a (7:6–9a had been a survey of what had been achieved to that point).[13] Three important elements occur, namely that Yahweh will make a great name for David (v. 9b), that he will appoint a 'place' for Israel (v. 10), and that he will give 'rest'. Only then (v. 11b) will a dynasty follow. In short, David's greatness must be established, Israel's problem of living space be determined, with the blessing of 'rest', as associated with dynasty, then to follow.

In all of this the appeal to the underlying theology of the Abrahamic covenant and the understanding of it by the writer of 2 Samuel is clear. Certainly 2 Sam. 7:9b–11a has in mind the establishment of Israel's ideal Abrahamic borders (note the 'place' of 7:10 – the Abrahamic borders of Gen. 15:18ff are defined in Deut. 11:24ff as Israel's 'place'). This would bring David a 'great name' (2 Sam. 7:9 with Gen. 12:2), and this conjunction of a great people, ideally governed, living in pre-determined geographical dimensions will result finally in the experience by Israel of the tantalizing but biblically fundamental promise of rest. The logic of the chapter recognizes that only when this ideal result has been achieved should a sanctuary be built. This will then mark out the promised land as 'holy space' and will point to the kingship of God which undergirds the whole Davidic programme. These are the implications of vv. 9b–11a. What is also emphasized in these verses is that this ideal result will be a divine achievement, for the emphasis upon the 'I' who will provide the promised result is paramount. Once David has fulfilled his task as the extender of the boundaries to the Abrahamic dimensions, and the Messianic line of David has been secured (note the reference to 'seed' in v. 12 and the Abrahamic connections to which it points, cf. Gen. 15:3–4), then a temple for Yahweh's name (v. 13) would be built by Solomon.

(e) The nature of the indwelling divine presence

Before the question of how such an idealization was translated into reality is explored, we note that it has often been suggested that the formula, 'for my name', of v. 13 is a weakening of the dwelling concept which has been raised by David in v. 5. There is thus, it is suggested, a conscious adjustment in v. 13 (the parallel to v. 5) of the somewhat more bald view of Yahweh's immanence which has appeared in v. 5. Not Yahweh himself will sit enthroned in the new temple, but only a reflex

---

[13]. *David the Chosen King*, pp. 111–114.

of himself (a sort of *alter ego*) will take his place there in the shape of the 'name' (v. 13 is often considered to be a 'Deuteronomistic' addition whereby older immanistic views of God's presence are corrected by this notion of the 'name' only as resident. This is supposedly a feature of Deuteronomic theology). We have already raised this question, however, in discussing the name formula in connection with the book of Deuteronomy. There we pointed to its use as a term indicating divine ownership of the sanctuary and thus finally the land. The use of 'name' therefore in v. 13 is the assertion, by means of the temple, of Yahweh's kingship over Israel. It is only (v. 13b) within the proper context of that continued assertion that David's line will be perpetually established. The very close connection of the two kingships expressed in v. 13 must not be lost sight of and bears upon what follows.

(f) Eternal Davidic kingship

The eternal character of Davidic kingship is referred to in absolute terms in v. 13b. Though the line may be chastised (v. 14) these new covenant promises (cf. *ḥesed* v. 15) will not be withdrawn. The Davidic house (v. 16) will stand for ever. This divine pronouncement appears to contrast markedly with the historical realities which began with the reign of Solomon whereby the dissolution of the Davidic empire was brought about. Yet the unconditionality of the promises to David is not confined to 2 Sam. 7. (Cf. 23:5, where that verse must be rendered, in view of 7:13, 'He has made an eternal covenant with me', and not, as some suggest, 'The Eternal has made a covenant with me' – note also the extraordinary lengths to which Ps. 89:33–37 goes to emphasize the unchanging character of the Davidic covenant.) On the other hand, the Davidic covenant is often viewed as though it were conditional (cf. Ps. 89:29–32; 132:12; 1 Kings 2:4; 8:25; 9:4–5). By these two sets of references a distinction is being made between the generality and the particularity of the promises to David. In general terms the line would not fail. Yet in particular terms, benefits might be withdrawn from individuals. In physical terms, the virtual failure of the Davidic line occurred in 587 B.C. but in spiritual terms we cannot but read 2 Sam. 7:13 finally in terms of New Testament Christology.

(g) Summary to this point

So far, we have dealt principally with the kingship implications of 2 Sam. 7 and we have noted how the Davidic line was ultimately to reflect the Kingship of God. But the related matter of covenant is what the first half of chapter 7 is referring to and we now take up this question. The chapter contains a series of promises with David in view. But this is David as Israel's representative and the interweaving of the fortunes of David with the unfolding of the history of Israel is clear in vv. 6–16.

Moreover David is the agent through whom the Exodus deliverance (rest in the land of promise) is finally achieved. Sonship terms applied to Israel (Exod. 4:22) are now applied to David (cf. 2 Sam. 7:14). It is thus generally clear that the covenant with David lies within the framework of the Sinai covenant with Israel ($b^e r\hat{\imath}t$, though it does not occur in 2 Sam. 7, occurs in the expositions of the chapter, cf. 2 Sam. 23:5; Ps. 89:34, cf. Ps. 132:12 and note how that Psalm operates as a poetic commentary upon 2 Sam. 6 & 7.) Yet we have seen also that the chapter contains extensive Abrahamic allusions. The promised land has now been secured from the river of Egypt to the Euphrates, the Abrahamic borders. Further, the sanctuary presence of God in the midst of his people, which the temple will provide, would secure the blessing of 'rest' in God's presence. In the book of Deuteronomy this had constituted the ingredient by which the land might become a second Eden. The full covenantal play of 2 Sam. 7 by which Israel under David returns to a Gen. 1 – 2 position is thus clear.

iv. 2 Sam. 7:18–29: the charter of man

The tenor of David's prayer in 2 Sam. 7:18–29 indicates that he well understood this covenantal significance of the divine promises and their effect upon humanity as a whole. We cannot treat this prayer in detail. It is introduced in v. 18 and summarized by the important and difficult v. 19. Puzzling in v. 19 is the Heb. phrase $w^e z\hat{o}'t$ $t\hat{o}rat$ $h\bar{a}'\bar{a}d\bar{a}m$ (literally, 'and this is the law of man' – we have already, however, drawn attention to the wide – reaching nature of Heb. $t\hat{o}r\bar{a}h$). There is some doubt, firstly, whether 19b is to be taken as a statement or a question and the English translations express this uncertainty. By carefully analysing occurrences of the Heb. phrase $w^e z\hat{o}'t$ $t\hat{o}rat$ + genitive, W.C. Kaiser[14] has shown clearly that v. 19b must be taken as a statement, and that the Heb. phrase concerned serves to introduce or to summarize (as here) a set of divine instructions. Under 'this' the promises of the first half of the chapter are being referred to, while under 'the law of man' their implications as David understood them are contained. This curious Heb. expression, 'law of man', has been shown to have parallels in the similar Akkadian phrase $t\bar{e}r\iota t$ $n\bar{\iota}sh\bar{e}$, which carries the meaning of a 'fateful oracle for man'.[15] What is conveyed by the Akkadian term is the notion of an utterance by which the destiny of mankind is controlled or provided for. Such a concept fits the Samuel context admirably and with more than some probability Kaiser suggests that the sense to be given to 2 Sam. 7:19b is, 'This is the charter by

---

14. W.C. Kaiser, 'The Blessing of David, The Charter for Humanity', in *The Law and the Prophets. Old Testament Studies in Honor of O.T. Allis*, ed. John H. Skilton, (Nutley, N.J.: Presbyterian and Reformed, 1974), p. 311.

15. Cf. the references cited by Carlson, *David the Chosen King*, p. 125, n. 4.

which humanity will be directed.'[16] That is to say, in the oracle delivered to him, David rightly sees the future and destiny of the human race as involved. The promises to David have built upon the broad history of the covenant concepts as, from creation onwards, they have covered divine intent for human development, and David has seen the connections which Nathan's oracle has offered.

v. Priest after the order of Melchizedek

In the light of the fuller covenantal exposition of this chapter, more may be said about the role of Davidic kingship which it introduces. Here the interpretative contribution of a Psalm whose content is consistent with the era of David, Ps. 110[17], can be brought into play. That Psalm asserts the priestly nature of David's Jerusalem kingship. It will not be strictly cultic, just as Melchizedek's, with which it is compared, was not (cf. Gen. 14:18). In its contemplation of a priestly kingship (cf. Ps. 110:4), the psalm appears to suggest that in the person of the king, the demand contemplated for all Israel in Exod. 19:3b–6 has been embodied. Only kingship of that character, the Psalm seems to imply in its second half, will guarantee the political extension of the Jerusalem kingdom, which it anticipates (Ps. 110:5–7). David's line is thus to reflect, in the person of the occupant of the throne of Israel, the values which the Sinai covenant had required of the nation as a whole. David therefore is operating as Yahweh's vice-regent, operating, as the general covenantal connections to which we have pointed seem to make clear, as the 'divine image'. For while the links are tenuous and need to be pursued more vigorously than is possible in this brief survey, the Davidic covenant as the 'charter of humanity' seems to prefigure in political terms the establishment of divine government through a human intermediary, so that the full intentions of the divine purpose for the race, expounded in Gen. 1 – 2, might be achieved. The way in which the Old Testament proceeds with these connections (i.e. king/son of God, primeval man, image, etc.) is outside the scope of our present purposes. They were eventually brought together in the person of Jesus of Nazareth who as son of David was son of Abraham and son of God.

---

[16]. Kaiser, *The Blessing of David*, p. 314.

[17]. F. L. Horton, *The Melchizedek Tradition* (London: C.U.P., 1976), surveys opinions held in regard to the dating of Ps. 110 and himself concludes that it belongs to the Davidic period (cf. p. 32).

D. THE DEVELOPMENT OF DAVIDIC ESCHATOLOGY

i. *The dissolution of the political empire and the emergence of*
Jerusalem/Zion as a symbol

The wars of David (2 Sam. 8 – 10), by which the idealized conditions of 2 Sam. 7 were apparently to be achieved, established an impressive empire. It is suggestive, however, that the Abrahamic borders were not in fact established by them.[18] This fact serves to remind us that the political forms of chapter 7 remained a hope and that there still remains therefore, 'a rest for the people of God'. In fact the Old Testament, as we have pointed out, is always torn between the tensions of what is projected for Israel and what is realised. Under Solomon's reign Israel achieved the height of its political splendour and this fact is recognized by the application of Abrahamic terminology to its times (cf. 1 Kgs. 4:20 which alludes to the united kingdom in Abrahamic terms, as multitudinous and happy, and note the 'rest' concept of 1 Kgs. 5:4). 1 Kings 8, on the occasion of the dedication of the temple recognizes, again in ideal terms, that a 'place' has been found for Israel. The Exodus traditions were henceforth to be centred upon the Jerusalem temple, with the setting of which the second book of Samuel had fittingly concluded (2 Sam. 24:18–25; 1 Chr. 22:1; 2 Chr. 3:1). Now invisible in the midst of his people, Yahweh was no longer to move throughout Palestine. The divine presence was now associated with the holy hill of Zion (the point on the Jerusalem hill on which the temple had been built, the part which was to give the spiritual name to the whole). What had been held out in anticipation in 2 Sam. 6 and 7 had now materialized in 1 Kings 8. From this time onwards Zion would be the point of contact between heaven and earth, and as such, the location of the Sinai traditions (the chapter indicates that these had been consciously moved to Jerusalem, cf. 1 Kings 8:21).

But the conduct of Solomon's reign, the ruthless display in 1 Kings of oriental-type kingship into which it developed, was a pointer to the fact that not only had the ideal not been fully politically realised, not only had the ideal structure of a 'promised land' not been erected, but also that the politics of the kingdom of God in terms of the platform of 2 Sam. 7 still lay ahead as a promise. We may only touch upon the way here in which Solomon's kingship developed. It began with the ruthless elimination of all opposition and it ended with the kingdom divided. It had initiated a new set of social changes which probably at that time brought into being a land-owning aristocracy, thus cutting across older Israelite democratic ideals (cf. the administrative divisions of 1 Kings

---

[18]. Y. Kaufmann, *The Biblical Account of the Conquest of Palestine*, (Jerusalem, Magnes Press, 1953), points out that the Davidic Empire never included Tyre and Sidon, p. 54, and included of course East Jordan territories which formed no part of the promised land.

4:7–19 which appear to have been a determined assault on the old tribal entities).

Such a presentation is characteristic of the Old Testament. The high–water level of Israelite achievement, the time when there might have been hope of Israel's occupying a world position which could have fulfilled its Abrahamic charter, was the Solomonic period. But this is the very point in the history when the fortunes of the political institutions which were the external carrier of the people of God concept began to lapse into serious decline. We shall have occasion to note that the books of Kings are really concerned to display the decline and fall of the Davidic empire and that thus the grandeur which was the age of Solomon was, by the very nature of its rise, ephemeral. We now turn to a brief survey of the fortunes of the Davidic kings.

As we might expect, we hear no more of the ark after 1 Kings 8. The place of Jerusalem and the function of the Davidic line were now firmly established, and the touchstone by which the northern kingdom was judged, after the split between north and south, was its attitude to Jerusalem. Thoughout the monarchical period, the concepts of Zion as a divine centre and kingship which was of the line of David, were issues which were prominently kept before the nation, particularly by the prophetic groups. Thus Amos, the first of the written prophets, writing about 750 B.C., prefaces his judgement upon the foreign nations and then on Judah and Israel by the notion of God, in a visitation of divine judgement, 'roaring' from Zion (Amos 1:2). The nations which are the object of this judgement stemming from Zion (the historical review of the first two chapters appears to extend, to judge by the interspersed present and past tenses of the verbs used, over a considerable period of time) have one common factor, namely that they were all once members of the Davidic empire. The book of Amos also ends on a pronounced Davidic note with the restoration of what seems to be the Davidic dynasty (under the image of the 'booth of David' to be repaired, 9:11).[19]

Expectations concerning the Davidic kingdom were fairly quickly translated by the prophets into eschatology. In Isaiah 1 – 39 particularly, the concept of the Davidic covenant, linked with a royal Zion theology is heavily featured. Isa. 2:2–4 (and the parallel passage in Micah 4:1–4 from about the same period) is the first prophetic passage to develop a thorough-going idea of Davidic eschatology in which Zion is to be the centre from which blessing emanates in the last days. Then the chosen city of Jerusalem will become the redemptive centre of the world. This passage looks forward to a reversal of the historically depressed condition which Jerusalem occupied in Isaiah's time (late 8th century B.C.), and Jerusalem becomes the world pilgrimage resort to which all nations will pay court. Zion, in reality only a fairly small hillock,

---

[19]. Cf. G. F. Hasel. *The Remnant*, (Berrien Springs, U.S.A.: Andrews Univ. Press, 1974), p. 211.

becomes exalted in the last days into a world mountain, this extravagant reversal of nature as bound up with the introduction of the new age being a feature which we find elsewhere in the prophecies of Isaiah (cf. Isa. 11). The world will then come to Jerusalem to find out the divine will for conduct of its life and to gain wisdom and guidance for the conduct of each nation's affairs. Everlasting peace will have been established, for the nations having been to, and returned from Jerusalem, with minds thus renewed, will convert their weapons of war to instruments of peace. The law (*tôrāh*) will flow forth from Zion like a life-giving stream, not merely as a prescriptive code, but, as the parallel with the more generalized concept, 'the word of the Lord', (v. 3) suggests, as divine instruction conceived of in the broadest terms. Though no obvious connections with Sinai are established by Isa. 2:2–4 it ought to be remembered that the Sinai traditions had become centred on Jerusalem (1 Kings 8). In any case, law conceived of in general terms as the divine will, could hardly do other than what the ten commandments had done, namely offer the same broad outline for relationships within covenant that they had offered. Since Zion theology is so prominent in this passage, Davidic theology and kingship could hardly be absent, all the more so since the future of Davidic kingship is a particular concern of the early chapters of Isaiah. Yet there is no reference to any such intermediate kingship such as a Messiah would have exercised, since it is Yahweh himself who is presented as king and as exercising the royal function of arbitration (cf. Isa. 2:4). There is nothing in 2:2–4 (though the passage is often associated by commentators with the feast of Tabernacles) to associate it with a typical pilgrimage situation which is to be repeated. Rather the language of v. 2 suggests that the consummation of history is in view, with the nations coming for final judgement and then returning to keep the peace which this final judgement will bring.

Speculation as to what might have triggered off this eschatological presentation probably ought to be centred on the older concept of the Davidic empire which has lingered on in prophetic thinking. The full flowering of this empire was reached under Solomon and the world recognition of that empire's significance is to be seen in the visit of the Queen of Sheba to Solomon's court, recorded in 1 Kings 10. The importance of this visit by the leader of perhaps the greatest trading empire of the time is to be seen in the fact that 1 Kings virtually, and Chronicles definitely (cf. 2 Chr. 9), end the reign of Solomon on this note. In the coming of the Sabaean queen to the royal court, all the riches, wealth, wisdom and honour which God had promised to Solomon (1 Kings 3:10–13) had been displayed to the world, and the world in the shape of the queen acknowledges the grandeur and the influence of the Solomonic court (1 Kings 10:4–9). Her visit, we are in fact told, is merely typical of 'world' attitudes taken to the Solomonic court for such was the splendour of the Jerusalem royal court that the whole world 'sought the presence of Solomon to hear his wisdom, which God has put into his mind' (1 Kings 10:24).

Though Isa. 2:2–4 replaces the economic pilgrimage of Solomon's day with a purely religious and final gathering of the nations, a connection between the two motives for a world journey to Jerusalem is not lost in prophetic thought. In chapter 60, which expands 2:2–4, Jerusalem is presented not only in terms of world significance but in a series of dazzling pictures in which wealth, beauty and world pilgrimage are all associated. We might further note that Zion in Isa. 2:2–4 has assumed the force of the world mountain, the sanctuary from which the torah will proceed and this has clear covenantal associations with Sinai. What is thus being said is that the redeemed community of the last days, which Zion represents, the Israel of the end-time, is the catalyst by which the world is brought into the sphere of blessing which divine association with Israel has brought about. The fuller presentation of Isa. 2:2–4 in chapter 60 is thus set within a final context (in 60–62 particularly, but also more broadly within 56–66) of a New Creation whereby all things have become new. Zion symbolism has so developed that it anticipates the later presentation of Revelation 20–22 in which the new Jerusalem comes as the onset of the New Creation. With the coming of that New Jerusalem the indwelling presence of God is related, and with it therefore comes the awareness that the full realization of all the covenant promises stands achieved. This gradual development in the Old Testament of Jerusalem as a symbol gathers force in the exilic period and after, particularly in the symbolism of Ezek. 40–48 whereby a transformed Jerusalem is presented. As it does so, interest in the Davidic line seems to decrease, probably because of the more direct political associations with which Davidic kingship had been bound up, and probably also as part of a process in which national hopes become increasingly spiritualized.

ii. *The emergence of the 'people of God' notion*

A transference of national hopes to spiritual expectations is seen within Isaiah 1–12, indeed within the call narrative by which Isaiah is commissioned in Isa. 6. The vision which Isaiah then received in the year that Uzziah, king of Judah, died (6:1) was of Yahweh enthroned as king, apparently in the Jerusalem temple (cf. the word 'house' in v. 4, which in the Old Testament is never used of Yahweh's heavenly residence). The mention of the death of Uzziah after a very long and prosperous reign by which the fortunes of Judah had been restored, serves not only to locate the prophecy in time (i.e. c. 740 B.C.) but also to remind the prophet that the course of the future is bound up with Yahweh's decisions, and not with whatever arrangements for royal succession might be made in Jerusalem. The very frequent association of Yahweh as enthroned while judgement is proceeding (Ps. 45:6ff; 1

Kings 22:19; Dan. 7:9ff etc.), together with the strong support which may be drawn from a very similar passage at 1 Kings 22:19, indicates that the task of the royal assembly at whose head Yahweh presides in Isa. 6, is that of pronouncing judgement upon Judah. As has been pointed out,[20] the awed response of the seraphim, plus the response of the prophet as an auditor of the divine proceedings, is consistent with a message of dire judgement having been proclaimed. In professing himself to be a man of unclean lips and to be living in the midst of a people of unclean lips, the prophet seems not merely to be identifying himself with sinful Judah, nor merely expressing the need for personal cleansing before he can become the bearer of the word. Rather, by reference to 'lips' he seems to be contrasting the worship responses which have characterized Judah and himself with those which he has just seen taking place within this temple vision. In that vision he has seen a response to Yahweh's kingship and since so many of Isaiah's early prophecies have been given over to a denunciation of current Judaean political policies, he is probably identifying himself with a wrong attitude to Yahweh's leadership which has been principally expressed in Judaean foreign policy. Isaiah then accepts (v. 8) the commission to convey the content of the judgements (cf. vv. 9–10), not specified in detail, but apparently overheard by Isaiah. This judgement will have its durative and quantitative limits (vv. 11–12) but it will result in a purified community of faith (v. 13). Such a community will not be able to be identified merely with those who live through the disasters which have been foreshadowed, though even those survivors will be few. Only the stock of a once national 'tree' will remain (v. 13) but from that stock the community of faith, likened to a holy seed, will be productive.

By the content of Isa. 6, for the first time in the Old Testament, a clear wedge had been driven between the nation and a community of faith which will emerge from it. In short, as a new[21] theological initiative, the doctrine of a godly remnant now appears. We have met previously in the Old Testament the notion of a remnant which lives through a particular set of catastrophes which have afflicted an age but with rare exceptions (the Elijah narratives in which the prophet is reminded that there are still in Israel some seven thousand who have not bowed the knee to Baal, 1 Kings 19:18; and the reference at Amos 5:15 to a remnant of the house of Joseph as a part from a wider whole) we do not meet until Isaiah the distinction between a nation and the believing community who will constitute a godly remnant (for this latter in Isaiah cf. 1:27–31; 4:2–3; 7:3; 10:20, etc.).

This development of a remnant notion in Isaiah meant a correspond-

---

[20]. By Rolf Knierim, 'The Vocation of Isaiah', *VT* 18 (1968), p. 54.

[21]. Hasel, *The Remnant*, pp. 394ff. convincingly demonstrates this. We also follow, later, the substance of his conclusions on Isa. 7.

ing depreciation of faith in a national political order. We may see this particularly in the treatment of the house of David in Isa. 7 – 11. The historical context of chapter 7 is the Syro-Ephraimite war on Judah of c. 734–733 B.C. Fearing an Assyrian move against the West, Syria and Israel attempted to coerce Judah into a coalition. Isaiah thus meets the Judaean king Ahaz as the king is inspecting the Jerusalem defences and confronts him with a challenge to give up national politics and to accept the offer of divine protection which Isaiah bears. In this encounter, Isaiah had been required by God to take with him his son *Shear-Yashub* (suggestively, 'a remnant shall return'). Here the Hebrew order in this combination name is important, since the usual order of predicate + subject is reversed in the interests of emphasis. The noun element is thus clearly thrown into relief and therefore the meaning of the name of the son appears to be, 'only a remnant (i.e. nothing but a remnant) will return'. But here again we need to note the ambiguity in meaning of the Hebrew verb, which in the Old Testament has a well-identified metaphorical as well as literal meaning. The run of the context in Isa. 7 favours the metaphorical sense of 'repent' for the verb in the name combination and thus a further reference to the community of faith which the coming historical events will bring into being.

In v. 11 Ahaz is offered a confirmatory sign by which the prophet's word will be validated. Invited to 'ask a sign of the Lord thy God', he piously refuses to tempt the Lord. The reply of Isaiah is significant for the change in the use of personal pronoun in combination with the appeal to the Lord which occurs. Ahaz is told that he has not only wearied men, but that he has wearied 'my God' (v. 13) also, a change thus occurring in the personal pronoun which seems to exclude Ahaz from the developing community of faith. The sign which is given is the sign of the child, shortly to be born, and to be given the name Immanuel (i.e. God with *us*). This sign is associated with the prospective Assyrian invasion of Judah (cf. chapter 8:5–8) and its intent is thus double-edged, namely judgement upon Judah generally (i.e. God-with-them in judgement), yet salvation for the remnant (i.e. God-with-us—the prophetic group forming around Isaiah, cf. Isa. 8:16 – in salvation).

At the same time as political leadership is depreciated in chapters 7 – 8, clear links between the house of David and the future are constructed in 9:1–6 and 11. The extravagant character of the language of Isa. 9:1–6, the four-fold throne name of v. 6 (a divine reference if we may see in it an allusion to the five-fold Egyptian throne names by which the deity of the king was asserted), and the promise in v. 7 of world-wide rule as established for the king by Yahweh, all look beyond the current political scene. The suggestion, therefore, that Isa. 9:1–6 looks forward to the birth of Ahaz's son Hezekiah, the 701 B.C. deliverer of Jerusalem, is not to be entertained. In chapter 11:1–9 Davidic expectations continue. God will one day begin again the Davidic line, unobtrusively, with a 'shoot from the stump of Jesse' (a reference to the initial choice of David). Such a reign will be the Spirit–directed reign that Israelite kingship was to have been (vv. 2–5) and will result in inner harmony and world significance for Israel, and a return to the peace of paradise. A harmony between all created orders will then occur and thus the purposes of creation will be fulfilled (cf. vv. 6–9).

iii. *Attempts at covenant renewal to the exile*

Davidic monarchy continued its political degeneration down to the exile. Not even the profound reforms of Josiah (622/621 B.C.) could avert the end (since they were only superficially received), which finally came for the southern kingdom in 587 B.C. That disaster left the city of Jerusalem devastated, the theology of Zion's invincibility in tatters, the nation in exile and leaderless. Josiah had reaffirmed a covenant at the temple in the presence of the people as the text of 2 Kings 23:1–3 reminds us. This renewal is conducted on lines similar to that of all Israel assembled and addressed at Sinai and the document which backed Josiah's covenant is described as the 'words of the book of the covenant' (2 Kings 23:2). Such a description relates both document and renewal specifically to the Mosaic legislation. Whether the contents of the 'book' can be described more accurately is a moot point, but the identification with Deuteronomy is tempting, in view of the Deuteronomic character of the measures which Josiah took.[22]

Covenant renewals during the monarchical period were few. The most famous was that which came about as a result of the challenge presented by Elijah to the syncretistic policies of the Israel of his day, and king Ahab in 1 Kings 17 – 19. We shall deal with the history of the covenant concep during this period, and prophetic reaction to the concept, when we discuss the exilic New Covenant. But it will now be helpful to refer briefly to covenant as bound up with the political history.

Apart from the reforms of Hezekiah, which were remarkably similar to those of Josiah but which were not ostensibly based upon a document, the only further real matter of interest was the covenant renewal effected in the south after the short reign of the usurping queen Athaliah. Here again the temple is central to the course of events, for again the covenant is renewed 'in the house of God' (2 Chr. 23:3), between king, people and Yahweh. Like that concluded under Josiah, this renewal is followed by the purging of foreign cults and the renewal

---

[22]. If the Chronicles account (2 Chr. 34) is to be followed on the Josianic reforms, it needs to be noted that the reform measures of Josiah were actually substantially taken *before* the book of the law was found. Thus the book found may have had no intrinsic connection with the reforms. It may have been as some have suggested a Judaean royal court covenant document or the like. On the question cf. J. R. Lundbom 'The Law Book of the Josianic Reform' *CBQ* 38 (1976), pp. 293–302.

of temple worship. The covenant is said to have been 'cut' on this occasion (2 Chr. 23:16) and this appears to give the character of a new beginning to what results. There is some warrant for this, as we shall note below, though the associated requirement that Judah should be the Lord's people, serves in its own way to indicate the continuity with Sinai (cf. 2 Chr. 23:16).

The common factor in the three southern covenant renewals (one can safely include Hezekiah's though the word $b^e r\hat{\imath}t$ does not occur) is that covenant violation and temple neglect had gone hand in hand. That is to say, the rejection of the covenant or its studied disuse really amounted to a search for political alternatives. On the people's side, however, rededication to the concept of Davidic kingship was not common during the period, though the covenant renewal in Athaliah's time by which king Joash received the throne provided the exception. Athaliah's seven year reign had seen a determined attempt to eliminate the Davidic dynasty in the south. In this case the anointing of Joash (2 Kings 11:12, 2 Chr. 23:11) and the giving to him of the 'testimony', was a virtual re-establishment of Davidic covenant promises. Since the Heb. word 'testimony' (Heb. $^c \bar{e} d\hat{u}t$) in its early biblical usage refers to the ten commandments in their abiding significance, particularly as preserved in the ark (Exod. 31:18, Josh. 4:16 etc.), what appears to have been put into the king's hands at this time are the covenant statutes. It is by no means surprising that the accounts which follow in both Kings and Chronicles emphasize that on Athaliah's overthrow a covenant is made between God, king and nation. It is difficult to be certain whether 2 Kings 11:17 speaks of a second covenant between king and people which follows a first between God, king and people or whether 2 Kings 11:17b merely emphasizes the effect of the general covenant re-establishment of the first half of the verse, and thus the popular re-commitment to the Davidic line. The association, however, of the 'testimony' with the anointing, speaks for the continued recognition of Davidic leadership within the wider Sinai framework. Mention here should be made also of the supporting evidence for the association of covenant renewal with temple reforms which can be drawn from covenant renewal which took place during the reign of the Judaean king Asa (2 Chr. 15:12). The language of that renewal—to 'seek the Lord, the God of their fathers' (Heb. $d\bar{a}rash$ 'seek')—refers in such contexts to the directed worship of Yahweh through the cult.

This close association of temple with covenant renewal and the continuance of Davidic kingship makes it fitting, therefore, that when Davidic kingship is politically withdrawn by the events of the 587 B.C. exile, the temple should have been destroyed. Such a destruction of the temple is clear evidence of Yahweh's refusal to maintain any longer the political institution of kingship. As Jeremiah makes clear in his famous temple sermon (chapter 7), while the people of Judah have inferred from the continuance of the temple, the continuance of divine protection of the nation and thus, the continued existence of Jerusalem, the reverse really ought to have been the case. They ought to have protected the temple and thus the divine link by conduct which would have been appropriate to the relationship. They had not, and Jerusalem and the temple will fall as Shiloh had fallen. So Davidic kingship and temple both fall and the period of the monarchy is brought to a close.

iv. *The assessment of the period in 1 and 2 Kings*

How then is the period of monarchy assessed by Israel and Judah? The exilic materials bearing upon the nature of the New Covenant will further help us to answer this question, yet it is virtually answered for us by the editor of the books of Kings. The second book of Kings closes on the note of the release of Jehoiachin in exile by Amel-Marduk of Babylon in 562 B.C. It is noted that subsequently, for the rest of his life (his death thus being presupposed), he dined regularly at the king's table, received an exalted position and as a sign of the change of personal fortunes received a change of clothing. For many this account serves to continue the note of hope which the editor of Kings (writing probably for the exiles and perhaps towards the end of the exile), reposes in the continuance of the Davidic dynasty. Thereby is continued the Davidic and Jerusalem emphasis which has characterized the two books of Kings from 1 Kings 11:13 onwards when the effect of the division upon the Davidic line is first discussed. On this view the books of Kings conclude with the assurance of the continuance of the promises of 2 Sam. 7 and are thus a commitment to the exilic community of restoration and political continuity. No such hope is reposed in Jehoiachin personally, for his death is presupposed, but on the foundation of the Davidic house, it is suggested, the new community of the return will take shape. Such a concept also, it is suggested, explains the high concentration of hope in a Davidic return that we find in early post-exilic prophecy.

We doubt, however, whether the concluding verses of 2 Kings are to be construed in this way. We feel bound to agree with those who argue that these closing verses are too weak a foundation on which to build such hopes. We agree with those who argue that the presentation of the books of Kings was designed to explain to the exiles the reason for their present plight. The united monarchy under Solomon with which 1 Kings commenced was already a severe defection from Davidic ideals and progressively the books of Kings lead us forward into the details of Israel's and then Judah's decline and fall. There is point, here, in the contrast offered between the position of Jehoiachin as elevated and that of a somewhat similar exilic figure, at least a noble if not royally connected, namely Daniel. The first chapter of the book of Daniel presents Daniel displaying the piety which ought to have characterized the typical Israelite in exile. Actually the first chapter of Daniel presents us with a clash between two markedly different world views. It is a carefully presented account of how the values of the Kingdom of God will persist when confronted with a totalitarian world power. We are told that they persist because its representatives refuse to compromise on principles, fix their hopes on Jerusalem temple ideals, and possess a deep conviction that it is the God of heaven who controls the destinies of men. Thus, the first chapter concludes with the laconic comment that Daniel continued until the first year of Cyrus the Persian (v. 21), i.e. that he outlived his Babylonian captivity and saw the exile through to its conclusion, and therefore it was conduct of the character exhibited by him which was calculated to preserve Israel's ideals.

One cannot help feeling that the epilogue to the second book of Kings, in which the Davidic representative Jehoiachin is treated as a puppet figure, eating as Saul's survivor Mephibosheth did in David's time (2 Sam. 9:13) at an overlord's table (and this time at a pagan table!), eloquently expresses in a picture of total dependency the final historical demise of the Davidic monarchy. Unlike the contemporary picture of Daniel, which is sketched with feeling and with prospect, the portrait of Jehoiachin comes before us with a hopeless finality that the plaintive 'all the days of his life' (2 Kings 25:30) serves only to underscore.

In short, the history of covenant under the Kings of Judah was not a happy one. Of course the Davidic concept was taken further during the exile and underwent considerable modification. Davidic kingship was not in fact restored after the exile, nor was such a restoration ever seriously contemplated. The reasons for this, as we shall see, were associated with changed attitudes to Israel's political forms which the exilic writings display, and even more significantly with the eschatological hope associated with the doctrine of the New Covenant, a concept to which we must now turn.

Summary

The spiritual and political decline of Israel, which the book of Judges emphasizes, exercised its influence on Israel's request for a king, not only in the timing, but also in the nature of the request. The incompatibility of the request for a king 'to judge us like all the nations' is met by 1 Samuel on three levels. Firstly by a renewal at that stage of the notion of divine kingship over Israel (1 Sam. 11:14), secondly by the distinct emergence of the prophetic office, and thirdly by the construction, on the occasion of the choice of Saul and David, of a theology of earthly kingship.

Passing on to the more particular treatment of 2 Sam. 6, and especially, of 2 Sam. 7 we noted the importance of the order of these chapters, the choice of the divine dwelling site taking precedence over the election of the Davidic line. The refusal of divine permission to David to build the temple was, we noted, due to the need for David firstly to establish the Abrahamic borders of the promised land, a task to which he devoted most of his reign. The absolute character of the promise to David and thus the eternal covenant with David was found not to be inconsistent with the rejection of particular individuals within the line. 2 Sam. 7:18–29, with its notion of the Davidic covenant as 'humanity's charter', provided for the future of the race under the leadership of the Davidic house and thus foreshadowed the fulfilment of the Abrahamic promises.

The political hold of the Davidic line on the land (never under David the 'promised' land) was quickly lost and as this progressively occurred there increasingly came to the fore (particularly in Isaiah) the emergence of Jerusalem as the end-time centre of world government. With this a doctrine of the 'remnant' went hand in hand, with promises seemingly politically orientated when given, clearly being interpreted in terms of the emergence of a 'people' within a 'nation'. The source of this eschatology in the magnificence of the Solomonic establishment and its function as spiritualizing the political grandeur of the Solomonic period, was observed.

The various political and prophetic attempts to arrest this national decline by covenant renewal, down to the exile, were then examined, and finally the theology of the Books of Kings was interpreted as dealing with the decline and fall of the physical dynasty of David to the exile.

5

The New Covenant.
The shape of Biblical Eschatology

A. THE EFFECT OF THE EXILE

This chapter will be concerned to evaluate the effects of the Babylonian exile upon the shaping of covenant theology and, in particular, to consider the way in which New Covenant theology is presented in the books of Jeremiah, Ezekiel and Isaiah 40 – 55. Since the Sinaitic covenant together with the Davidic covenant, which was attached to it, had provided a political base for Israel, the removal of this base which occurred at the exile demanded that covenant theology assume a new direction. It involved also, as this chapter will endeavour to show, a closer integration of covenant and eschatology as theological ideas. This connection of themes brought about in Jeremiah, Ezekiel and Isaiah a doctrine of a New Covenant which looked forward to the realization in the new age of the political forms originally developed at Sinai for Israel. At the same time the notion of Israel as a centre of world blessing was not lost and thus we are not surprised to find, particularly in the books of Ezekiel and Isaiah, that a strong connection is established between covenant and a doctrine of the new creation.

Turning now to the events leading to the exile, the deportation of king Jehoiachin and the governing elite in 597 B.C. saw the beginning of an end which came to the Judaean state with the destruction of the temple and the capture of Jerusalem in 587 B.C. The question of the future political condition of Judah/Israel was raised. For by the exile all the effective machinery which could have been adduced to identify empirical Israel during the monarchical period had disappeared. Davidic kingship, with which the covenant had come especially to be associated, had gone. Though the book of Lamentations presumed the continued operation of a priesthood, bound up with the temple site, and something of that nature continued until the return from exile, it is clear from the post-exilic writings that the essence of the priesthood, the expression of its continuity, had gone into exile after the fall of Jerusalem. Then, the famed temple of God, which had been the focus of

Israelite worship, and with which the concept of the divine presence had been actually and theologically related, had been totally destroyed. This had been a possibility which the Judaeans to whom Jeremiah had preached, as well as the exilic community among whom Ezekiel had ministered, had refused to entertain. A doctrine of the inviolability of the temple and Zion had grown up. This had not sprung up, as some suppose, because of the miraculous preservation of Jerusalem at the time of the Assyrian siege under Sennacherib in 701 B.C. It had arisen rather out of the choices which 2 Sam. 6 and 7 had expressed. Such a doctrine of the temple's sacrosanctity appears in the early chapters of the book of Isaiah and in Psalms such as Psalms 46 and 48. It is very clearly appealed to by the Judaeans at the end of the monarchical era, as the temple sermons of Jeremiah 7 and 26 imply. There was at that time a blind and dangerous trust reposed in the security of Jerusalem which was thought to be preserved by the fact of divine choice expressed in the building of the temple. Ezekiel, however (Ezek. 8 – 11), had made it clear that the rationale for worship in Jerusalem, namely the presence of Yahweh there, had been withdrawn from the temple before its destruction – in fact, the destruction of the temple had been engineered by Yahweh! Palestinian interest in the Jerusalem sanctuary site continued, however, as is clear from Jer. 41:5 which appears to report a pilgrimage directed towards Jerusalem.

The result of all this was that the final base upon which the Abrahamic promise structure had rested, the promised land itself, was also removed. We have noted how the possession of the land was regarded in the Old Testament as the spiritual index of Israel's political health. The ultimate blessing for Israel had been conceived of in terms of a good national life in the promised land, the enjoyment of the divine presence associated with it, and the material blessings which the land offered. Since we are dealing in the Old Testament, for the most part, with a national entity whose growth in spritual terms must be able to be monitored, the use of some such index as the possession of the land is understandable. Covenant obedience, Israel knew, would result in the retention of the land, covenant disobedience in the temporary withdrawal of its gifts and in its final loss.

In 587 B.C. all the tangible marks of the empirical Israel had thus vanished and the question which the exile raised was really, what was the nature of the true Israel and was such a body tied to any necessary political forms? Had Israel come to an end in 587 B.C. and did the destruction of the temple mean the end of Abrahamic election? Of course it did not, for all that was lost in 587 B.C. were the means by which national Israel could be located and identified. But none of these had, by themselves, made Israel the elect people of God. What had made Israel so, was not the land which had been inherited, for that came to Israel already *as* Israel. What was lost was the political framework which had been forged at Sinai and expanded by the addition of monarchy. But long before Sinai, Israel had existed as an independent social entity. All the exile did, therefore, was to remove the accoutrements and make clear to Israel wherein its true nature could be seen.

One would expect, as we have indicated, that losses of this character would lead to covenant reassessment. In the mind of the average Israelite, church and state had been indistinguishable. In one sense this was correct, for this is what Sinai had projected. On the other hand, the popular understanding of the Sinai arrangement had been progressively so perverted as to make the political institutions etc., with which the life of Israel prior to 587 B.C. had been bound up, the necessary carriers of the Sinai traditions. Thus the events of 587 B.C. called for a popular reassessment of the basis upon which Israel's faith rested. If Israel was to continue to be defined as a people with a common language, sharing a common geographical area, bound together by a common set of historical experiences etc., then an Israel of that character could be reconstituted only by a return of the type which was in fact the popular exilic hope, namely a return to conditions obtaining before 587 B.C.

Israel, however, could not be defined that way. There could not be a return to pre-exilic conditions, if pre-exilic attitudes could be revived, for they had brought about the destruction of visible Israel. When the return from exile finally occurred, it was clear that some at least of the returners accepted the fact of change. The ease with which the post-exilic society accommodated itself to the loss of monarchy made it clear that the post-exilic community, or significant elements within it, now recognized that not political forms, but ultimate responsibility to Yahweh would ensure Israel's survival. Israel's special position depended in the last analysis on Yahweh's elective purposes. This had been the burden of the exilic preaching, particularly Ezekiel's. The future of Israel would be determined by the activity of God as it had been in the past and would be ultimately bound up with the divine activity which, as we shall see, would write divine law on the hearts of the faithful.

It is often suggested, and it is bound up with the course of the discussion which has preceded, that it was the appeal to individuality which the exile brought with it, which accounted for much of the change in covenant expectations. We shall need perhaps to look at this possibility a little more closely when we come to Ezekiel, but it can be said somewhat summarily of the exilic period that while the individual comes into clearer focus, this is so only because by the very nature of the altered times the older corporate and national notions had gone. With the exile, however, we are certainly on the threshold of the New Testament age. Such emphasis upon individual reponse as we now encounter is consistent with the view of the later New Testament proclamation. This was that nothing short of the advent of God himself would bring about the existence of the type of society which for many centuries the Israelites presumed to exist in the state which Sinai had called into being.

B. COVENANT EXPOSITION IN THE PRE-EXILIC PROPHETS

i. *1 Kings 17 – 19 and Elijah*

Before we turn to the exposition of the New Covenant in Jeremiah directly, we must undertake a brief survey of the activity of some of the more significant northern and southern prophets so far as their ministry bears upon the course of covenant theology. Here we shall find the common factor operating, that prophetic activity was, and had always been based upon and directed by, covenant aims. We may commence with Elijah, the prophet of the north, whose activities serve for the later Old Testament and New Testament writers as a sort of prophetic paradigm. In the narratives of 1 Kings 18 and 19 he is pictured very much in Mosaic guise and as thus seeking to re-establish covenant values in the face of the opportunist political kingship of the house of Omri. At the Carmel assembly (1 Kings 18:20ff) Elijah placed before Israel virtually the Sinai prescription of the decalogue in the shape of the first and controlling commandment, by calling upon Israel to choose which deity, Yahweh or Baal, they were prepared to serve and by calling for an unqualified choice. By building a twelve-stoned altar, as he does at that time on Mt. Carmel, a twelve-stoned altar he makes it perfectly clear that (1 Kings 18:31) he is appealing to the theology which supported the older twelve-tribed confederation. The Sinai note is further emphasized by his flight south in chapter 19 when he returns to Horeb (1 Kings 19:8), since it is probably to be conjectured that he returns in fact to the cave (v. 9, Hebrew *the* cave cf. Exod. 33:17–23) of the Mosaic experience. There he sees himself as the second Moses, the founder of a new Israel, since at that time in dialogue with the Deity, he stresses the complete apostasy of all Israel. Of course he is then reminded by God that he does not stand alone, there are yet seven thousand in Israel who have not forsaken the covenant (v. 18) and that in effect the covenant will be maintained, notwithstanding the unpromising nature of the contemporary political situation. The manifestation which comes to Elijah at Horeb is not in the unrepeatable Sinaitic terms, the Lord is not in the natural manifestations of earthquake wind and fire by which the presence of the Deity at Sinai was demonstrated (1 Kings 19:9–12). The imperceptible voice ('voice of an attenuated silence' v. 12), by which he is alerted, serves by the paradox of the expression to emphasize that God has nothing to add to the Sinai revelation. Thus chastened, he returns with a threefold commission to set in train a series of political judgements upon Israel, and is reminded

by the notion of the remnant, introduced in v. 18, that the business of
upholding the covenant really belongs to God alone.

ii. *Amos*

When we come to the course of written prophecy, in the middle of the
8th century B.C., little more than a century after Elijah's time, the
prophetic attitude to covenant is clearly set forth by Amos, a southerner
and the first of the classical (written) prophets. In Amos, though his
preaching is covenant centred, the word *b^{e}rît* does not occur in this
sense. Some have suggested that the concept had not yet been defined,
that *b^{e}rît* was a notion which later 'Deuteronomic' preaching called
forth. This is an extreme position and the answer for the absence of the
term must be sought in other areas. Perhaps the word is not mentioned
because the covenant as a concept was so axiomatic as to be the base
from which Amos' and all prophetic preaching proceeded. At any rate,
when he turns his particular attention to the North (3:2) he reminds
them that it had been divine election operating from the Exodus
onwards which had accounted for Israel's present position and had thus
been responsible for the platform from which Amos would now speak.
The book of Amos, it is true, is very much given over to social breaches.
But the exploitation of class by class, the manipulation of justice, the
economic ills to which Amos refers, are all the result of covenant breach.
If he thus does not appeal directly to the covenant, but is aware of the
traditions on which it is based, he is saying that the denial of covenant
obligation has been manifested in social conduct whereby Israel has
simply become like one of the surrounding peoples (Amos 9:7),
forfeiting thus her elective status and inviting divine punishment in the
form of the threatened exile. His insistence upon positive demonstration of covenant relationships takes principally the form of the demand
for righteousness, a demand which we may rightly regard as covenant-
based, since righteousness is in the Old Testament was primarily a
relational term and only secondarily forensic. We may conclude then,
that although Amos does not refer to the covenant explicitly, the entire
approach which he makes presupposes it.[1]

---

[1]. Notwithstanding the omission of particular terminology the Book of Amos is entirely
covenantally centred. Amos made free use of general terminology which related to the
covenant framework (*yādā^c, tôrāh, pesha^c, hôq* etc.), the types of offences denounced by
him were those for which covenant stipulations provided, while the use of curse formulae
by Amos alludes to the disaster about to befall the north for covenant breach. cf. F.H.
Seilhamer, 'The Role of Covenant in the Mission and Message of Amos' in *A Light to My
Path: Old Testament Studies in Honor of Jacob M. Myers*, (Philadelphia: Temple Univ. Press,
1974), pp. 435–451. *B^{e}rît* in Amos 1:11 is difficult to assess. It may in the context refer to a
treaty between Solomon and Tyre, cf. 1 Kings 5:12, or to Tyre as a member of the Davidic
empire.

iii. *Hosea*

Hosea is much more obviously covenant oriented than Amos, at first sight, appears to be. The word $b^e r \hat{\imath} t$ occurs explicitly (some five times) in the book. More importantly, however, the image of marriage with which he commences and continues for the first three chapters sets the tone for the book as a whole, which thus develops into an arraignment of Israel for infidelity. Both historical and eschatological perspectives are involved in the use of the imagery, since in the first three chapters the metaphor illustrates both the temporary disruption to and yet the essential permanence of the relationship (note this blend in Hos. 1, where at 1:9 Israel's rejection is followed [1:10] by an appeal to the Abrahamic promises – Israel numberless, back again in the promised land). Verses 2–13 of chapter 2 specifically contain an indictment directed towards Israel's breach of covenant, with the operation of the typical covenant curses of Deuteronomy 28 being invisaged. Verses 14–15 point to the possibility of restoration and to a re-enactment of the Exodus, while verses 16–23 offer something like an anticipation of the exilic New Covenant teaching. Verse 18 refers specifically to a prospective covenant ($b^e r \hat{\imath} t$) which will lead to a harmony of created orders, universal peace and secure occupancy of the land, together with (vv. 19–20) a perfected and therefore an indefectible marriage relationship. The blessings of this New Creation are enumerated in vv. 21–23.

That Hosea should have thought so inclusively about the renewal should cause no surprise in view of his fondness for referring to Israel's (and Judah's) older traditions (cf. 2:3, 9:10, 11:8, 12:4). His explicit uses of $b^e r \hat{\imath} t$ normally have significance. Thus at 6:7 the breach of the Sinai covenant by Israel is likened, as we have had an earlier occasion to note, to a breach of a similar character—'like Adam'. We have previously suggested that it is possible, though not probable, that Hosea had the Gen. 3 breach in mind. At Hosea 8:1 the association of 'my covenant' with 'my law' shows clear acquaintance (if that were in doubt) with Sinai. The references to $b^e r \hat{\imath} t$ in Hos. 10:4 and 12:1 are not as covenantally specific. They refer to compacts with foreign powers (cf. 12.1, of Assyria).

Important also in the book of Hosea is the direct reference to the covenant by the use of the language of relationships to which the covenant gave rise. Notable here is Hosea's fairly frequent use of *ḥesed* (2:19, 4:1, 6:6), a closely associated covenant word, the significance of which we have already referred to. A close parallel is drawn by him between *ḥesed* and 'knowledge'. This latter term appears to be used to refer to the basic deeds of salvation performed by Yahweh in the formative period of Israel's history, together with the commitment which stems from that content. In all, Hosea is a book thoroughly covenant based, ringing with appeals founded upon God's love for Israel and indicating the countless ways in which this love had been demonstrated, but pointing also to the corresponding lack of response from Israel. The marriage metaphor explicitly sets the tone of the book and highlights the broken relationship. Chapter 14 ends with Israel re-established and with that harmony achieved, towards which chapter 2 had pointed. The movement therefore in thought is from covenant breach to covenant renewal.

C. JEREMIAH

i. *The reaction of the prophet to his times*

Before moving directly to Jeremiah we need note only that Isaiah 1 – 39 begins with a long invective against covenant breach (Isa. 1:2–20), which is typical of the juristic form which the written prophets seem freely to have used to document covenant fault.[2] Not unexpectedly Isa. 39 ends with a prediction of the exile of the Davidic house, just as the first chapter had begun with the prediction of the destruction of Jerusalem. It is the book of Jeremiah which takes both of these issues further. If we accept Jer. 1:2 to refer to the beginning of his ministry (and not to his birth, though that is equally probable), then Jeremiah began to preach in 627 B.C. in the priestly centre of Anathoth, his birthplace, the town to which Abiathar, the final survivor of the house of Eli, had been exiled under Solomon (1 Kgs. 2:26). That would place the beginning of Jeremiah's activity some five years or so before the beginning of Josiah's reforms, about which he appears to have little to say. There is mention in Jer. 44:19 of worship which had been offered within living memory by 'our fathers' to the Queen of Heaven, and there seems little doubt that the cessation of the practice referred to there was bound up with the reforms of Josiah. By the time of Jeremiah's ministry, the major emphasis of which was directed to the regulation of Judah's foreign policy, the Josianic reforms had fallen into desuetude, for there is plenty of evidence within the book of Jeremiah attesting official policies which cut right across the spirit of the reforms (Jer. 7:8ff, 22:20ff). Perhaps Jeremiah's relative lack of interest in the reform movements may have stemmed from the fact that he merely considered them good as far as they went. In his judgement they may have seemed to be superficial, politically directed, and thus failing to deal with the real issue of the national heart. Negatively, the reforms seem to have resulted in a more elaborate cultus, with more weight attached to the temple and its supposed role as a talisman by which the inviolability of Jerusalem was ensured. This certainly blocked, as Jeremiah saw it, any return to the ancient paths (cf. Jer. 7:21ff).

---

[2]. We are referring here to what has become known as the Prophetic Lawsuit or *rîb*. Kirsten Nielsen, *Yahweh as Prosecutor and Judge* (Sheffield: Univ. of Sheffield Press, 1978), reviews the literature relating to the *rîb* and refers to Isa. 1 on pp. 27–29.

The shape of Jeremiah's early preaching indicates his shocked attitude towards the prevailing apostasy which he found. There was a
spirit of ingratitude for past deliverances which Jeremiah regarded as
quite without analogy among the nations of the world (2:4–13). Under
King Jehoiakim (609–598 B.C.) the situation rapidly deteriorated. Non-
Yahwistic cults seem to have been multiplied and these were accompanied by a simpistic trust in Zion and the presence of the Davidic line.
Under these circumstances, at the beginning of the reign of Jehoiakim,
Jeremiah in his famous temple sermon (cf. chapters 7 & 26) displayed
his contempt of the indifferent Yahwism which prided itself upon the
retention of its present institutions as sufficient bastions against foreign
aggression. As 1 Kings 8 had made clear,[3] the temple was the focus of
the Sinaitic and the Davidic traditions. Since it was the focal point of
the land, and represented the cumulative revelation which had been
offered to Israel, it was, Jeremiah argued, the responsibility of the
people to protect the temple (and thus basically the land whose focal
point it was), whereas its destruction was imminent if they did not
mend their ways. In this temple sermon an easy attitude to the covenant
is condemned. Just as the renegade cultic establishment of Shiloh had
been destroyed in Samuel's time when a similar attitude had been
displayed to what should have been an appropriate covenant response,
so the Jerusalem temple would go (Jer. 7:12–15). They could not,
Jeremiah preached, expect the temple to protect them, unless their
conduct had been protective of the temple.

Not merely the temple and land, however, are involved. The entire of
Israel's religious traditions is subjected to careful evaluation. In Jer.
7:21ff, the whole system of institutionalized worship bound up in the
means of national response, namely the cult, is condemned. This
prophetic protest against sacrifice, however, cannot be pressed to mean
that sacrifice was no part of the earlier Israelite system of response.
Probably in underscoring the fact that sacrifice was not commanded
(7:21) the prophet is saying no more than that sacrifice was not primary.
It was responsive and supplementary to the decalogue but not intrinsic
to it. In 3:16 the prophet goes even further. The ark, the most solemn
and most ancient symbol of all, the symbol which stood at the heart of
covenant worship, will be superfluous in the future kingdom. Pilgrimages which have been directed to it, the national festivals which had
been temple and ark orientated, will be replaced (v. 17) by international
pilgrimages to the divine seat in Jerusalem. That is to say, in the new
age, the temple will be seen to display God's cosmic rule. Under these
circumstances there will be no more room for merely national objects of
worship. Israel will then become part of a general worshipping company of nations.

---

[3]. 1 Kings 8 is regarded as the product of a Deuteronomistic redaction. Whatever our
assessment of the sources underlying this narrative may be, the clear connection between
Sinai and the Davidic covenant is a fact which emerges from the narrative.

Jeremiah's attitude to the sacrosanct Davidic kingship is also to be noted. In Jer. 22 a review of kingship exercised by the sons of Josiah is conducted. There is universal failure. It is said even of the boy king Jehoiachin, a son of the infamous Jehoiakim, and soon to be exiled, that if he were a signet ring on Yahweh's hand, Yahweh would pluck him off and commit him to exile. He would be written in the genealogical registers as childless (Jer. 22:30—although there is evidence from the period which suggests that Jehoiachin was the father of five sons in exile). If in the uncertain future (23:5) God were to persevere with the throne of David, it would not be by way of linear connection, for God would raise up for himself a righteous branch, a divine offshoot of the type which had been already been referred to under other but similar terms in the earlier Messianic prophecy of Isa. 11:1. Kingship of that type would stand in stark contrast to the present kingship of Zedekiah (who succeeded Jehoiachin from 597–587 B.C.), since the name to be given to the future Messianic ruler (the Lord is our righteousness, v. 6) was a direct reference to the meaning of the name that Zedekiah bore (Yahweh is my righteousness). Thus Messianic rule would be re-established in Israel, but not directly linked to the historical line of David. It will be divinely imposed in theological fulfilment of the Davidic promises. Only in this way and at this time (vv. 6–8) will salvation come. The Davidic covenant is in no sense abandoned by Jeremiah, however. In Jer 33:14ff the prophecy of 23:5ff seems to have been expansively reiterated. Interestingly enough, there the attribute of righteousness which the Messiah will display (23:5ff.) is transferred (and the same descriptive phrase, 'the Lord our righteousness' occurs) to Judah and Jerusalem whose righteousness is the result of Messianic intervention. In Jer. 33:20ff the irrefragability of the Davidic covenant is dealt with at length. This is a remarkable assent by Jeremiah to the basic direction of 2 Sam. 7 in a political context in which his own criticism of empirical kingship has been both searching and trenchant.

ii. *Jeremiah 31:31–34. The New Covenant*

(a) The context of Jer. 30 – 31

The most well known institution which comes up for review in Jeremiah's treatment of Israel's institutions is the Sinai covenant. Before we discuss this in detail we need to ask ourselves more generally why such a comprehensive treatment of Israel's institutions should have been conducted by Jeremiah. We may put it down, as we have earlier indicated, to the failure of the Josianic reforms and Jeremiah's disen-chantment with the total reform movement. We would be correct to do this but we must not ignore the more fundamental reasons suggested by the call narrative of Jeremiah in Jer. 1. We cannot do more here than refer to the nature of his call and the watershed which it provides in the history of Old Testament prophecy. He is uniquely called to be a prophet to the nations (1:5, 10). This is a fact which the first chapter of the book underscores. Any attempt to come to terms with the purpose of Jeremiah's ministry must therefore keep the purpose of his call in mind.

In substance the message of his book is that the time of the gentiles has arrived with the hegemony of Babylon. The end of the political history of Israel has thus virtually come. The facts of the exile will bear this out. The political connections which were established with Israel by covenant thus stood in need at this time of theological restatement. Above all there was a need that the underlying significance of the Sinai covenant be recognized since the political connections which had been popularly imposed upon the doctrine of election stemming from the Sinai encounter now required reinterpretation. Jeremiah's New Covenant theology was therefore intended to provide for the necessary transition from Israel as a nation to Israel as a theological ideal.

Of course, Israel had always been that, but the loss of nationhood in exile would be exploited by the exilic prophets to clarify the more basic character of her connection to Yahweh. Hence at and during the exile emphasis would be placed upon the theological purpose of Israel and the function as a world centre of Jerusalem in the divine economy. Both Ezekiel and Isaiah 40–66 will draw out the consequences of this new theological internationalism to which the book of Jeremiah commits us. In entering upon a detailed discussion of the New Covenant in Jeremiah we merely note at this stage the set of historical occurrences which made it necessary.

Jer. 31:31–34 contains the prophet's statement about the inauguration of the New Covenant, a passage which is set within chapters 30 – 31, chapters dealing with the return of the divided nation from exile and the consequences of that return.

Jer. 30:1–3 asserts the certainty of a return, 30:4–11 promises restoration under Messianic leadership, vv. 12 – 17 indicate the disciplinary nature of the punishment received by the exiles, vv. 18–22 treat of the restoration of Jerusalem/Zion. Jer 31:1–6 draws support for the projected return from the unexpected grace displayed to Israel in the first Exodus, vv. 7 – 22 specifically relate to the return of the North, vv. 23 – 26 deal with the restoration of the South, while vv. 27 – 30 which lead into the New Covenant section have in mind the restitution of the total nation. Jer. 31:31–34 deals with the New Covenant, vv. 35–37 locate the certainty of such a renewed covenant within the purposes of creation itself (and the impossibility of their being frustrated), while vv. 38 – 40 logically conclude the subject of the renewed people of God, with which these chapters have been dealing, by referring to the building of the New Jerusalem.

The New Covenant passage, whatever may be its relative date within the ministry of Jeremiah, provided the link in that prophet's thought between Israel's past and future. It effected a junction between Israel and the new Israel, between political Israel and the people of God. What is striking and what cannot be missed in Jer. 31:31–34 is the theocentric character of the new arrangement, to which our attention is directed by the sustained series of first person divine addresses during the course of the verses. From first to last the New Covenant rests upon divine initiative, and is constituted solely by a divine pardon which permits a new beginning.

(b) Jer. 31:31–34

(i) Is the immediate or the remote future in view? A point of importance, however, is the question of the inauguration of the New Covenant. When will it begin? What is to be its starting point? The section is simply introduced by the phrase, 'Behold the days are coming', familiar in Jeremiah (occurring some fourteen times), but rare in the remainder of the Old Testament. Outside the book of Jeremiah, this phrase (1 Sam. 2:31; 2 Kgs. 20:17; Amos 4:2; 8:11; 9:13) refers to the indefinite future. In Jeremiah the reference is to the uncertain future, near or remote.

> In the interpretation of such a phrase one must recall that the expectations of Jeremiah's New Covenant are also in effect handled by Isaiah and Ezekiel (cf. especially Ezekiel 37:15–28 where the reunion of the two segments of the old undivided kingdom is contemplated, again in the land). The problem which occurs in regard to these prophecies is to determine what refers to the immediate future, and what is eschatology, and how we may make such distinctions. However, in the view of the exilic prophets (whose enthusiasm was like that of the early New Testament writers), in the new movement by God which would inaugurate a new phase of Israel's history, the end had prospectively come. The expectation of what is thus about to happen, particularly in the matter of the return from the Babylonian exile, is couched by the exilic prophets in grandiose terms which see in what is imminent the ushering in, or a paradigm of the end. It is thus true that Jeremiah in chapter 31:31–34 is speaking to his contemporaries of their present expectations, but through an address to that situation he is at the same time propounding a doctrine of a New Covenant as an ideal. If the ideal is not in fact presently realised, such a present non-realisation will not vitiate the note of final purpose which Jeremiah saw as inevitable. In the anticipated return from exile Jeremiah saw the inbreaking of the end. If the actual return did not correspond to the ideal, this did not falsify the prophetic conception of the end. Nor did it alter the nature of the end: it simply postponed it.

There is thus little merit in arguing whether Jeremiah is speaking of the remote or the immediate future, for in the sense that the return from exile restores to Israel the potential to which Jeremiah draws attention in chapter 31:31–34, both are true.

(ii) In what sense is the New Covenant New? There is no difficulty in understanding the sense of $b^e r\hat{\imath}t$ in this passage. It is that of unilateral promise and its content will be imposed by Yahweh. No hint of mutuality is contained in the proposals. In what they regard as a new emphasis in covenant conclusion, some have seen the 'newness' as consisting of this lack of mutuality. We have noted, however, that what is made explicit in this formulation here obtains in all divine covenants in the Old Testament and we must therefore look elsewhere for what newness is to be found in this new arrangement. As noted, the New Covenant's unilateral nature is emphasized by the constant first person divine address which occurs throughout the episode (cf. v. 31 'I will make', v. 33 'I will put', 'I will write', 'I will be their God' and note the significant concluding statement of v. 34, 'I will forgive ... I will remember no more').

We may ask ourselves as we consider the question of the 'newness' of the New Covenant whether what is contemplated is absolutely new or whether it is simply a fresh dispensation or enactment of the covenant arrangement repeated already at significant episodes in Israel's history. What therefore, is the precise sense of the word 'new' in this section, since Heb. *ḥādāsh* 'new' can have both meanings of 'renewed' (Lam. 3:22–23) or 'brand new' (Exod. 1:8, Deut. 32:17, 1 Sam. 6:7)? In the immediate context of this chapter, the same adjective occurs in v. 22 where it is used in conjunction with the verb to 'create' (Heb. *bārā'*) to indicate a totally new set of circumstances (as indeed we might expect by the use of this Heb. verb which always refers to the creative newness of the experience, i.e. to an experience for which there are no antecedents). These have been brought about by God's intervention to effect a return from exile. In the revolutionary new age now being ushered in, Jeremiah tells us that inrooted human tendencies will be reversed, for (v. 22) 'the Lord has created a new thing on the earth: a woman protects a man.' One would surmise therefore that a radical discontinuity with the past is attached to the adjective in Jer. 31:31. Yet the Greek Old Testament translates Heb. *ḥādāsh* by Gk. *kainos* at this point, using an adjective which refers to a qualitatively new dimension being added to the covenant experience and not merely or necessarily to a totally new divine initiative which has no temporal reference to the past. In the element 'new' then, we are probably being asked to look for dimensions which will add a creative qualitative addition to an old arrangement, a fresh dispensation of the covenant to which the elements of both continuity and yet radical discontinuity belong. There is thus continuity in the arrangement under consideration since the association of Yahweh with Israel will continue, but there is a radical discontinuity as well, since a new element is introduced which has not so far been part of Israel's experience. The relative balance of these two factors in the New Covenant must now be assessed.

(iii) With whom is the New Covenant made? This New Covenant is to be made (v. 31) with the 'house of Israel' and 'with the house of Judah'. 'House of Judah' (v. 31) is often regarded as an editorial addition because only the 'house of Israel' appears in v. 33, but to adopt such a view is to misunderstand the nature of the argument which is being detailed here. The twin reference to the existing geographical divisions of Israel and Judah in v. 31 recognises the realities of the present national position or the position as it has existed since the division of the united kingdom into two entities after the death of Solomon. The New Covenant will heal this breach and we thus have here a parallel to the view of Ezekiel (Ezek. 37:15–28) that in the new age the two houses of Judah and Ephraim (i.e. Israel), will be joined together by a divine grafting operation which will make them one. The point that Jeremiah is making here is a common exilic emphasis. There can be only one people of God and this concept will be exhibited in an inner harmony which will transcend the present geographical divisions.

The use by Jeremiah therefore of the terms Judah and Israel occurs throughout the passage with complete consistency. When the new age is described by him in v. 33 (note the 'after those days' of v. 33) and the content of the covenant then concluded is referred to, it is naturally in those circumstances made only with the 'house of Israel'. In using his terms in this way Jeremiah is maintaining a consistency which is to be found elsewhere throughout his work.

When in the book of Jeremiah the term Israel specifically refers to the old northern kingdom, the context always makes that reference clear. Of about one hundred and twenty references to 'Israel' in Jeremiah at least two thirds of these refer prospectively to the united people of God. Typical of such usage is Jer. 19:3, 'Hear the word of the Lord, O kings of Judah and inhabitants of Jerusalem. Thus says the Lord of hosts, the God of Israel …'. In Jer. 18:1, where the possibility of a new beginning for the nation is being explored under the parable of the visit to the house of the potter, it is the house of Israel (18:6) which stands addressed, though when the prophet is commissioned to explain the parable and expound its meaning it is to the men of Judah and the inhabitants of Jerusalem that he is sent. The picture of the prophetic consciousness of an undivided people of God is clearly presented in Jer. 50:17: 'Israel is a hunted sheep driven away by lions. First the king of Assyria devoured him, and now at last, Nebuchadnezzar king of Babylon has gnawed his bones.'

The general context of Jer. 30 – 31 places, moreover, strong stress upon the reconstitution of the united people of God and in doing so virtually ignores the monarchical period divisions.

Thus 30:1–11 appears to contemplate the restoration of Israel as a whole. This is made clear by the reference to the division only at v. 4 (cf. Israel and Judah) after which the passage then goes on to treat of the wider issues of Davidic kingship which is (v. 9) to be exercised over a united people. In these circumstances the reference to Jacob and Israel (v. 10) must be theologically and not geographically applied and must refer to the reconstitution of the undivided people. In vv. 12–17 the same eschatological picture seems to be in view (cf. the reference to Zion, v. 17). Verses 18–22 continue the same note with particular reference to the rebuilding of Jerusalem (and note the Abrahamic promise implications of v. 19 with its allusion to the multiplicity and glory of the people). There is an oscillation in Jer. 31:1–6 between the theological (v. 1, 2, 4) and the geographical uses (cf. 5, 6), showing how closely the two concepts are bound up together. Verses 7 – 22 refer to the return of the North, vv. 23 – 26 speak of the return of the South, but the emphasis in vv. 27 – 30 (though the geographical terms are still used of both entities) is upon a merger after restoration. In these circumstances the combination of the older, politically independent kingdoms of Israel and Judah in the New Covenant (vv. 31–34) is expected, while the remainder of the chapter (vv. 35–40), as we have previously noted, deals with the results of restoration, a united people of God worshipping in the eschatological New Jerusalem.

(iv) What constitutes the continuity and the discontinuity of the New Covenant? In v. 32, Jeremiah then refers to the Old Covenant, the Sinai arrangement which is the point of departure for the New Covenant. Here, the points conveyed are those of its foundation by divine initiative, the redemption which gave rise to it, and the relationship ('I was their husband') which flowed from it. Since this parallelism is being employed to provide an analogy for the New Covenant, the new arrangement will be preceded by a redemptive movement of the same character as that to which Jeremiah has so far referred, and to which the exilic prophets refer under the imagery of the New Exodus. Just as the Sinai covenant had been preceded by a divine intervention into Israel's history at that point, so now in the exilic age we may, Jeremiah implies, look for similar parallels. Here the element of continuity is thus expressed; a fresh demonstration of divine grace will occur, the nature of which may be as analogous to perceive the initial divine intervention which secured Israel's political existence.

At the same time, however, in v. 32 the element of discontinuity is stressed in the reference to the Old Covenant as one which had been breached. Like the imposition of the covenant, the breach was one-sided. They broke it (v. 32), Yahweh had imposed it ('my covenant which they broke'). The indivisibility, however, of the covenant from the divine point of view is referred to in v. 32 by its depiction in marriage terms. Yahweh had been a 'husband to them'. The use of this marriage imagery, so extensive in Jeremiah as a figure for Israel's apostasy, ought to be carefully noted in this New Covenant section. It is saying that by its very nature the covenant arrangement could not be sundered. Divorce on the divine side could never be contemplated. Within the human situation in the Old Testament divorce within the marriage relationship was possible, since the hardness of the human heart necessitated that (cf. Deut. 24:1–4). Even within this situation, however, this was a concession and not a realisation of any divine intention (note God's attitude to divorce in Mal. 2:16 where in a difficult text and context divorce seems to be in view). The language of the marriage relationship, therefore, as applied to the Sinai arrangement, underscores its permanency and provides thus the counter to the discontinuity of 'my covenant which they broke' (v. 32). In short the element which will characterize the New Covenant and thus render it 'new' will be its irrefragability. It will not be new because of new conditions which Yahweh will attach to it, nor because it is the product of a new historical epoch, nor because it will contain different promises, for indeed those attached to the Sinai covenant could hardly have been more comprehensive, but what will make it new is that in the new age *both* partners will keep it. In that age there will be no possibility of the new arrangement being breached unilaterally. Thus what is being said in this dialogue of continuity and discontinuity is that discontinuity takes its rise in the nature of the human problem, in the human inability to maintain the older Sinai arrangement. Nothing short of an inward and transforming arrangement, to which Jeremiah will now refer in vv. 33–34, will guarantee continued human fidelity within the new arrangement. Divine continuity would continue, divine consistency, as it has been expressed in the successive arrangements with Abraham, Israel, and David, will be expressed in the new age and within a New Covenant, the model for which will apparently be the Sinaitic. The tendency to see the covenant of Jeremiah as a New Covenant because it replaces obligation by promise drives a wedge between promise and law. This division is not consistent with the relationship of those entities in prior Old Testament covenants such as the Sinaitic. Covenant and promise are essentially inseparable as we have consistently seen. Covenant simply confirms promise, recognizes the existence of a relationship to which promise and obligation are attached.

(v) What is the place of 'law' in the New Covenant framework? If the newness of the New Covenant is thus not simply covenant construed in the new age as promise, because obligations are also attached, is its newness to be found in the way in which the obligations of the covenant are to be realized? Here we refer to the question of law or 'torah' which is raised in v. 33. This provides a further point of contact with the Sinai code to which it seemingly refers—specifically, one presumes, to the decalogue by which the Sinai covenant was primarily expressed. We are now informed that in this new age the law will be put in the hearts. Is this therefore in opposition to the old age in which the law was externalized on two tables of stone (cf. Exod. 24:12)? Or is it in opposition to covenant reformulations such as Josiah's which were

based upon appeals to a 'book of the law'? Will the torah then in the new age be written upon the *heart* of the individual, interiorized, personalized and thus denationalized? Here we briefly note the place of the word 'heart' in the psychology of the Old Testament as comprehensive of all inward personal states. Most frequently, it is used of thought processes as directive of the total attitude and the actions which stem from them. It can be used also for moral awareness in the sense of conscience, and thus of a responsibility for personal decisions and their implementation.

Whether law is hereby interiorized for the first time in the Old Testament is debatable. In broad terms, in the book of Deuteronomy presents torah as the divine direction giving Israel guidance about how the saving event which put Israel in the land, is to be reflected. It served also to identify the saved community as one who would express torah. It is therefore wrong to think, as some have supposed, that torah did not provide for God's maximum requirements but represented only the minimum which in that period was practicably achievable. Law exhibited the relationship in practice. It had no meaning in fact outside the presuppositions of such a relationship. It is difficult to suppose, under these circumstances, that law could be, in intention, something merely external, any more than salvation could have been thought of as some simply external act. Human achievement had neither accounted for the existence of Israel nor could it guarantee its existence. Once law became externalised, then equally salvation would come to be thought of in quantitative, mechanical, political terms, as bound up with the blessings of salvation, i.e. the land, and not with the experience of salvation, i.e. liberation. It can be very plausibly argued that the failure of the national experiment was occasioned by externality at both levels, namely that salvation became externalized as law became externalized. But certainly this does not seem either the national nor, we must deduce, the personal intent, of the book of Deuteronomy. The oscillation between the second person plural and the second person singular address in Deuteronomy, a fact which is often supposed to offer evidence for the composite character of the book, reflects the concern shown by the author to address both nation and individual. The fact remains, however, that in Deuteronomy, on whatever level the address is based, the law is required to be lodged in the heart, presumably in both the national and the individual heart (cf. Deut. 6:4–6, 11:18). Admittedly such references are imperatives, but they do point to the ideal state. In the context of obedience, circumcision of the heart is required (Deut. 10:16), but likewise in the context of 30:1–14 (a passage which envisages recall from an exile which has taken place as a result of apostasy), the circumcision of the heart is something which is divinely wrought (30:6), as a result of which love will proceed from the heart. This latter passage is thus an indication of the ideal which is there at the beginning, and the inwardness of the work of God is a factor which is not confined to the new-birth narratives of the New Testament. It is in fact a presupposition of the Old Testament relationship, even if, nationally concerned as the Old Testament primarily is, it is not sufficiently or repetitively individualized.

The demand, moreover, for the purification of the heart, for the creation of a clean heart within, for contrition as a heart exercise, is an entirely Old Testament one (cf. Ps. 51:10, 17; 73:1, 13; Prov. 22:11; Isa. 57:15). A return to Yahweh is the result of a change of heart (Jer. 3:10, and note the use of the earlier imagery in regard to the need to circumcise the heart, Jer. 4:4, cf. 9:25; Ezek. 44:7, 9). The law in the heart is essential for the possibility of covenant experience, as Ps. 37:31 clearly implies, and we may similarly refer to Ps. 40:8, where the possibility of doing the will of God is related directly to the state of the heart. It is deemed axiomatic by Isa. 51:7, where the exiles are addressed and the prospect of a return is under review, that to know righteousness, to understand the true nature of the covenant relationship, is to have the law in the heart. This matter of the heart relationship must be taken further when the New Covenant passages of Ezekiel are considered, but the law in the heart as a precondition of law in action is as plainly Old Testament as it is totally biblical. Of course, the Old Testament calls upon the individual to ensure that the law is in the heart. This does not mean, however, that the individual puts it there, the cumulative evidence argues in the opposite direction. Whatever tensions may exist between calls to lodge the law in the heart and the implication that only God may put it there, they are not peculiar, as we well know, to the salvation experience of the Old Testament. Under these circumstances, Jer. 31:33, closing as it does with the conventional covenant formula of 'I will be their God, and they shall be my people', seems merely to outline the operation of covenant as we have come to recognize it in its Old Testament forms up to this point. Of course that God purposes in the new era to put his law in their hearts recalls us to an ideal position. We may contrast with this the externality which increasingly characterised Israelite religion in the Old Testament period, but when we have done that, Jer. 31:33 seems to be saying no more than that in doing what is planned, God is returning to the original intent of the Sinai covenant.

Such an attitude to continuity in respect of v. 33 is supported also by the tenor of Jewish exegesis. Traditionally this looked upon Yahweh as initiating and the maintaining the covenant. The maintenance of the covenant was not conditional upon Israel's obedience, as though God would cancel it if that was not displayed. Rabbinic theology seems to have believed that a person could withdraw from the covenant, but that this would not cancel the obligation. Even when faced with national disobedience, God would remain faithful to his covenant promises. Intentional rejection of God's right to direct the affairs of the nation entailed rejecting the covenant, but God's covenant in Israel was finally not contingent upon Israel's obedience.[4]

The New Covenant like the old, is thus God's gift. Jer. 31:33 makes this clear. With the New Covenant, like the old, the element of law is necessarily connected. The prophetic assertion that the demands of the covenant can be met only by the infusion of divine grace, merely preserves the connection between covenant and law which had been made explicit at the earlier Exod. 20:2ff. The problem to which Jeremiah refers has been Israel's inability to keep the covenant. Thus, the stipulation of v. 33 that the law will be put in the heart is presumably a stipulation that the same law which was inserted into the national and personal consciousness of Israel earlier at Sinai will be reapplied in the same way in the new age.

(vi) The 'no longer' of v. 34. The conditions for spiritual experience described in v. 33 could with some plausibility be generalized, as we have argued, to provide the basis for all spiritual experience. But they are given a new significance by the content of v. 34 where the intention to interiorize the divine will (v. 33) is seen to result in the transformation to which the verse refers. This does not, as we have pointed out, depend upon the insertion of the law in the heart alone, but it is consequent upon other factors taken up in v. 34. Thus v. 34 begins with Heb. $w^e l\hat{o}$ ... $^c\hat{o}d$ (and no longer) indicating by the w^e (Heb. 'and') an affirmation of the material of v. 33 and a continuance of it. With the 'no longer' of the verse however, we do presume the emergence of a new situation. There is emphasis in v. 34 on the immediacy of the new relationship. No longer will there be need to preserve the instructional framework in which intermediaries such as priests and particularly prophets had operated under the Old Covenant. In the new situation all will know God, knowledge will be direct and totally personal. The emphasis upon the need for instruction, by which the old alliance was characterized (Deut. 6:7; Josh. 1:8; Ps. 1:2 etc.), pointed to the imperfect character of the old relationship as it had in fact been personally and nationally apprehended. This tension in the Old Testament between the concept that the law ideally was in the heart and the concept that it needed to be put there by instruction is, as we realise, a problem which confronts New Testament writers also. The parallel to which we may refer in the New Testament, is that of the believer who is in the sphere of the Spirit, but who at the same time must recognize the need to strive against the carnal realities with which he is faced. Yet the immediacy of the new situation to which v. 34 refers us seem to take us beyond all biblical personal experience; the limitations of the purely human

---

[4]. The Rabbinic evidence is referred to and assessed by E.P. Sanders, *Paul and Palestinian Judaism* (London: S.C.M., 1977), cf. pp. 95–96.

situation have been transcended. The era to which Jeremiah points here and its characterization by the absence of the need of any human instruction, brings with it the concept of changed natures, indeed perfected human natures.

Lest we think that this democratization of approach, whereby all in effect have become prophets, is simply a projection of the New Testament era and thus looks to the democratization of the gift of the Spirit, the remainder of v. 34 adds elaboration and clarification. The final and important factor which controls the era of the New Covenant, Jeremiah tells us, is that it is the era of the forgiveness of sins. God, he tells us, in the new era, 'will forgive their iniquity, and ... will remember their sin no more'. The forgiveness of sins in the Old Testament was, as we have seen, bound up, other than in exceptional instances, with the system of institutionalized approach through sacrifice. God forgave on the condition of repentance, and this was the very basis of forgiveness. There is no mention, however, in v. 34 of any such preconditions in the new age. In fact a situation seems to be envisaged in which sin has been once and for all dealt with. No more action in the new age will be called for against sin, for, remarks Jeremiah, 'I will forgive their iniquity, and I will remember their sin no more.' That parallel statement is not simply the language of prophetic hyperbole nor merely a reference to the psychological attitude of God in the new age, namely that he will 'forgive by forgetting' sin. It refers rather to the new age as one in which no action (in this biblical sense of remembering) needs to be taken against sin. The contrast in v. 34 is not between the wide measure of the divine grace in the new age versus a limitation in its display in the old, namely that the mercy to be extended under the new covenant is so extensive as to create in itself a new situation in which sin can be totally overlooked as it could not in the old era. What is rather meant is that in the new age sin will not be required to be dealt with at all. This is a supposition of unfettered mutual fellowship between God and men, the creation of a community in which not only is there no need for instruction but no breach of fellowship occurs, no divisions within the new community are expected. All this presupposes a degree of harmony within the new society which prevents the possibility of any tensions threatening the new relationships.

(vii) The eschatological view which characterizes the New Covenant. We have not in all this simply looked ahead to the New Testament age, for in that age the recipients of the Spirit, the redeemed, the church of the post-resurrection age are all bound up in the types of tensions to which we have referred. Injunctions to seek forgiveness of sins committed within the new relationship established for the believer through the death of Christ, abound in the New Testament and do not here need to be detailed. Jeremiah is not simply looking forward to the Cross and Resurrection as ushering in the new age, though of course they do that.

It is not a Christological point of view which is being offered here, as though we are being specifically presented with the series of covenant contrasts which the death of Jesus, as ushering in the New Covenant, will resolve. In Jeremiah, we are looking beyond the New Testament age to the community of the end-time, to a situation when the kingdom of God has finally come and God is all in all. In such a situation the blessings of Jeremiah's New Covenant will be achieved. Not only will sin not be imputed, in the new age it will not be a factor.

In speaking of the renewed house of Israel Jeremiah would then have been speaking typically about the redeemed people of God. The New Covenant age is something which lay not merely beyond the circum-stances of the return from exile to which Jeremiah immediately spoke, but, we suggest, beyond the New Testament age as well. One must briefly mention at this point the important exposition of the New Covenant by the writer of the Epistle to the Hebrews. Institutionally, as that writer points out, the Old Covenant has becoming obsolete (Heb. 8:13). The imperfections of the old to which he points in chapters 8 – 10 are clear at all points (repeated sacrifices, etc.). Encouraged by the cloud of witnesses (chapters 11 – 12), the readers are exhorted to 'draw near' to the new situation, i.e. to recognize what is their present position. Analogies are then drawn to the Sinai situation (Heb. 12:18–24), yet the readers are already in the New Covenant framework whose mediator was Jesus. That has been concluded, and the blood of the sacrifice which ushered it in does speak far better things than the blood of Abel. This blood speaks of reconciliation, whereas Abel's blood spoke of the divisions which were the manifestation of the disharmony which the fall was bound to produce. It needs to be noted, however, that the argument of the epistle stops at this point in its eschatological presenta-tion. Believers have come to the counterpart of Sinai, the heavenly Zion. They are redeemed and perfected, i.e. able to draw near, and they have drawn near. The New Covenant has been concluded, but in Heb. 12:18–24 we deal only with a counterpart to Sinai. We have not yet advanced on this schema to the promised land, we have not yet advanced into Canaan. There still remains – and this has been the presentation of the argument of the Epistle from chapter 3 onwards – the 'rest' which the full experience of the New Covenant will yield.

In short, the superstructure of the New Covenant has been erected, the basis on which it will operate, namely the vicarious and representa-tive death of Christ, stands secure. Access to the presence of the Deity is now assured, the veil of the temple has been rent, etc. But the point which the Epistle underscores is a common New Testament one, namely, that the full content of the new age still beckons us on. It is a 'let us go on' situation to which Hebrews and the New Testament sum-mons us. The New Testament age thus surveys the tensions of the 'now' and the 'not yet'. Jeremiah, however, goes beyond this. He looks to the completion of the historical situation, as does the post-exilic New

Covenant prophecy. In the Upper Room Jesus shared with his disciples the concept of a New Covenant which his death would inaugurate. The future nature of the arrangement is emphasized also by St. Paul, who, in pointing to the New Covenant aspects of the Lord's Supper, sees that the Supper proclaims the Lord's death 'till he comes', with which process the finality of the New Covenant will be bound up (1 Cor. 11:25–27).

(viii) The question of prophetic 'realised' eschatology. The question of the 'when' of the fulfilment of the New Covenant is one which the exilic prophets did not take up. But Jeremiah's view of the future will be confirmed when the content of Ezekiel and Isaiah is considered. They spoke of immediate fulfilment in terms of the return of a united Israel to the land, and of the perfected people of God in the age before which they believed themselves immediately to stand. In doing so, however, they did no more than the New Testament church did in its expectation of the Second Coming. In every age of stage or the early church this was a matter of great imminence. They were right to see in their age the signs of the last days and they were right to apply to those signs the theology of the final end to which New Testament eschatology refers. They saw the end as a return to the situation as it was in the beginning with an overplus, and in this they were correct also. In like fashion the post-exilic prophets saw the end refracted through the great event before which they stood, namely the return from exile and the reconstitution of the people of God. And to this event they applied the ideal covenant theology of the ultimate end. They were not wrong to do so, just as the earlier prophets had not been wrong in attempting to idealise in national experience the Exodus redemption. We are able to see that the New Covenant prophecies of Jeremiah, Ezekiel and Isaiah remain to be fulfilled. But for them the Sinai covenant had always contemplated the ideal life in the land. They look for the secure dwelling of Israel, the people of God, in a position of universal influence in the land which God had given them. More than that, it was the dwelling of God with them which would accomplish this end. Thus the Sinai covenant always had parodisiacal implications. If these were not realised progressively in the Old Testament this did not mean that prophecy would not coninue to expect a final fulfilment in New Covenant terms!

In all this we do not mean to spiritualize the Old Testament promises, unrealised in Israel's experience in the Old Testament, by transferring them to the people of God in the New Testament. The exilic prophets, particularly, drew attention to distinctions between the nation and the community faith, though these distinctions, as we have noted, had always been there. When therefore, the exilic prophets prophesied of Israel's return, it was of the return of an ideal Israel that they spoke. We cannot thus construe their prophecies in narrow nationalistic terms, since they are operating within the framework of ideals. That is why when we turn to the New Covenant concepts of Ezekiel and Isaiah we see that the notion of the New Covenant in both books is tied to a notion of the renewal not only of the land, but of creation itself, to a new heaven and a new earth. This is as we should expect, for the New Covenant can mean only the Sinai covenant completed in Israel's faith experience or (putting it in a different way) the Abrahamic promises effected in Israel's experience and thus the fall reversed.

D. EZEKIEL AND THE NEW COVENANT

i. *Ezekiel's blue-print for the return of Israel (33:21 – 39:29)*

At first glance Ezekiel does not seem to accord the concept of the covenant a prominent place, for in the key passages which relate to the return, the term $b^e r\hat{i}t$ is not frequently found (though it occurs in total some eighteen times in Ezekiel). It would not, however, be too much to claim the whole of the prophecy of Ezekiel is New Covenant orientated. The remarkable throne vision of Ezekiel 1 with which the prophecy begins, contains imagery and language, as the commentators have frequently noted (referring also to the very similar Isaiah 6 call narrative),[5] which point to clear Jerusalem temple associations. Chapters 1 – 3 of the prophecy determine the tone of the first twenty-four chapters which have to do with judgement pronounced upon Jerusalem and upon the object which expressed and symbolized its election – the temple. The oracles against the foreign nations (chapters 25 – 32) seem to find their logic in the removal of any political impediments to the return of Israel from the erstwhile foes to whom reference is made in those chapters. The watchman call to Ezekiel in 33:1–20, initially delivered to him in chapter 3, reinforces by its repetition the new phase of Ezekiel's ministry to which he is directed at this point. Ezek. 33:21—39:29 is then a series of six messages delivered to the prophet during the course of the night preceding that on which news of the fall of Jerusalem had been delivered to him, messages which then deal with the shape of Israel's ultimate future.[6]

The first address to Ezekiel (33:23–33) concerns the validity of the Abrahamic promises (cf. v. 24), a question much in the minds of the exiles consequent upon the fall of Jerusalem. The reply given by the prophet is that for Israel the physical enjoyment of the land was conditional upon obedience. In chapter 34 the problem of faulty leadership which led to the exile is under review (vv. 1– 6). In the future age Yahweh himself will shepherd (i.e. rule) Israel, though in the new economy there is room for a Davidic figure who as 'prince' (Heb. *nāsî*, not 'king' – Heb. *melek*) will be an under-shepherd (vv. 7–24). Condi-

---

5. As W. Zimmerli, *Ezekiel I* (Philadelphia: Fortress Press, 1979), pp. 119ff. notes.

6. The detail of these six messages is examined by Ralph H. Alexander, 'A Fresh Look at Ezekiel 38 – 39', *JEvTSoc* 17 (1974), pp. 157–169.

tions of wonderful peace will follow this (vv. 25–29) with thus a return
to paradisiacal conditions. It is stressed, however (vv. 30–31), that the
new arrangement will obtain solely as a result of divine leadership. The
position of David, or the Davidic figure, in the proposed situation is
clearly a subordinate one and certainly this conforms to the general
tenor of post-exilic prophecy in which the Davidic covenant merges
more closely into its Sinaitic background. Ezek. 35 deals with the
removal of Israel's enemies or enmity conceived in the shape of Edom,
who might have been seen as a threat to the return. This discussion of
possible threats continues in a more general form in the further address
of 36:1–15.

At Ezek. 36:16ff the question is raised as to how the ideals set before
the nation are to be effected. The factors which led to the loss of the land
are reviewed (vv. 16–20), but there is no suggestion of the Deut. 30:1–10
situation where the operation of such covenant curses leads Israel in
exile to repent. The restoration which is pursued in vv. 21–23 is
Jeremianic in its emphasis, namely that the restoration and renewal of
the covenant are contingent not upon performance by Israel but upon
divine fidelity. Three great issues provide the basis of divine action on
Israel's behalf in these verses. They are firstly a concern by God that 'his
holy name' (v. 21— his character displayed) should be honoured by
integrity of divine action which continues in accordance with a divine
intention to honour promises to Israel. Secondly, the reversal of Israel's
situation provides no ground for national pride but is due simply to
God's constancy (v. 22). Thirdly, what will happen in the sight of the
nations will be an open divine demonstration to them of God's
purposes for the world, so that divine holiness might be vindicated
among the nations also (v. 23). In vv. 24ff the catalogue of individual
acts by which such a restoration is to be effected are then announced.
People and land will again be bound together by an exodus (v. 24), the
taint of contaminating influences (as befits the restored sanctuary
situation of Israel) are then removed by ritual cleansing (v. 25), thereby
expressing a formal separation between Israel and her environment.
These are characteristics of the New Covenant, the more so when we
compare the cleansing here with the sprinkling effected at Sinai which
was then designed to bring about the inauguration of Israel's covenant
(cf. Exod. 24:6).

Mere separation, however, from the past will not account for the
shape of the future, and this great passage then goes on to explain (v.
26) the inwardness of the transaction by which the new arrangement
will be effected. Unlike Jer. 31, it does not state that the law is put in the
heart, though a new (i.e. renewed) heart is given to Israel for life in the
new age. Since obedience to the divine will is at issue, Ezekiel regards
the law as a matter for the heart in both dispensations, new an old.

The explanation, then, becomes a little more detailed than that which
was provided in Jer. 31:31–34, for v. 27 goes on to explicate what was

meant in v. 26 by referring to the programme as effected by a renewed spirit in man. In the Old Testament the spirit of a man is the point of divine contact, or put differently, man viewed as spirit is man looked at from the point of view of divine possibility, as opposed to man viewed as soul where man appears as mortal and as exposed to disintegration. The correspondence between this position and the Pauline one of 'spirit' versus 'flesh' is thus a close one. In the new age the emphasis is hereby placed upon the enabling direction of God within the human situation which promotes and prompts response. Not the reformation of man in spiritual terms, but the insertion of the divine nature into man seems to be the emphasis here. In the Old Testament, prior to this point, the gift of the divine Spirit was spasmodic and associated with Israel's leadership[7] but here Ezekiel is extending this notion of directed inward guidance to the people of God as a whole. This can mean nothing less than a democratization of leadership, the establishment of a kingdom of priests in the distributive sense, a position which is taken up by Peter in his Pentecost speech in Acts 2.

In making God the author of this new obedience, Ezekiel expands and illuminates Jeremiah's New Covenant concept. The goal is the same, however, and we move on in this chapter to reflect upon the new life in the Edenically restored land (cf. v. 35). Thus we come in vv. 28–38 to the virtual consummation of the original divine promise to Israel at Sinai, of rest in the land. The point is made in these verses that the transformation of the people of God proceeds concurrently with, and indeed effects, the renewal of their environment. As we should have expected, the renewal of the creature in Israel begins progressively to effect the renewal of creation. In Ezek. 37:1–14 the process of renewal is further reflected upon. At the beginning of the chapter the prophet is taken to 'the valley', that is to say, apparently to where judgement upon Israel was originally pronounced (3:22) on the commencement of Ezekiel's commission. In Ezek. 37, the nation is viewed as merely lifeless bones—is the result of the execution of the prophetic commission. The prophetic response to the divine question as to whether life in exile may yet come into these bones recognizes the inadequacy of human judgement to pronounce upon such a question, but also contains the prophetic recognition of the power of God to begin again. With a clear allusion (v. 5) to Gen. 2:7, the new creation then follows in two stages, until not only form, but also life is given to the national body. The significance of this in political terms is recognized in the next address (Ezek. 37:15–28), where the union of Judah and Israel, with the entire nation again in the land, is broached (v. 22). The place of the Davidic representative in the new era is also adverted to (v. 24).

In the new circumstances, a covenant of peace, an everlasting

---

[7]. Cf. my article 'Spirit and Kingdom of God in the Old Testament', *RefTR* 33 (1974), pp. 1 – 10.

covenant will be made with Israel (v. 26). The Abrahamic promises in v. 26, or indeed the creation promises, of being blessed and multiplied are reinvoked, and the sanctuary character (and thus the Edenic character) of the divine presence as dwelling with Israel follows (v. 27). The resulting witness to the world and the wider consequences of Israel's election (v. 28) then come into play. There follows the last of the six addresses, chapters 38–39, the assault upon the people of God, dwelling securely, by Gog from Magog. The chronological relationship of Ezek. 38–39 to 40–48 is uncertain. Ezek. 38–39 may be a reference to the conflict following upon the Messianic age and preceding the final ushering in of the New Covenant (cf. Rev. 20:4–15), but the issue must remain open.

ii. *Ezekiel 40 – 48: the New Creation*

Following this, the blueprint of the end is delivered in Ezek. 40 – 48. The cosmic character of the visionary experience is underscored by the prophet in his allusion to the very high mountain to which he is spiritually transported in 40:2 and from which vantage point he views the transformed land and the new holy city. It is thus clear that we are to be given a vision of the world sanctuary, the end-time Zion (cf. 40:2). Chapters 40 – 42 describe the temple complex which is very carefully marked off from its surroundings. The design is based largely upon that of the Solomonic temple but with visionary additions which project ideal relationships. The lack of exact correspondence to the Solomonic form, the immaculate symmetry of the proposed new complex, the centrality of the temple structure in the new age, are all apocalyptic summarizations. By this note of discontinuity with the past they point prophetically to the fulfilment of what the historical institutions had symbolized. The elaborate attention in successive chapters that is given to temple consecration and priestly courses and rites adds further stress to the prominence given in these chapters to the centrality of worship, and thus finally to divine kingship, in the new age. We need not for our purposes elaborate on the details by which the institutional framework of the new age is introduced between chapters 43 – 46, though the absence of any mention of an Israelite king in these chapters cannot be overlooked. Such an absence belies also by its further insistence upon the primacy of priest over prince in the new arrangement, what are sometimes seen as forward projections here of the attempts to restore the Davidic dynasty in the post-exilic period. Particularly we think here of the Messianic hopes which are often associated with Haggai and Zechariah. These are said to stem from the temple programme of Ezekiel 40 – 48. No Messianism would be expected, however, in these chapters which are given over to the question of *divine rule* in the end-time. We shall note later that such a lack of Davidic emphasis is consistent with what is in fact found in the restoration programme of the post-exilic prophets which similarly has the final end in view.

More to the point for our covenant considerations is the vision in Ezekiel 47:1–12 of living waters issuing from the temple. We are clearly back within the symbolistic framework of Gen. 2 and thus with the New Creation at this point – the use of similar imagery in Rev. 22 makes this patent. Important also is the new land division to which Ezek. 47:13ff then refers. Here, in a tribal order which closely resembles the battle camp order of the tribes grouped around the symbols of the divine presence in the book of Numbers (cf. Numbers 2), the twelve tribes are grouped four-square in groups of three around the sanctuary. Thus the holy city which is set in the midst of the tribes is in the territory of none. The earthly Jerusalem emphasis and the associated Zion theology of the Davidic house are apparently rejected. On the other hand, the order of these tribes around the shrine corresponds to no Old Testament antecedents. We are therefore presented with Israel once again on the threshold of its conquest era, with a return to Israel's Sinaitic and immediately subsequent wilderness situation. Thus the conquest traditions and Israel's later history, particularly that of the monarchical period, are seen by Ezekiel as a distortion of the original divine intention as one gathers from the studied avoidance within these chapters of any Davidic or Zion parallels. This latter rejection theme, so strongly asserted by Ezekiel, is further reinforced by the closing reference of the prophecy to the direct rule of God in the new age (Ezek. 48:35), for the name of the city so surrounded is again, not Davidic Jerusalem, but, 'The Lord is there' (48:35).

iii. *Ezekiel and Davidic monarchy. New Covenant and divine kingship*

The rejection of monarchical traditions in these chapters serves merely to reinforce the interpretation of Israel's history that Ezekiel has offered elsewhere in the book. Principally Ezek. 20 had operated as a review of Israel's past to that point. As has been shown,[8] the history of Israel is divided in that chapter into three stages, namely the sojourn in Egypt and the first and second generations in the wilderness (20:5–10, 11–17, 18–26). It is significant that the great events in Israel's history, the conquest and the settlement, the establishment of the united monarchy, the question of the divided kingdom, are unceremoniously passed over by the prophet. As in Ezek. 47 – 48, Israel is placed once again over against a wilderness possibility, for the life in the land is referred to in Ezek. 20 simply as a series of national apostasies (cf. vv. 27 – 31). In exile, apparently, they can raise their thoughts no higher than the goal of assimilation with the nations among whom they have been dis-

---

8. By W. Zimmerli, 'The Word of God in the Book of Ezekiel', *Journal for Theology and the Church* 4 (1967), pp. 1 – 13.

persed, and they thus contemplate the obliteration of the very notion of
Israel as a divine foundation. God interrupts in Ezek. 20, however,
asserting that he will effect a second separation from the peoples and in
a situation analogous to that at Sinai, to which the Exodus language of
v. 34 makes reference, he will reaffirm his kingship over them (v. 33). He
will lead them once again through a wilderness chastisement of exile
until a purged remainder re-enters the land. There is no explicit
mention of the New Covenant there, but that is clearly implied.

The New Covenant, however, is explicit in a further review of the
past appearing in Ezek. 16. In 1–52 the initial call of Israel and the
fortunes of the divided kingdom are pursued. All these led ultimately to
the breach of covenant to which v. 59 refers. God then pledges himself
in vv. 60 – 63 to remember, i.e. to reactivate, the covenant concluded
with them 'in the days of their youth' by establishing it (Heb. hēqîm, i.e.
maintaining it) as an everlasting covenant. Verse 61, which mentions
the reception of the two erstwhile wayward daughters into the new
arrangement, adds, somewhat puzzlingly, that their reception will not
be 'by covenant'. Perhaps this presumes in essence the New Covenant
situation to which Jeremiah has referred, namely that the renewal of the
covenant so transcends the older and well-known bond that it cannot
therefore be regarded as its automatic continuance or extension.

Ezekiel's emphasis has thus been upon Yahweh's kingship. Between
the poles of judgement with which the book has commenced and
redemption in new creation terms with which it ended, this kingship
has been manifested. But kingship and covenant are correlates and we
have noted that the restoration passages in Ezekiel 34 – 37, themselves
concerned with the imposition of the New Covenant, found a fitting
conclusion in the new temple prophecy of Ezek. 40 – 48. Those chapters
were concerned with the renewal of creation itself, and yet with the
admission of Israel's special role, and thus its holy city as the world
centre in which God as king is present as the end-time begins.

E. THE NEW COVENANT THEOLOGY OF ISAIAH 40 – 66

i. *Re-creation through the divine word – covenant renewal*

This same New Covenant theology presents itself equally clearly in
Isaiah 40 – 66, with the same relative emphasis upon divine kingship
and the same virtual absence of Davidic Messiahship. In Isa. 40 – 55 the
theme is the recreation of Israel through the divine word, which has as
its aim the establishment of an everlasting covenant (55:3). This
emphasis upon the creative power of the word, and thus the setting of
this message of consolation to Israel in the widest possible of Old
Testament frameworks, is clearly marked by reference to the power of
the word in Isa. 40:1–11, as an introduction to the whole section and in

chapter 55:6–13, where the word is again potent. The redemption from Babylon, to which 40:1 refers, will take the character of a second Exodus (40:3–5) and will thus (this second Exodus motif is pervasively expressed throughout these chapters, cf. Isa. 42:16; 43:16, 19; 49:9, 11; 51:10 etc.) presumably lead to a re-institution of the covenant and certainly to what the prophecy always has in view, the ideal occupation of the land. This return is effected (Isa. 40:6–8) not by human achievement, for all flesh is admittedly 'grass', but by the power of the divine word, which is nothing less (Isa. 40:9–11) in its proclamation than the presence of God himself. There is thus an easy transition in these chapters from the use of the theology of creation as the grounds of the appeal (cf. Isa. 40:12–31; 41:20; 42:5; 45:12 etc), to the redemption from Babylon which exemplifies New Creation power and thus covenant renewal.

Important appeal, therefore, is made by Isa. 40 – 55 to the continuity of the Israelite covenant traditions which operate as the assurance for the new action God is about to take. The New Exodus had had implicit Sinai references, and the employment of the further election material relating to the patriarchal promises (Isa. 41:8; 51:1) serves to underscore what will be the tenor of God's intervention on behalf of his people. Abraham, who was once without prospect of heirs or land, became, by a call received in an area in which the exiles were now actually dwelling, the father of a great nation who eventually found themselves in the land which had been promised (cf. Isa. 51:2). The prophet thus reminds Israel that she is the offspring of Abraham who was Yahweh's friend (41:8). Israel shall become a great people (cf. 49:20ff; 54:3), and shall dwell in the land (49:19ff; 49:8) and shall become a blessing (cf. 49:5–6). We should note, however, that Israel in Isa. 51:1ff is faithful Israel, i.e. those 'who pursue deliverance', who 'seek the Lord'. Already in the prophecy the use of the double name Jacob/Israel (cf. 48:1) has indicated the validity of the old election motifs and thus the belief is clear that the disaster of 587 B.C. has not cancelled out the ancient promises. The prophetic reasoning in Isa. 51:1–11 bears noting. Because (v. 3) Yahweh will move to comfort Zion, to make her like Eden, the centre of world blessing (v. 3), the redeemed people are to look unto the rock, Abraham, from whence they were hewn. That is to say, the restoration of Zion means for Isaiah the direct continuity of the Abrahamic promises.

This leads in vv. 4–6 to the incorporation of the nations into the new sphere of salvation. In this way the second arm of the Abrahamic promises, Israel's function in respect of the world, is referred to. In some sense again, these verses must, in view of their marked similarity to the eschatology of Isa. 2:2–4, refer to divine activity emanating from Jerusalem and thus directly continue the thought of v. 3 has raised. After an address of reassurance to the redeemed in vv. 7–8, direct links between Creation, Exodus and second Exodus are forged in vv. 9–11. The implicit link between creation, Sinai and Davidic covenants (cf. the specific mention of Zion in v. 11) is therefore offered. All occurs within the more specific Abrahamic framework with which the chapter has begun. In Isa. 51:9, under the figure of the 'arm of the Lord' which had earlier served to 'cut Rahab in pieces', we have an appeal to the ancient near Eastern mythology of the slaying of the chaos dragon and the resulting creation of the universe, and thus to the act of creation itself. Verse 10 moves directly to the Exodus redemption in language reminiscent of Exod. 15, while finally in v. 11 the return of the redeemed to Zion heralds the fulfilment of the second Exodus prophecies to which reference has earlier been made.

The extensive use of creation motifs in this prophecy (some fifty allusions to creation, eleven of them referring to the creation of the world, with the other forty referring to the redemption from exile)[9] serves to stress not only God's sovereignty in these chapters but also the constancy of his covenant purposes. The prophet delights to appeal to older traditions to emphasize the continuity that he seeks to promote. Thus phrases such as Creator of Israel (43:15), Redeemer (49:26), King of Jacob (41:21), abound.

ii. *Servant and covenant*

Covenant and election motifs, vocational purposes for Israel etc., are conveyed probably most emphatically in the prophecy by the use of the concept 'servant', especially in passages such as Isa. 42:1–4 (with which vv. 5–9 are closely connected); 49:1–6; 50:4–9; 52:13 – 53:12. A connection between the servant and Israel is forged directly by Isa. 49:3, while that between the servant and covenant exists by virtue of 49:6 when compared with 42:6. The role of the servant in these passages is a contested one. The language of 42:1–4 contains, as has been recognized,[10] both kingly and prophetic features, and the servant is thus clearly an ideal figure who rightly finds his final biblical explanation in the ministry of Jesus in the New Testament. In the context of Isaiah 42:1–4 he is charged to bring forth 'justice' and to 'establish' it. This language must serve, in the light of the total argument of Isa. 40:12 – 42:4, to indicate Yahweh's direction of the whole of the historical process, encompassing both the work of creation and redemption.[11] The achievement of this goal is conceived to be by a ministry which lacks superficial impressiveness (42:2), a point which is more thoroughly elaborated in the extensive servant disclosure of Isa. 52:13 – 53:12 in

[9]. I am reliant here on the analysis by F. Holmgren, *With Wings as Eagles, Isaiah 40–55, an Interpretation* (New York: Biblical Scholars Press, 1973), p. 25.

[10]. Though kingly features dominate in the presentation of the servant in Isa. 42:1–4, prophetic traits are not absent, cf. W. A. M. Beuken, 'Mišpāṭ The First Servant Song and its Context', *VT* 22 (1972), pp. 2 – 4.

[11]. As H. C. Spykerboer, *The Structure and Composition of Deutero-Isaiah*, (Groningen: Univ. Groningen Dissertation, 1976), p. 88, notes.

which the sufferings of the servant community which led to the salvation of the wider people of Israel[12] are on view.

It is the link between the servant and covenant, however, which is more germane for our purposes and we turn now to consider Isa. 42:6 which is closely linked with 49:6. The difficult phrase 'covenant to the people, a light to the nations' continues to puzzle.

Of this phrase, *berît ʿam*, unique in the Old Testament, four explanations are commonly offered. Popular has been the notion of the servant community as the 'covenant people'. But this is ruled out grammatically since the intent to depict the servant community as the carrier of the covenant traditions would have necessitated the reversal of the Hebrew phrase; i.e., *ʿam berît*, would have been expected. Secondly, 'covenant of the people', with the servant as a pledge for Israel as a whole, is very possible, as is thirdly, 'covenant of the people', with the Israel in view a pledge for the world as a whole (cf. the 'light to the nations' of 42:6 which stands in a parallel relationship). The fourth suggestion, which takes *berît* as referring not to covenant, but as having been derived from some other Heb. root and thus referring to 'splendour' or 'brightness' or the like, provides an attactive parallel to 'light to the nations'. It fails, however, to do justice to the context of 42:1–9 which firstly stresses the servant's role in vv. 1–4 as bound up with torah (and thus finally covenant) with the nations in view, and which then continues in vv. 4–9 to underscore the nature of the redemption which he will effect. It is moreover too much of a strain on probability that in using this important word the prophet would have had something else in mind other than covenant, given the emphasis that covenant relationships receive throughout the course of Isa. 40 – 55.

The notion of the servant as a covenant pledge for the world seems commended by the distinction between 'people' and 'nations' of Isa. 42:6 and therefore the third suggestion offered above best fits the context. The servant thus embodies the covenant and perpetuates it for the true 'Israel', who are to recognize that the covenant with whatever Israel may be on view in this context has its point of final reference in its wider application to the nations. However, the reconstitution of the Israelite *nation* by the ministry of the servant (if the *nation* is in mind) would not in any case be an end in itself but merely a guarantee that the divine intention for the world at large would be finally achieved.

In regard to the ministry of the servant, however, the point to be noted is the close connection which is established between the ministry of the servant and the return to Jerusalem. This cannot be developed here but it is noteworthy that Isa. 52:7–12, which deals with the climactic return of Yahweh to Zion, is followed by a detailed appraisal

---

12. The language of Isa. 52:13 – 53:12 is traditionally difficult to interpret. Since the servant is specifically identified with Israel (Isa. 49:3), the suffering language of Isa. 53 (which may be typical of the ideal sufferer) which seems so personal, is best taken corporately.

of the servant's role. Only then, as we shall note, are the covenant implications of his ministry drawn out in completely Zionistic terms in Isa. 54–55. Zion thus stands ready as the centre to which nations will come in pilgrimage. This is a prospect which the first servant passage (Isa. 42:1–4) has alluded to with its mention of 'tôrāh' (42:4) for which 'the isles will wait' (cf. Isa. 2:2–4).

iii. *Isaiah 54 – 55: a review of covenant theology*

The elaboration of the servant's activity takes place principally in Isa. 53. By that action national deliverance has been effected. The covenant passages of 54:1 – 55:5 which follow this, thus do so logically. They describe the results of that deliverance in terms of the new relationships which are to arise from it. Thus in terms of the marriage relationship, 54:1 takes up the language of reversal, a theme which the whole chapter will develop at great length. Verses 1–3 with their notion of children to be borne by the barren woman, who will in their turn possess the nations, are obviously Abrahamic in their character, but the mother image of these early verses changes in vv. 4–6 to that of the widowed and forsaken wife, who is then given assurance in the divine speech which follows in vv. 7–8. This is equally clearly the imagery of the Sinai covenant, not solely because of the characterizing marriage metaphor, but also because of the occurrence of the phrase 'everlasting ḥesed' in v. 8. The term ḥesed is one which we have seen to be firmly anchored within the Sinai covenant and to be used usually with reference to it.

At first sight the imagery of vv. 1–3 (mother/children) seems distinct from that of vv. 4–8 (husband/forsaken wife) and the covenant appeals mixed. Verses 1–3 are clearly Abrahamic – verse 3 with its promise of descendants who will possess the nation and then people the desolated cities is a clear reminiscence of Gen. 22:17. Sarah, moreover, had been an auditor in her tent of the Gen. 'seed' promise (Gen. 18:9), making the reference here to the need to enlarge the tents etc., of v. 2 a particularly apposite one. Vv. 4–8 just as clearly bear Sinai references (cf. v. 6 'wife of your youth' etc.). However, the husband of vv. 4–8 is identified in v. 5 as the creator of Israel, a notion which carries us back to the Abrahamic promises, while in the same verse the Sinai terminology of 'Lord of Hosts', 'Holy one of Israel', 'Redeemer', is also applied. The ease with which these basic covenant motifs can be blended points to the underlying connections between all Israel's covenant/election notions which were so apparent to the prophetic thought of the period.

The Noah comparison which begins in v. 9 adds to the bewildering complexity of covenant interplay upon which the prophet has drawn. By such a comparison the exiles are being invited to parallel their situation with the period of the flood when the deluge was merely an interlude within an everlasting covenant on the basis of which Noah, after the flood, was invited to begin again. The appeal in v. 10 to an everlasting covenant of peace which is indissoluble, must, within the exilic thought framework, be an appeal to the New Covenant to emerge from the exilic situation. Taking the form as it does of a self attestation of divine fidelity (cf. *ḥesed* again occuring in v. 10), it is at the same time an affirmation of divine covenant constancy. Never again (v. 10) will Israel be disturbed by the threat of exile; in the new order their position will be as unchangeable as the most fixed elements of the fixed natural order (v. 10).

The flood imagery seems to continue in v. 11 where Israel is addressed as 'tempest tossed'. But the theme of reversal of fortunes with which the chapter had begun is taken up afresh in vv. 11–12, in which the resplendent foundations of the New Zion are referred to. The mother image of vv. 1–3 reappears in v. 13, but this time in combination with the husband/wife symbolism of vv. 4–8, for the children referred to are those to be given to the Zion wife. There is, then, in verses 11–13 a similar combination of covenant interplay as occurred in vv. 1–3, 4–8, and we are thoroughly within the New Covenant framework in v. 13, for all Zion's sons (v. 13) 'shall be taught by the Lord'.

At the same time the eschatological direction of vv. 11–13 is clear. The new city is one whose maker and builder is God, whose foundations are divinely laid (cf. v. 11, and therefore unshakeable in the terms in which v. 10 has referred to them). The splendour of the city (vv. 11–12) and the prosperity of Zion's sons make it certain that we are dealing in these verses with the notion of the New Jerusalem, to which all the world will resort, the city for which the sojourner Abraham looked (cf. Heb. 11:10). The consequences (i.e. the blessings) of the new arrangement are drawn out in vv. 14–17, an address as W.A.M. Beuken[13] has noted, enclosed by the concept of 'righteousness' (vv. 14, 17) which will be the characteristic of the new age. The attachment of this notion of righteousness to the concept of the New Covenant (v. 13) is what might logically have been expected. This righteousness is not, however, Israel's response to the New Covenant relationship, but rather the display of divine fidelity which will be declared in fidelity to old commitments, a righteousness which guarantees therefore Israel's continuance in the new age (cf. vv. 14 and 17).

Verse 17 sees the fulfilment of what has been contemplated in v. 11–17 as Israel's 'inheritance' (Heb. *naḥᵃlah*). By taking up this term, which we have seen already to be so much an integral part of the theology of the ideal occupation of the land which characterized the book of Deuteronomy, Isaiah 54 implicitly concludes the note of 'rest' which will be the heritage of the restored Israel. The chapter thus ends by pointing to a New Covenant edifice which will be erected upon the structure of the

---

[13]. Cf. W.A.M. Beuken, 'Isaiah liv: The Multiple Identity of the Person Addressed', *OTS* 19 (1974), p. 61. He has perceptively noted the combination of covenant imagery in Isa. 54 to which we have referred.

older promises. The appeal to the flood at the mid-point of the chapter had within it the notes of discontinuity/continuity whereby we may understand that the Old Covenant will come to an end and the New Covenant be ushered in. Thus the chapter dealing with Abraham/Sinai (vv. 1–8) and the New Jerusalem (vv. 11–17), holds forth the perfection of Israel under the multiple series of Old Covenant promises with which it has dealt.

Within the framework of Zion theology to which the latter section of Isa. 54 has directed us, we might have expected prominent mention of the role of the Davidic covenant in the new age since the eschatology with which the New Covenant is surrounded is Zion–centred. That in fact comes in Isa. 55. Verses 1–3 deal with a further invitation issued to faithful Israel to participate in the new life which will flow from the New Jerusalem (cf. 'waters' and Ezek. 47:1–12). The abundance of water, wine and milk herald the blessings of the new paradisiacal age. All this is to be based (vv. 3–5) upon the introduction of the everlasting covenant foreshadowed through David.

The promises to David and through him to all Israel, had been made in order to provide Israel with Spirit–directed leadership. The benefits of Davidic kingship in the new age, however, are democratized since the Davidic sure mercies will then be given to faithful Israel (v. 3). By this older Davidic promises are evacuated of all political significance and are transferred to the redeemed people of God as a whole. In the new age, what was true in terms of Davidic political influence in the day of the empire (v. 4) will be true of the extent of Israel's leadership in the new era (v. 5), a leadership which will be recognized by a world pilgrimage to Zion (cf. v. 5).

The remainder of Isa. 55 continues on the same note of assurance. Verses 6–9 appeal to the people of God to turn back to the Lord now on the basis of the promises outlined. Verses 10–11 assure fidelity to the divine commitment by affirming the dependability of the divine word. Verses 12–13 close the chapter as an inclusion by reasserting the paradisiacal nature of the restored age and speak of the harmony between the created orders. The whole of creation will respond to the redemption which the return from exile will effect as it ushers in the new age. Thus the curse of exile, which the proclamation of Isa. 40:1ff was designed to relieve, has given way at the end of chapter 55 to the blessings of restoration.

iv. *Universalism and particularism in covenant emphasis in Isa. 40 – 55*

In Isa. 40 – 55 'nationalism' and 'universalism' have gone hand in hand. By nationalism we mean, of course, the prophetic concentration upon Israel's position. In a covenant sense this has been made particularly clear by the content of chapters 54–55. Universalistic Noachian and Abrahamic promises have been employed in the interests of narrower

Zionistic theology. This in its turn was designed to offer to the redeemed Israel the leadership of witness (cf. 55:4) to the world. Such a leadership is to be exercised, however, within the strongly nationalistic guidelines that chapters 40–55 have provided. In chapters 40–48 nationalism has been particularly paraded in the series of prophetic law suits by which the nations have been put on trial for their attitude to Israel. On the other hand, the mood of Isa. 49–55 has been far less political and more international. Since within these chapters the so-called great missionary passages of the prophecy occur, we might be tempted to suppose that rigid nationalism has given way after the return (which Isa. 49–55 presupposes – it is only in prospect in chapters 40–48), to a more relaxed internationalism. The Servant passages, however, to which we have briefly referred, deal primarily with the redemption of Israel and though Isa. 49–55 are more international in their character, it is an internationalism which sees Israel and Zion at the centre of the world stage.[14] Such an internationalism sees Israel's covenant goals won, for it is recognized that the nations will also be beneficiaries in the final age, when, and only when, they have adopted a proper stance to the Israel to whom the servant's message is directed. For the shape of this general world scene to which chapters 40 – 55 refer, the embracive covenantal arguments which chapters 54 – 55 have provided, have forged the necessary connections between retrospect and prospect.

v. *Survey of Isaiah 56–66*

The remainder of the book of Isaiah (chapters 56 – 66) expands upon the nature of the relationship between the redeemed Israel and her world. Only a brief summation of the thought of these chapters is presented here. Much in them seems given over to the difficulties arising within the Israelite community after the return. They are often seen as presenting inverted domestic concerns which contrast starkly with the grander pictures of Isa. 40 – 55. Yet within these chapters the same world view prevails of Israel at the centre of her world.

This is particularly so in Isa. 60 – 62 which entertains the idea of the manifestation of the Lord of the second Exodus who will glorify the new Zion by his coming. The tribute of the world comes to Zion (60:11), the promised land is possessed for ever (60:21), and all this is in obvious fulfilment of the Abrahamic promises which are referred to in 60:22. As Paul Hanson has shown,[15] the essential features of Isa. 40–55 are

---

[14]. Israel's designation as 'servant' is a term of elective privilege. No missionary connotations can really be read into the term. D. H. Odendaal, *The Eschatological Expectation of Isa. 40 – 66 with Special Reference to Israel and the Nations* (Nutley, N.J.: Presbyterian and Reformed Publishing Co., 1970), p. 126, offers a very balanced treatment of particularism and universalism in Isa. 40–66.

[15]. In his *The Dawn of Apocalyptic* (Philadelphia: Fortress Press, 1975), pp. 32 – 46.

expounded in chapters 56–66. Salvation, therefore, is not for all Israel, but for a community of faith. In these chapters there is no mention of a Davidic figure, total emphasis being placed upon God's intervention by which the new age is introduced and upon his kingship to be exercised in it. Thus the renewal of Israel in 40–66 is not presented from the standpoint of national revival, but as being in fulfilment of the Abrahamic promises. It thus operates as a guarantee of world salvation, and it is based upon the prospect of a New Creation (cf. Isa. 65:17–25).

F. THE QUESTION OF THE FULFILMENT OF THE EXILIC PROPHETIC REDACTION

The point has often been raised that the extravagant promises of these chapters, the expectations which they raised, the end which they had in view, were not fulfilled in the return from exile. But a return from exile is never exclusively in view in such references. Two points by way of addition need to be made. The first is that the use of Israel's older traditions (creation theology, Abrahamic covenant, Exodus, David, even Noah and Eden) makes it clear that basic Israelite theological directions have been adhered to. The second is that Israel in the wider sense of the reconstituted people of God, loosed from the bonds of nationalism, is always in the prophet's mind. In Isa. 40 – 66 the return of Israel has been spiritualized into the advent of a new age[16] and thus into association with the ushering in of a New Covenant, the realisation of a New Creation.

Nothing less is on view in these chapters than the renewal and extension of theocratic government over Israel and the world. The aim of these chapters, and the note upon which Isa. 66 concludes, is the renewal of creation and its submission to divine rule. The submission of the nations is presented in these chapters not as the triumph of Jewish nationalism, but as a result of the establishment of the Kingdom of God, where God himself rules from the reconstituted centre of Zion.

Of course, a return from Babylon is also in the mind of the prophet. But this great historical act, now to take place before the eyes of the exiles, is in itself a harbinger of the future of redeemed Israel. There is in fact an indication that we have moved beyond literal history by the way in which the return from exile is extravagantly and constantly presented (a transformed wilderness, mountains levelled etc.). The paradisiacal shape of the promised land upon the return, moreover, is a further indication that something more than a physical national return is in the mind of the prophet.

This means, correspondingly, that the shape of the New Covenant, in which Israel will be involved, will necessarily transcend any arrangement completed with Israel during the historical process. The covenant

---

16. Odendaal, *Eschatological Expectation*, p. 126.

orientation of all these chapters has been remarked upon, but particularly noticeable are the covenant inclusions formed by the beginning and end of Isa. 40 – 55, since with Isa. 40, the note of consolation to 'my people' from 'their God' is at once struck, while 54 – 55 display the full breadth of covenant imagery as operating.

The New Covenant theology of Jeremiah received therefore its elaboration and confirmation at the hands of both Ezekiel and Isaiah. This theology was never merely national. Therefore in none of the three prophets does Davidic kingship really figure in the new arrangement. The New Covenant is seen by Jeremiah as the fulfilment of the Sinai covenant, though Ezekiel and even more Isaiah take us much further. They associate with the New Covenant the distinct predominance of New Creation features, for the expectation that the exile forced upon the prophets of the time was that the only political solution for the disordered world of which Israel was a part was the inbreaking of the reign of God. This, as we well know, is a view which is thoroughly consistent with the eschatology of the New Testament.

Covenant theology in the Old Testament reached the limits of its exposition and expectations in the doctrine of the New Covenant. The post-exilic writings which will be briefly surveyed in the subsequent epilogue take us no further. They are, however, illuminating as endeavours to implement in the period after the return from exile the programme of the exilic prophets to which this chapter has referred. Messianism, particularly, recedes into the background at this time. It is replaced by a very heavy emphasis upon the kingship of God, beginning with the book of Daniel, a product of the Persian period. Haggai and Zechariah are endeavours to implement the platform of Ezekiel, while Chronicles, Ezra and Nehemiah are, in their own way, attempts to realise the theology of New Covenant expectation.

Summary

The effect of the disaster of 587 B.C. was to transfer attention away from the institutions which had supported the concept of Israel to the idea of Israel itself and to make it clear that the continuance of the people of God depended solely upon God's covenant grace. Before the question of the New Covenant in Jeremiah was considered we devoted some space to the way in which the concept of the covenant, of covenant breach and covenant renewal had been dealt with in the pre-exilic prophets. Jeremiah 31:31–34 is set within a context of two chapters dealing with the restoration of North and South, the concept of a second Exodus and a re-occupation of the land. We have noticed that in Jer. 31:31–34 elements of continuity and discontinuity were present. The 'new' covenant appears to have had in mind a fresh dispensation of the Sinai covenant, or better, a re-writing of the provisions of the Sinai covenant on the individual heart. The search for the element of 'newness' in the

New Covenant leads us to conclude that the covenant was not 'new' because it now contained the element of obligation as well as promise, nor because God in the 'new' situation would put the law in the heart, though that latter phrase did refer to what had been the ideal expectation under the old Sinai covenant. The new element in the New Covenant appeared to us to be the forgiveness of sins which was to be so complete that sin would no longer be remembered. Put otherwise, in the parlance of the Old Testament, sin would not be a factor in the new age under consideration. This led us to conclude that the New Covenant would operate fully only in the end-time age or the eschaton. We had noted also the irrefragability of the Sinai covenant on the divine side. God had not broken it, in fact the image of the marriage relationship had pointed to the impossibility of his doing so. *Both* partners in the new age would keep it.

The exilic prophets had also in mind the operation of this new arrangement in their own age as the consistent language of Ezekiel and Isaiah 'second Exodus' indicates. But this oscillation between present and future in terms of fulfilment we found to be characteristic of the biblical presentation as a whole. Ezekiel carried the New Covenant theology a stage further with his doctrine of the 'new heart', indicating at once what ought to have been the case under the old covenant and what would take place under the new. His concept of the gift of the Spirit to the individual pointed to a democratization of leadership (with which the notion of the gift of the Spirit was bound up in the Old Testament) in the new age, a fact which Pentecost takes up later. Ezekiel thus goes a stage further than Jeremiah, making God the author of the new obedience. The eschatology of Ezek. 40–48 stresses the concept of Kingdom of God rule in the last days. There is hardly any emphasis upon the concept of Messiahship in the book of Ezekiel.

Isaiah 40–55 is a repository of covenant traditions. The New Exodus emphasis of those chapters presupposes a new Sinai and also a New Conquest. The Abrahamic traditions are combined in Isa. 51:1–11 with both the Sinai and the Creation covenant traditions. Covenant motifs are especially associated with the figure of the servant who was a pledge that the ideal of Israel would continue with the welfare of the world finally in view. On the basis of the Servant's atoning sufferings fuller covenant materials were introduced in Isa. 54–55. Isa. 54 contained an amalgam incorporating materials from the Abrahamic, Noachian and Sinai covenants, whereby those are presented as interrelated and as leading to the concept of the New Covenant with which the chapter ends. Chapter 55 refers to the democratization of the leadership of Israel (under the imagery of the Davidic covenant) in the new age. The chapter concluded with a brief survey which indicated that Isa. 56 – 66 consistently presented material relating to the renewal of Israel and the resulting renewal of creation in chapters which expanded the eschatological detail of chapters 40 – 55.

Epilogue

THE POST-EXILIC DEVELOPMENTS

In the post-exilic period there is no advance upon the theology of the New Covenant developed by the major exilic prophets. Yet the literature of the post-exilic period reveals a measure of reaction to their teaching, and certainly in some instances, an attempt to implement it. While therefore what follows is to some degree unrelated to the main theme of this book, it may be helpful to indicate summarily post-exilic developments within the community of faith, as a preparation for the New Testament era in which the theology of the New Covenant is so heavily appealed to.

A. DANIEL

This is a book in which kingdom and not covenant is the prominent concept, though it was pointed out at the beginning of our discussion that kingdom and covenant cannot be dissociated. It is a striking feature of the book of Daniel that the context of the Abrahamic covenant is recalled at the very beginning of the book. We refer here to the very conscious way in which the Babylon of Nebuchadnezzar is seen by the author to manifest a re-incarnation of the Babel mentality of Gen. 11:1-9. The book of Daniel commences with an assault on Jerusalem, the carrying into captivity of members of the seed royal and the seizure of some temple vessels. Put into the language of that day, we may see this as a pagan assertion of dominance over Jerusalem/Zion and its God. Notable is the use in Daniel 1:2 of the phrase 'land of Shinar' as the locale to which the temple vessels were carried. It occurs in only three other contexts in the Old Testament, two of them strikingly significant.[1] In Zech. 5:11 it is the place where a 'house' (i.e. a temple) could be built for 'wickedness', while for the direction of the book of Daniel the use of the phrase in Gen. 11:2 of the Babel incident is important. In Dan. 1 Nebuchadnezzar's monochrome policy for his empire of one language, one common culture, one educational base etc., all emanating from the 'land of Shinar', recalls vividly Gen. 11. We have previously noted that the book of Daniel is the account of the clash of two imperiums, world

---

[1]. The phrase is also found at Gen. 10:10 in a purely geographical sense.

power structures of one form or another, and the kingdom of God. We are left in no doubt by the laconic conclusion to Dan. 1 ('Daniel continued until the first year of King Cyrus' – i.e. Daniel lived through the entire exile and saw the downfall of Babylon), which imperium will prevail. It thus comes as no surprise that Daniel, which commences with the 'church in chains', ends with an account of the 'church triumphant' (Daniel 12). While the book is given over to the way in which the kingdom of God will break into human history and bring it to an end, the connection between covenant and kingdom, to which we have previously drawn attention, requires us to understand that Daniel is a presentation of the clashes which must occur within the course of history before the New Covenant age can be ushered in.

B. HAGGAI AND ZECHARIAH

Both of these books presuppose the theology of Ezekiel, particularly the platform of Ezekiel 40 – 48. Both are temple–centred in that both lay very heavy stress upon the need for the rebuilding of the temple. Haggai 1 with its theme of sin and the operation of the covenant curses (Hag. 1:4–11), the people's repentance and the divine acceptance of this response (vv. 12 – 14), is very much covenant renewal orientated.[2] In chapter 2 the eschatological picture is sketched in which the temple, as the centre of the royal presence, attracts the world (2:1–9), all of which will demand a 'purified promised land' (2:10–19), in connection with which subdued Davidic expectations are raised in the form of Zerubbabel, the physical legatee of the Davidic claims. We should note direct contrast that the elective terms used of Zerubbabel (2:20–23) provide to the way in which Jehoiachin, the last Davidic king, was unceremoniously rejected (Jer. 22:24).

In the book of Zechariah the rebuilding of the temple is raised within Zech. 1 as the prime concern for the returnees. At the end of chapter 8 (8:20–23), at the conclusion of the first half of the book, the rebuilding of the temple has been coupled, as in Haggai, with Jerusalem assuming its role as a world pilgrimage resort. In that section it is of particular interest that the asseveration of the foreigner as he takes hold of the robe of the Jew ('Let us go with you, for we have heard that God is with you') echoes distinctly the words of Abimelech (Gen. 21:22), the first foreign contact with whom Abraham had been regularly associated. God's fidelity to the Abrahamic covenant thus completes the cycle of promises with which the first eight chapters of Zechariah have been concerned. It must be added that the note which the initial verses of Zech. 1:1–6 had struck was, like Haggai, that of covenant renewal. The

---

[2]. Cf. W. A. M. Beuken, *Haggai-Sacharja 1–8* (Assen: Van Gorcum 1967), pp. 42ff., who draws parallels between Haggai and Old Testament covenant renewal passages.

sustained use of the Heb. verb *shûb* ('return'—Zech. 1:3, 4, 6), a verb frequent in covenant contexts in the Old Testament in the transferred sense of 'repent', points in that direction. In covenantal use by the prophets, *shûb* always involves a return, the goal of which is Yahweh, and the call to return has as its purpose the renewal of the covenant.[3] Following upon the covenant renewal, the visionary programme of the first six chapters is then put forward. This has in mind, not only the rebuilding of the temple, but also the return of God to Jerusalem/Zion and the political rule in the new age, shared, as Ezekiel had foreshadowed, between priest (Joshua) and prince (Zerubbabel).

The second half of Zechariah (chapters 9 – 14) begins and ends as the first half has done. Paul Hanson's approach[4] may be followed here and chapter 9 be seen as a royal progress from the northern limits of the old Davidic empire to the temple (v. 8) in the course of which a progressive judgement is delivered upon the traditional enemies of the covenant people. Zech. 14 ends the second half of the prophecy in much the same way as 8:20–23 had the first half. Jerusalem (14:1–2) is again under threat but Yahweh's intervention heralds the inbreaking of a new age and notes are introduced of a New Creation in which the binary divisions of the old creation cease (vv. 6–7). The Edenic symbolism of Ezekiel in terms of living waters is taken up (v. 8) and Jerusalem becomes, as expected, a compulsory pilgrimage resort for the nations (vv. 16–19). This pilgrimage is in response to Yahweh's kingship (v. 17). The aims of the Abrahamic covenant by which the world comes through Israel into contact with blessing are thus also realized.

It seems clear that the second half of Zechariah forms a theological commentary on the first. The function of the temple in the Old Testament was to be the divine dwelling place from which covenant blessings would flow out to the world. Zechariah thus deals with covenant realization, i.e. divine rule exercised in the New Covenant age. Such a rule would usher in the New Creation and thus complete in full finality the biblical concept of purpose. We know, however, that the confident expectations of Haggai and Zechariah were not realised. This did not mean, as we have noted in the case of similar material in Isa. 40 – 66, that their final projections required adjustment. What they proclaimed as imminent for their own age would surely happen. They were not wrong to see the return from exile as charged with possibility. They were right to see the return from exile as at least the beginning of the end and the eschatology which they endorsed will surely come to pass. Neither in Haggai nor Zechariah do we see the disappearance of prophecy with a whisper. Indeed the movement bows out on a very high note, for Zechariah particularly, by his symbolic re-interpretation

---

3. The arguments are presented by A. Petitjean, *Les Oracles du Proto-Zacharie* (Paris: Gabalda, 1969), pp. 29–37.
4. Cf. *The Dawn of Apocalyptic*, pp. 290–401.

of history in chapters 9–14, compels the expositor to recognize that nationalistic interpretations of Old Testament promises, never an important element at any stage of Old Testament history, had now no further part to play.

C. MALACHI-EZRA-NEHEMIAH

Ezra-Nehemiah are best seen as implementing the reform programmes of Malachi, a fifth century book written on the eve of their return. Malachi takes up the catalogue of social evils of the day and with his expectation of the final return of Elijah, the twelve-tribed–covenant revivalist, ends with a direct reference to covenant renewal as that which will precede the ultimate end. Priestly disorders, problems of mixed marriages, non-payment of what appears to have been the Levitical tithe, are all referred to. It is interesting to speculate that the messenger of the covenant of Mal. 3:1, while it undoubtedly has its final fulfilment in the figure of Elijah, may have pointed in its times more immediately to the figure of Ezra. Ezra's action was temple–centred and did aim at the abolition of the malpractices to which Malachi had referred.

Ezra returned, with Persian permission, in 458 B.C. Traditionally, but incorrectly, he has been seen as the 'Father of Judaism', bringing back with him from Babylon the newly completed Pentateuch. The facts of his mission, however, point in another direction. Certainly his mission was covenant orientated as indicated by the renewal ceremony of Neh. 8–10 which brought his work to a close. We cannot see him, however, as an inaugurating law-giver, for Ezra 7, which reports his commission, makes every effort to stress the antiquity of the law which Ezra brought with him (cf. Ezra 7:6, 10, 25). As Klaus Koch has pointed out,[5] the emphasis in chapter 7 is upon Ezra as the regulator of temple practice. The parallel between the commission given to Ezra and that given a century earlier to Zerubbabel is therefore striking. In view of the emphasis upon cultic purity and a cleansed people that the book of Ezra promotes, we should do better to see in his return a fresh national commencement. The impediments to the implementation of second Exodus theology which the return from exile of 538 B.C. ought to have made possible have now been removed.

Nehemiah, a layman, builds upon Ezra's work and is associated with him in bringing it to fruition. It is noticeable that in the covenant renewal ceremony which Neh. 8 – 10 reports, laymen and not priests are prominent. Certainly the High Priest is not mentioned. A review of Israel's history in terms of covenant relationships occurs in chapter 9.

---

[5]. Klaus Koch, 'Ezra and the Origins of Judaism' *JSS* 19 (1974), 173–197.

The plea for renewed mercies with which that chapter ends (cf. v. 32) is based upon God's covenant–keeping nature. The detailed sufferings of the people are rehearsed within the chapter and at its end there is virtually a return to the Abrahamic covenant base from which Israel's fortunes in this prayer have been traced (v. 8). What is asked for is the reversal of the present situation in which they are slaves in the land which was given to their fathers (v. 36), that is for the restoration of Israel's influence in the land which was promised to her.

Ezra and Nehemiah are illuminating for the insight which they give into the community of their day. Their relationship to the books of Chronicles is disputed and there are dissimilarities in the emphasis of these books. But like Chronicles they propound a form of realised eschatology by which the cleansed people of God dwell in an idealized concept of Jerusalem. Chronicles, of course, is even stronger in this stress and if the community after c. 400 B.C. lapses into tight priestly control until the Advent despite all these reform efforts, this might have been predictable from the failure that the history of Israel throughout the Old Testament had demonstrated.

D. THE WISDOM LITERATURE

Though much of this literature clearly predates the exile, it is convenient to refer to it at this point. It is beyond the scope of this present work to take up the question of covenant as a regulating factor for Old Testament theology. But the point is briefly made in this general summation that traditional covenant theologians have tended to leave this literature to one side as unrelated to the redemptive purposes of the Old Testament. On the view of covenant as based upon creation itself, the wisdom literature provides no difficulty for us if wider issues of the Old Testament are being taken up. It is true that the narrower redemptive themes bound up with Exodus, Sinai, Messianism etc., find no place in the wisdom books. We are not discountenanced to admit this, however, for the widom books are concerned with the daily life of the people of God within the broad experience which life in the created world provided. In fact, the thought of the wisdom literature reflected a theology based upon the fact of creation.[6] On this wider level, the nature of conduct as based upon existing relationships cannot be lost sight of. The essence of wisdom is thus the 'fear of the Lord' (cf. Prov. 1:7; 9:10; 15:33; Ps. 111:10; Job 28:28). This note of fear is not to be identified with a psychological or emotional response to Yahweh, but with one of total commitment within a framework of covenant rela-

---

[6]. For a recent survey of attempts to integrate Wisdom into a Biblical Theology cf. J. Goldingay, "The 'Salvation History' Perspective and the 'Wisdom' Perspective within the context of Biblical theology" Ev.Q 51 (1979), pp. 194–207.

tionships which Israel knew had been established. In the sense that such a response is a reaction to and a reflection of *tôrāh*, the identification of 'wisdom' with 'law', though not overtly made until the end of the biblical period, is something which is implicit from the beginning (Deut. 4:6).

E. KINGDOM AND COVENANT

We commenced this chapter with a reference to the book of Daniel and in particular to the philosophies of world rule with which that book was bound up. We suggested that the manifestation of the kingdom which that book primarily had in mind was the precursor to the community of the New Covenant of the end time. We have returned throughout this book to the interplay of kingdom and covenant, though we are conscious that the connections offered have been summary and perhaps allusive. Kingdom, of course, would require a separate and detailed treatment. But we have emphasized that in any treatment of covenant the parameters within which covenant operates must not be lost sight of. It is this implied connection between these two important biblical themes which has encouraged us to sketch the general course of the development of the community of faith in the post-exilic period, in this brief epilogue. Our study must end at this point, though its proper conclusion would be in the New Testament revelation. While that is more directly concerned with the question of Kingdom, the conclusion of the general kingdom exposition which the New Testament offers is the virtual return to Genesis 1–2 which closes the book of Revelation.

The Old Testament is a record of national failure. It shows how Israel succumbed to the danger of attempting to institutionalise spiritual traditions. Within a covenant structure, the Old Testament held out a programme of ideals for a perfected people of God. But the Old age did not reach that goal. Now did the New. Neither has our own. The kingship of God sought expression through a whole web of relationships which successive covenants both pointed towards and also exercised over the people of God and their world. But this kingship presupposed a return within history to the beginning of history. As we have repeatedly noted, nothing less than a new creation – and thus a new covenant – would achieve this goal. In that sense, the notion of the kingdom of God, controlling as it does the whole of biblical thinking, was always a theological assertion pointing towards a future reality – the New Covenant.

INDEX OF AUTHORS

INDEX OF REFERENCES